Mastery motivation in early childhood

All children possess a motive to 'master' the various tasks and problems that they face. Without mastery motivation, it is doubtful whether children would make progress in cognitive, social, communicative and other domains. Although all children possess this motivation, it will vary according to inherited dispositions and to environmental experiences. This makes mastery motivation a key factor in understanding later developmental and educational achievement.

Concentrating on pre-school children, the volume brings together current research work and thinking concerned with mastery motivation. New ideas are presented about the way mastery is related to other developmental processes such as self-concepts and attention. There are discussions and findings about innovations in the methods of assessing mastery. Another important theme present in this volume, is the way in which features of social interaction, attachment and the environment influence the development of mastery motivation.

With a broad range of international contributors, *Mastery Motivation in Early Childhood* will be of interest to developmental psychologists and educationalists, and advanced students in these fields.

David Messer is Reader in Developmental Psychology at the University of Hertfordshire.

International Library of Psychology
Editorial adviser,
Developmental psychology:

Peter K. Smith
University of Sheffield

Neo-Piagetian Theories of Cognitive Development
Edited by Andreas Demetriou, Michael Shayer and Anastasia Efklides

New Perspectives in Early Communicative Development
Edited by Jacqueline Nadel and Luigia Camaioni

Classroom Nonverbal Communication
Sean Neill

Mastery motivation in early childhood

Development, measurement and social processes

Edited by David Messer

London and New York

First published 1993
by Routledge
11 New Fetter Lane, London EC4P 4EE

Simultaneously published in the USA and Canada
by Routledge
29 West 35th Street, New York, NY 10001

Reprinted 1996

Typeset in Times by Intype, London
Printed and bound in Great Britain by
Antony Rowe Ltd, Chippenham, Wiltshire

British Library Cataloguing in Publication Data
A catalogue record for this book is available from the
British Library

Library of Congress Cataloguing in Publication Data
A catalogue record for this book is available from the
Library of Congress

ISBN 0-415-06956-4

Contents

Illustrations

TABLES

Contributors

Inge Bretherton, Child and Family Studies, University of Wisconsin, Madison, Wyoming, WI 53706, USA.

Terri T. Coombs, Department of Psychological Sciences, Purdue University, 1364 Psychological Sciences Building, West Lafayette, IN 47907–1364, USA.

Lois Brockman, Department of Family Studies, College of Human Ecology, University of Manitoba, Winnipeg R3T 2N2, Canada.

Nancy A. Busch-Rossnagel, Department of Psychology, Fordham University, The Bronx, New York, NY 10458, USA.

Karen Caplovitz Barrett, Human Development and Family Studies, Fort Collins, CO 80523, USA.

Robert J. Harman, Department of Psychiatry C268, University of Colorado School of Medicine, Denver, CO 80262, USA.

Penny Hauser-Cram, School of Education, Boston College, Chestnut Hill, Mass. 02167–3813, USA.

Jutta Heckhausen, Max Planck Institut fur Bildungsforschung, Lentzeallee 94, D–1000, Berlin 33 – Dahlem, Germany.

Kay Jennings, Psychophysiology Laboratory, Western Psychiatric Institute and Clinic, 3811 O'Hara Street, University of Pittsburgh, Pennsylvania 15261, USA.

Diana E. Knauf, Department of Psychology, Fordham University, The Bronx, New York, NY 10458, USA.

Jeannette Koks, University of Nijmegen, Psychologisch Laboratorium, Postbus 9104, 6500 HE Nijmegen, The Netherlands.

Robert M. MacTurk, Gallaudet Research Institute, Gallaudet University, Kendall Green, 800 Florida Avenue, NE, Washington DC 20002–3625, USA.

Christine Maslin-Cole, Rocky Mountains Marriage and Family Center, 1302 South College Avenue, Fort Collins, CO 80521, USA.

Hans Th. Meij, University of Nijmegen, Psychologisch Laboratorium, Postbus 9104, 6500 HE Nijmegen, The Netherlands.

David Messer, Psychology Division, University of Hertfordshire, Hatfield Campus, College Lane, Hatfield, Herts AL10 9AB, England.

George A. Morgan, Human Development and Family Studies, Colorado State University, Fort Collins, CO 80523, USA.

J. Marianne Riksen-Walraven, University of Nijmegen, Psychologisch Laboratorium, Postbus 9104, 6500 HE Nijmegen, The Netherlands.

Juchke van Roozendaal, University of Nijmegen, Psychologisch Laboratorium, Postbus 9104, 6500 HE Nijmegen, The Netherlands.

Maribel Vargas, Department of Psychology, Fordham University, The Bronx, New York, NY 10458, USA.

Theodore D. Wachs, Department of Psychological Sciences, Purdue University, 1364 Psychological Sciences Building, West Lafayette, IN 47907–1364, USA.

Chapter 1

Mastery motivation
An introduction to theories and issues

David J. Messer

Motivation to achieve and to improve skills is an important characteristic of our and other species. One can think of many vignettes of young organisms struggling to master problems: the young fledgling flapping its wings, jumping and hopping in its attempts to start to fly; the baby pulling herself or himself up on to chairs in the first attempts to start to walk, or the concentration and sometimes frustration of the toddler attempting to solve a puzzle. In all cases there is a strong motive directing behaviour, and the motive is not related to any immediate physical reward. Instead, the mastery of the task appears to be a reward in itself. The fascination of this type of behaviour provides the basis for the present volume.

The first section of this chapter provides an historical perspective about the growth of interest in mastery motivation. The classic papers by White, Hunt, Harter and others are outlined and discussed; differences between the formulations are highlighted. The second section considers more recent advances in the study of mastery motivation which are considered in the contributions to this volume.

THE GROWTH OF INTEREST IN MASTERY MOTIVATION

A number of terms have been used to refer to children's motivation to achieve objectives: mastery motivation, intrinsic motivation, competence motivation and, with older children, achievement motivation. These terms sometimes have been used interchangeably, but different perspectives can be identified within the literature. For this reason I will describe the ways in which these terms have been employed and consider distinctions between them. In doing so, I will outline the theories of White, Hunt, Harter and Yarrow. Particular attention is paid to four issues: the conceptualizations of the goal-directed nature of motivation, the description of the relationship between intrinsic and extrinsic sources of motivation, the relationship between motivation and cognition, and the types of behaviour influenced by motivation.

White's effectance and competence motivation

White (1959, 1963) used the terms 'effectance' and 'competence motivation'. 'Effectance' referred to a disposition of children to act on their environment, and the satisfaction associated with effectance was seen as the result of a 'primitive biological endowment' (White 1963: 35). 'Competence motivation' referred to children's motivation to master tasks, increase knowledge and perfect skills, or, as White expressed it, 'an organism's capacity to interact effectively with the environment' (White 1959: 297). Competence motivation was considered to be directed, selective and persistent. White believed that it resulted in satisfaction if there was a series of transactions which 'change[d] one's relation to the environment'.

White did not believe that it was useful to attempt to identify either the most important motive of an activity or the specific goal of this motive. He argued against dividing competence motivation into categories such as curiosity, manipulation or mastery because, he suggested, all these behaviours contained similar properties (although there is some inconsistency in this position, as he also proposed that, with age, effectance motivation becomes more differentiated). For similar reasons, he rejected the idea of distinguishing between behaviours according to their goals, such as the need for activity, the acquisition of knowledge, or the acquisition of mastery. White's ideas were developed further in subsequent articles; his later view was that effectance motivation and feelings of efficacy were related to single transactions with the environment, while competence and a sense of competence were the result of a series of successful transactions (White 1963).

White drew attention to the relevance of motivation to development, and indicated that some motives did not involve drive reduction. However, he did not provide a clear definition of his constructs. At his most specific he proposed that competence motivation could be inferred from behaviour that shows 'lasting focalization and that has the characteristics of exploration and experimentation' (White 1959: 323). White's conception of motivation was broadly based. Goal-directed behaviour was seen in general terms, the motive force being regarded as intrinsic rather than extrinsic. He also believed that these motive forces increased children's skills and abilities, and that it is a component of many child activities.

Hunt's cognitive-motivational perspective

Hunt (1965) was also interested in the relevance of motivation to our understanding of development. He provided a synthesis between the theories of Piaget and those of cognitive psychology by suggesting that motivated behaviour is initiated by incongruity with a standard. This could be a physiological standard as in the case of hunger and thirst, or a psychological standard as in the case of cognitive schemata. His distinction between intrinsic and other forms of motivation focused on whether motivation was a result of factors external or internal to the information-processing system; thus, intrinsic motivation was believed to be the result of cognitive processes and not physiological deficits. In Hunt's words, 'an optimal standard of incongruity supplies a motivation for behaviour change and learning that is inherent within the organism's information interaction with its circumstances' (1965: 227). It was also supposed that, because the relationship between motivation and incongruity was curvilinear, the highest degree of motivation would be elicited by an optimal degree of incongruity.

Hunt drew together different ideas to formulate proposals about the way intrinsic motivation develops during infancy. For the first five or six months he supposed that when a stimulus changes, attention is directed to the new event. Thus, young infants' standards of reference are extrinsic rather than intrinsic. In the second phase, infants make some progress to an intrinsic standard in the sense that they become motivated to maintain perceptual contact with stimuli or events which are recognized. A cognitive transformation is supposed to bring about the third phase, the result being a motivation to capture novel stimuli rather than recapture familiar ones. During this phase, motivation becomes influenced by the degree of incongruity between an internal standard and the external stimulus.

Thus, Hunt supposed that motivation is generated by homeostatic mechanisms, and that a motivation to investigate and find out is based on incongruity. Furthermore, Hunt's ideas suggest that resolution of incongruity will lead to a change in existing cognitive structures. In contrast to White's view that effectance motivation is a unidirectional force for competence, Hunt saw competence as being a product of cognitive processes. However, Hunt shared White's perspective in seeing intrinsic motivation as a basic process which could be expressed in a variety of behavioural forms.

Ulvund (1980) has discussed the relation between cognition and motivation in a way similar to Hunt. Ulvund also suggests that measures of competence reflect both cognitive and motivational processes and that 'cognition and motivation are two closely intertwined processes, and in early infancy they can probably not be identified as two separate processes in operation' (1980: 26). Furthermore, he suggests that development will be facilitated by a highly variable environment, which will increase the probability of infants encountering stimulation that is optimally discrepant with their cognitive schema.

Learning and motivational processes

A number of perspectives have considered motivation to be a product of learning (see also Heckhausen, this volume, chapter 4). Papoušek (1969) has reported that young infants will act in a way that produces effects on their environment even though there may be no reward except a successful outcome. Watson (1966, 1972) claimed that infants' recognition of the relation between their actions and some contingent response elicits pleasure. Watson also proposed that experience of such contingencies results in 'contingency awareness', which may increase motivation and facilitate learning in other circumstances. Karniol (1989) has emphasized that feedback must be seen in relation to infants' capacities. In particular, she proposes that changes in manipulative skills will, through feedback and contingency, also produce changes in the infant's awareness of his or her capacities.

A different emphasis has come from Lewis and Goldberg, who consider contingencies in mother–infant social interaction (Goldberg 1975; Lewis and Goldberg 1969). They hypothesized that when infants learn contingencies between their actions and some response, they are not simply learning a specific relationship, but are also learning that they can affect their environment. Lewis and Goldberg have suggested that learning, or a failure to learn, this relationship can influence cognitive development in two ways. First, learning the effect of their actions could increase infants' exploration and investigation, which in turn alters infants' experiences. Second, there may be a change in the way infants process sensory information, because they are aware of the possibility that their actions have an effect on the environment.

Some support for the idea that motivation is influenced by learning comes from intervention programmes. Tutoring families to foster children's feelings of mastery has been found to improve performance on a learning task (Ramey et al. 1975). Thus, the suggestion coming out of learning theories is that discovering the effectiveness of one's own actions may lead to a general motive that results in higher levels of investigation and of processing information, which in turn may lead to cognitive development.

Harter's model of motivation

Harter has employed the terms 'effectance motivation', 'intrinsic motivation' and 'mastery motivation' when discussing children's behaviour. 'Mastery motivation' is considered by her to be in part a product of social learning, and is defined as a 'desire to solve cognitively challenging problems for the gratification inherent in discovering the solution' (Harter 1975: 370). Behaviours which are claimed to exhibit this include curiosity, preference for challenge, internal criteria for success, and working for one's own satisfaction.

In later articles, Harter (1978, 1981) proposes a model in which effectance motivation leads to mastery attempts and in which different components of effectance motivation are identified: cognitive, interpersonal and motor competencies. It is suggested that effectance motivation has two sources, an instinctive desire to have an effect, and an acquired motivational drive. The latter is hypothesized to become internalized during development so that motivation is less dependent on the praise and encouragement of others. This is more in accord with traditional learning theory than White's and Hunt's formulations.

The internalization provides self-praise for a child's own attempts and successes, as well as providing mastery goals for which the child has been rewarded or punished. A lack of praise for independent attempts and for success is believed to result in some children failing to internalize appropriate motives, and as a result their continuing to be dependent on extrinsic sources of motivation. Harter, unlike White or Hunt, has emphasized the acquired nature of mastery motivation, and the way in which the development of motivation may be either fostered or inhibited. Unlike the previous learning theorists, Harter has emphasized the social basis of mastery motivation. In so doing she has provided one of the most comprehensive models of mastery motivation. In particular, she has drawn attention to the different components of effectance motivation and has identified a variety of behaviours that can be examined as indices of this motivation.

The mastery motivation of Leon Yarrow

Yarrow's interest in mastery motivation culminated in two longitudinal studies at the National Institutes of Health (NIH), and can perhaps be traced back to a study of his own (Yarrow et al. 1975) which revealed that restrictive home environments were associated with poorer cognitive outcomes. Yarrow sought to explain this relation, not by simple stimulus availability, but by the motivational opportunities provided in an infant's environment. He used White as a source of theoretical direction and, with his colleagues, developed methods to assess motivational processes.

Mastery motivation was operationally defined by Yarrow and his colleagues to refer to a motive which leads infants to 'explore and play with objects about them' (Jennings et al. 1979: 386). Gaiter et al. (1982) used persistence in mastery tasks as a major index of mastery motivation; this was defined as the proportion of time spent in task-directed activities. Jennings et al. (1979) coded both exploration and persistence in tasks as assessments of mastery motivation. In these studies, three components of persistence were investigated by using three corresponding sets of tasks which elicited different behaviours: those that produced immediate perceptual feedback, those that involved practising emerging skills, and those that concerned problem solving (Jennings *et al.* 1979).

A second study produced further developments in methodology. Yarrow *et al.* (1983) examined behaviour in relation to these three sets of tasks or components. The following behaviours were recorded: latency to task involvement; off-task behaviour; visual attention without manipulation of the task; exploration and persistence. In this study, exploration and persistence were seen as the most important indices of motivation. An investigation of thirty-month children has examined a number of dimensions of behaviour which could be influenced by mastery motivation, such as persistence, exploration, speech and visual attention (Messer *et al.* 1987). Thus, a central measure used in the studies of mastery motivation by Yarrow and his colleagues has been young children's persistence in their attempts to solve tasks, or, as it has sometimes been termed, their task-directed behaviour.

It should be remembered that measures of persistence provide information only about the duration of behaviour and not the sequence of behaviour. MacTurk *et al.* (1987) have presented findings that suggest the examination of transition probabilities of behaviour may help us to understand the overall structure of mastery motivation. MacTurk, Hunter *et al.* (1985), MacTurk, Vietze *et al.* (1985) have also examined what they have termed social mastery motivation in Down syndrome and non-delayed infants. They regarded social mastery as concerned with maintaining and influencing interaction.

The work at NIH provided an important focus and stepping stone for later investigations. The individuals working with Leon Yarrow have continued and developed this line of research and in doing so have produced new findings and ideas about the process of mastery motivation; some of their contributions are present in this volume (e.g. Harmon, Jenning, MacTurk, Messer and Morgan).

Motivation in school-aged children

Studies of older children have generally been concerned with achievement motivation. Mastery and achievement motivation are conceptually related characteristics of children, but it remains to be established whether the latter develops out of the former. Dweck and Elliott (1983) have defined achievement motivation as having three distinct goals: to increase competence by acquiring new abilities or knowledge, to obtain favourable judgements from others, and to avoid unfavourable judgements. Thus, motivation for competence may be directed towards attempting to reach a certain standard of excellence or a certain standard in relation to others.

Dweck and Elliott suggest in the beginning of their article that studies of achievement motivation are distinct from those of intelligence, as the latter are concerned with optimal performance, while the former are concerned with the reasons for performance departing from the optimum. However, by the end of the article they suggest that intelligence could be considered as the way an individual approaches problems, an implication being that intelligent behaviour requires an individual to be motivated.

Summary

From this review of the way that motivation has been conceptualized and measured, it is apparent that there is a variety of ideas about the goal towards which mastery motivation is directed. White (1959) does not believe that specific goals can be identified. He suggests that competence motivation is directed towards general feelings of satisfaction that emerge from a series of effective transactions with the environment. In contrast, Hunt (1965) uses Piaget's ideas to suggest that motivation is elicited by incongruity and that the child's goal is the resolution of incongruity. Harter (1981) appears to suggest that effectance motivation is the result of particular patterns of success and reinforcement in relation to goal-directed behaviour. In this sense, effectance motivation is seen not as motivation towards any one specific goal, but as an influence on goal-directed or exploratory behaviour in general. Similarly, the learning theorists suggest that contingency awareness or a feeling of effectiveness is the result of particular patterns of experience; these may influence the way that children approach problems, but this awareness will not establish a specific goal for the children's behaviour. Yarrow and his associates have operationally defined mastery motivation as persistence or task-directed behaviour towards goals which are contained in tasks presented to children. It is perhaps noteworthy that these latter studies, which have been concerned with measurement, regard mastery motivation as behaviour directed to an end state which is identified by the experimenter.

Thus, most of these perspectives do not appear to be concerned with the way that children identify goals towards which motivated behaviour is directed. Rather, they consider either the way that children approach tasks that confront them, or their persistence in activities presented to them. As a result, there are theories about the psychological basis of motivation, but no specific predictions about the goals or end states towards which motivation is directed. Though this may not be a theoretically satisfactory position, it is a realistic one. The many discussions of intentional behaviour (e.g. Bruner 1973, 1981; Kaye 1982; Trevarthen 1982) have failed to identify sufficiently general and precise criteria which can be used to identify young children's goal-directed behaviour.

A further issue concerns the intrinsic nature of mastery motivation. Mastery motivation could be thought of as being intrinsic in two ways (Yarrow and Messer 1983); in the sense that it is innate or in the sense that it is internalized. White implied that effectance motivation is present at birth. Similarly, Jennings *et al.* (1982) have proposed that mastery motivation is an innate capacity, and that environmental experiences will influence its development. Hunt suggested that motivation is intrinsic in terms of its being the result of the way information is processed. Harter has outlined the way that environmental circumstances can increase or decrease children's effectance motivation and the way these experiences can result in an internalization of the external influences. Thus, there appears to be agreement that mastery motivation is an intrinsic characteristic in both senses of the word. An implication of this is that mastery motivation will not be a stable characteristic, but is likely to change over the short term due to previous experiences of events like success and failure, and over the longer term as such experiences become internalized.

Another difference between perspectives is the relationship between motivation and competence. Yarrow and Pedersen (1976) have suggested that motivation and cognition are inextricably bound together. Ulvund (1980) has gone further with his statement that in infancy the two dimensions cannot be distinguished. In a similar way, Dweck and Elliott (1983) draw attention to the possibility that for intelligent behaviour to occur there must be motivation to perform the activities. The relationship between motivation and cognition, at the scale of a moment-to-moment experience of a problem, could occur so that both motivation and competence together result in the emergence of a response; and on a larger time scale, a high level of motivation by consistently influencing behaviour could ultimately affect competence. The possible presence of these interrelationships complicates the ways that mastery can be measured and the questions that can be asked about its effect on development.

RECENT ADVANCES IN THE STUDY OF MASTERY MOTIVATION

Up to now I have considered what can be thought of as the classic studies of mastery motivation. I will now turn to the more recent investigations and formulations which are present in the contributions to this volume. The volume has three parts, 'Developmental processes', 'Conceptualization and measurement' and lastly 'Attachment and social processes'. Some chapters deal with more than one of these issues, in which case they are allocated to the most appropriate section.

Developmental processes

One exciting feature of recent work on mastery motivation is the growing awareness that it should be placed in a broader developmental framework. This allows a better understanding and assessment of it, and a better placing of it in relation to children's overall development.

In the first chapter of the part on developmental processes, I discuss the possibility that mastery motivation is one component of young infants' attentional system, and is related to habituation and novelty preference. The argument is developed that infants' attentional systems may be influenced by adult–infant interaction, which provides a means of increasing the ability to process information and extending infant attention span in exploration and persistence. Several lines of evidence are identified which point to the developmental importance of these attentional processes.

The significance of the relationship between mastery motivation and self-concepts is highlighted by Jennings. Chapter 3 clearly shows that children's motivation to achieve objectives will change with their developing awareness of their own agency (the sense of 'I') and their awareness of themselves as an object that can be evaluated by others (the sense of 'me'). These developments lead to changes in goals as motivations become incorporated into a more complex social and cognitive system. The importance of this work is that mastery motivation is integrated with other major processes, and as a result we obtain a broader, more complex and more accurate picture of children's development.

The contribution of social interaction to the development of mastery receives attention in Chapter 4 by Heckhausen, who takes a different but not necessarily incompatible perspective to the one I have proposed. She argues that social contingencies provided by adults are fundamental to the early development of mastery.

Heckhausen also presents data about the way mothers scaffold infant development during the second year. This scaffolding provides assistance and emotional support. Heckhausen's careful analysis of social interaction shows that as children became more competent in tasks during the second year, maternal instructions about completing the task decrease. In addition, there are age-related changes in the use of affect. The age at which mothers are most likely to express positive affect about success, is the age at which infant positive affect was rare. As infant signs of pleasure increase with age, maternal positive reactions are reduced. Heckhausen also picks up themes discussed by Jennings, and emphasizes the developmental significance of secondary control which buffers children's self-concepts against the negative consequences of failure.

The presence of transitions in development is discussed in a number of chapters. Jennings believes a nine-month transition involves the development of higher levels of intentionality as infants identify goals, rather than simply respond to the possibilities of tasks. She also suggests that a transition at eighteen months involves, among a variety of changes, the beginnings of comparisons of outcomes with a standard.

A similar emphasis on these transitional ages is made, in the first chapter of the next part, by Barrett, Morgan and Maslin-Cole. Barrett *et al.* suggest that the eighteen-month transition point involves a recognition of behavioural standards. One consequence of this recognition is that children are most motivated for moderately difficult tasks. They also suggest a transition at about 9 months, and argue that infants younger than 9 months will engage in goal-directed activities on tasks with which they are *familiar*. Older infants are supposed to be able to engage in goal-directed activities with *unfamiliar* tasks. Supporting evidence comes from a study of infants who were learning to activate a display. Both 6-month and 12-month-olds could produce an effect by touching a manipulanda, and this was accompanied by similar pleasure at both ages.

I would put forward a slightly different perspective about the nine-month transition, which was implicit in an earlier formulation (Messer *et al.* 1986). My suggestion would be that the 6-month-old is unaware of the goals present in many of the mastery tasks that they are given. Consequently, they treat most objects equivalently, as things to be investigated and explored. Thus, at this age the duration of time spent in exploration will assess the child's emerging mastery motivation. I believe that following the transition at about 9 months infants become more able to identify goals, and their goals are more likely to coincide with those set by the experimenter. As a consequence, the 6- *and* 12-month infants, in the study by Barrett *et al.*, may have performed in a similar way because the task involved objectives that both age groups could identify.

In all the chapters discussed so far, there is the argument that mastery motivation needs to be seen in relation to other developmental processes. An implication is that mastery motivation is not a static characteristic, but changes and becomes more complex with advances in other areas of infant functioning. Such formulations call for new conceptualizations and measurement of mastery motivation.

Conceptualization and measurement

Persistence in goal-directed activities has been central to the measurement and conceptualization of mastery motivation; however, this position is being challenged. As we have just seen, new proposals about the development of mastery motivation suggest that persistence across different ages will be a product of increasingly complex processes. Measurement will need to take account of these possibilities.

Specific proposals about assessing mastery are made by Barrett *et al.* in Chapter 5. They suggest that there is a need to utilize a greater range of methods to measure the instrumental (i.e. goal-directed) aspects of motivation, and that there is a need to pay more attention to the affective aspect of mastery motivation, such as pleasure at success. Their study (and others in this volume) indicates that we still have much to learn about the relationship between instrumental motivation and pleasure. As yet, findings do not reveal a particularly strong relation between the two dimensions (Morgan *et al.* 1990), and consequently, there is much interesting work to be conducted in teasing out the relation between instrumental and expressive forms of mastery.

The possibility that the behaviour on a task is a function of task difficulty has been recognized for some time (e.g. Harter 1978). It is predicted that moderately difficult tasks will elicit the strongest motivation, and there will be less persistence on tasks that are too easy or too difficult for an *individual* child. Support for this prediction comes from a study by Barrett *et al.* (this volume, Chapter 5), who found that 15–30-month-old children persist less at extremely difficult tasks than at moderately difficult tasks, and it would seem that by 36 months children may be persisting less on easier tasks (Redding *et al.* 1988). There is the interesting possibility that mastery may be better assessed by persistence on difficult tasks, or by some combination of the measures of persistence on moderate and difficult tasks. The value of this new methodology is illustrated in Chapter 7 by Busch-Rossnagel, Vargas, Knauf and Planos, utilizing it in their assessment of children of Hispanic origin, and in Chapter 11 by Maslin-Cole *et al.*, who employ this procedure in their longitudinal study.

Chapter 6 by Morgan, Maslin-Cole, Harmon, Busch-Rossnagel, Jennings, Hauser-Cram and Brockman, provides a thorough review of the findings and psychometric properties of a questionnaire that has been developed to assess mastery during early childhood, the Dimensions of Mastery Questionnaire (DMQ). The advantage of the DMQ is that data are quicker and easier to collect than by the more usual laboratory observations. In addition, it may be possible to obtain more accurate information about typical behaviour when adults, who are familiar with the child, are questioned.

The DMQ has undergone a number of modifications and improvements. It assesses general mastery motivation, mastery pleasure, independent mastery attempts, and competence. It has satisfactory consistency, reliability and predictability. In addition, differences are found between children according to their developmental status, and correlations have been reported between the 'general mastery' scale and observed persistence.

Chapter 7 concerns the measurement of mastery motivation in children of Hispanic origin. In this investigation, techniques identified in the two previous chapters are utilized. Busch-Rossnagel, Knauf, Vargas and

Planos adapted both a standardized mastery task (see Barrett *et al.*, this volume, Chapter 5) and the DMQ for use with Hispanic children. Both adaptations proved to be successful. Their chapter also discusses the problems and the benefits of cross-cultural research.

The next two chapters concentrate on social processes, which are increasingly seen as an important and separate dimension of mastery motivation. In Chapter 8, MacTurk presents a complex picture of the different developmental patterns in children who can hear and children who are deaf. He suggests that these differences may partly reflect the need of children who are deaf to compensate for the lack of information from the auditory channel. These intriguing findings raise questions about the role of social processes both in the development of mastery motivation and in assessment situations.

As support has accumulated for the validity of mastery motivation, there have also been efforts to develop a more differentiated description of the global concept. Notable in this field has been the work of Wachs (1987), who has suggested that the mastery of physical tasks should be distinguished from the mastery and control of social processes. The findings presented in Chapter 9 by Coombs and Wachs provide support for this viewpoint. Their methodology for assessing social mastery is an important innovation.

The analyses by Coombs and Wachs suggest that social mastery involves attempting to obtain adult involvement in a task, initiation of social interaction, and more positive affect. Coombs and Wachs argue that there are issues still to be resolved in the study of social mastery. The most important of these are the effect of the identity of the child's social partner, the context of the activity, and the need to achieve even more precise definitions of social mastery.

Chapters in this part provide details about more differentiated conceptualizations of mastery motivation. There are proposals to examine affect as well as instrumental behaviours, and to examine social behaviour as well as play with objects. There are also proposals about innovations in measurement: the assessment of persistence in relation to competence, the use of questionnaires, adaptation of tasks for Hispanic samples, and examination of social behaviours. All this should provide the basis for further investigations in this research area.

Attachment and social processes

There has been a long-standing interest in the way that characteristics of the child, parents and the environment contribute to the development of mastery motivation. In Chapter 2, I suggest that certain characteristics of early social interaction will increase attentive and persistent activities. Heckhausen, in Chapter 3, emphasizes the importance of contingent relations in the first year, and of scaffolding in the second year. The placing of mastery motivation within a more clearly specified developmental framework has been accompanied by an increasing interest in assessing the influence of social and environmental variables.

Chapter 10, by Riksen-Walraven, Meij, van Roozendaal and Koks, examines the relation between mastery motivation and attachment. They predicted that there should be a relation between attachment and exploration, as exploration is typically believed to be activated when children feel secure. Because of this, it was thought that anxious-resistant infants would explore less than secure infants. In contrast, it was anticipated that anxious-avoidant infants would, because of their independence of the mother, turn to the world of objects but explore in a less focused manner.

However, their study revealed that only one measure was related to the child's security of attachment, and this occurred only for girls and not for boys. Thirty month-old girls who were securely attached were found to explore more than anxious-avoidant girls. Thus, despite theoretical predictions, mastery behaviour and the security of attachment do not appear to be closely related domains. One possible explanation is that the attachment system has the greatest influence on exploration of distant objects. As a result, exploration of objects which are comparatively near to the mother may be unaffected by the child's type of attachment.

A study by Maslin-Cole, Bretherton and Morgan (Chapter 11) examines the relationship of attachment, temperament, maternal scaffolding and social environment to mastery motivation and competence. Attachment security and the social environment were not found to be particularly helpful in predicting concurrent mastery or competence at 18 or 25 months. In contrast, maternal scaffolding activities predicted both mastery and competence. This suggests that the moment-to-moment interventions of adults in children's activities may be particularly relevant to mastery motivation.

A similar conclusion comes out of an excellent study by Hauser-Cram (Chapter 12) who found that certain features of social interaction between parents and children with Down syndrome may explain the lower levels of mastery behaviour in these children. High levels of parental involvement (a sub-scale of the Home Observation for Measurement of the Environment) during infancy was related to lower persistence measures at 3 years. This was interpreted as the result of a directive style of interaction that may impair the development of autonomy. In contrast, the provision of play materials and a cohesive and adaptable family structure predicted the presence of persistence and pleasure at a later age. The work by Hauser-Cram presents a neat picture of the way that intrusive parenting may interfere with the development of motivation, but that supportive family characteristics may promote the development of motivation and competence.

Somewhat surprisingly, the investigations in this section do not find particularly strong relationships between attachment and mastery (see also Coombs and Wachs, this volume, Chapter 9). As yet, the reasons for this failure are not entirely clear. In contrast, there are indications that features of adult–child interaction influence mastery motivation. In general, it would seem that a style which involves an emphasis on technical aspects, direction and modelling is associated with lower levels of mastery, while the provision of appropriate materials and social support are associated with higher levels of mastery motivation.

SUMMARY

In this chapter I have outlined different views about mastery motivation and the way that interest in this topic has grown. The classic views about mastery tended to present it as a dimension of children's activity which is only related to a few cognitive and social processes. More recently, it has been considered in relation to and interacting with a greater range of processes. As a result, we are beginning to see a fuller but more complex picture of children's development. An implication of this more recent perspective is that mastery motivation is the result of a variety of processes: attentional, social, contingent, cognitive and so on. This perspective has moved away from the traditional reliance on persistence as the main method of assessment; other dimensions of behaviour are starting to be examined, and other methods are being utilized to measure mastery. Finally, there continues to be an interest in the way that family processes are related to mastery motivation. These studies provide another broadening of perspective, because they examine the way that mastery is a product of the children's social and emotional environment.

Thus, our motive to find out about children's motivation is providing a fuller and more complex picture of development. There are still many uncertainties and many questions to be answered. This is, of course, the fascination of investigating this topic.

REFERENCES

Bruner, J. S. (1973) 'The organization of early skills action', *Child Development* 44, 1–11.

Bruner, J. S. (1981) 'Intention in the structure of action and interaction', *Advances in Infancy* 1, 41–56.

Dweck, C. S. and Elliott, E. S. (1983) 'Achievement motivation', in P. H. Musser (ed.) *Handbook of Child Psychology. Vol. 4: Socialization, Personality and Social Development*, New York: John Wiley.

Gaiter, J. L., Morgan, G. A., Jennings, K. D., Harman, R. J. and Yarrow, L. J. (1982) 'Variety of cognitively-oriented caregiver activities: relationships to cognitive and motivational functioning at 1 and 3.5 years of age', *Journal of Genetic Psychology* 141, 49–56.

Goldberg, S. (1971) 'Social competence in infancy: a model of parent-infant interaction', *Merrill-Palmer Quarterly* 23, 161–77.

Harter, S. (1975) 'Developmental differences in the manifestations of mastery motivation on problem-solving tasks', *Child Development* 46, 370–78.

Harter, S. (1978) 'Effective motivation reconsidered: towards a development model', *Human Development* 21, 34–64.

Harter, S. (1981) 'A model of mastery motivation in children', in W. A. Collins (ed.) *Minnesota Symposia on Child Psychology. Vol. 14*, Hillsdale, NJ, Erlbaum.

Harter, S. and Zigler, E. (1974) 'The assessment of effectance motivation in normal and retarded children', *Developmental Psychology* 2, 169–80.

Hunt, J. McV. (1965) 'Intrinsic motivation and its role in psychological development', in D. Levine (ed.) *Nebraska Symposium on Motivation, Vol. 13*, Lincoln, NE, University of Nebraska Press.

Jennings, K. D., Conners, R. E., Samkaranarayon, M. S. and Katz, E. (1982) 'Mastery motivation in physically handicapped and non-handicapped children', paper presented to American Academy of Child Psychiatry, Washington.

Jennings, K. D., Harmon, R. J., Morgan, G. A., Gaiter, J. L. and Yarrow, L. J. (1979) 'Exploratory play as an index of mastery motivation', *Developmental Psychology* 15, 386–94.

Karniol, R. (1989) 'The role of manipulative stages in the infant's acquisition of perceived control over objects', *Developmental Review* 9, 205–33.

Kaye, K. (1982) *The Mental and Social Life of Babies*, Brighton, Harvester.

Lewis, M. and Goldberg, S. (1969) 'Perceptual-cognitive development in infancy: a generalized expectancy model as a function of the mother-infant interaction', *Merrill-Palmer Quarterly* 15, 81–100.

MacTurk, R. H., McCarthy, M. E., Vietze, P. M. and Yarrow, L. J. (1987) 'Sequential analysis of mastery behaviour in 6 and 12-month-old infants', *Developmental Psychology* 23, 199–203.

MacTurk, R. H., Hunter, F., McCarthy, M. E., Vietze, P. M. and McQuiston, S. (1985) 'Social mastery in Down syndrome and nondelayed infants', *Topics in Early Childhood Special Education* 4, 93–109.

MacTurk, R. H., Vietze, P. M., McCarthy, M. E., McQuiston, S. and Yarrow, L. J. (1985) 'The organization of exploratory behaviour in Down syndrome and nondelayed infants', *Child Development* 56, 573–81.

Messer, D. J., Rachford, D., McCarthy, M. and Yarrow, L. J. (1987) 'Assessment of mastery behaviour at 30 months: analysis of task-directed activities', *Psychological Documents* 15, 21.

Messer, D. J., McCarthy, M. E., McQuiston, S., MacTurk, R. H., Yarrow, L. J. and Vietze, P. M. (1986) 'Relation between mastery behaviour in infancy and competence in early childhood', *Developmental Psychology* 22, 366–72.

Morgan, G. A., Harmon, R. J. and Maslin-Cole, C. A. (1990) 'Developmental transformations in mastery motivation: measurement and validation', in R. Enide and R. Hasmon (eds) *Continuities and Discontinuities in Development*, New York, Plenum.

Papoušek, H. (1969) 'Individual variability in learned responses in human infants', in R. J. Robinson (ed.) *Brain and Early Behaviour*, London, Academic Press.

Ramey, C. T., Star, R. H., Pallas, J., Whitten, C. F. and Reed, V. (1975) 'Nutrition, response contingent stimulation and the maternal deprivation syndrome: results of an early intervention program', *Merrill-Palmer Quarterly* 3, 89–96.

Redding, R. E., Morgan, G. A. and Harmon, R. J. (1988) 'Mastery motivation in infants and toddlers: is it greatest when tasks are moderately challenging?', *Infant Behavior and Development* 11, 419–30.

Trevarthen, C. (1982) 'The primary motives for cooperative understanding', in G. Butterworth and P. Light (eds) *Social Cognition*, Brighton, Harvester.

Ulvund, S. E. (1980) 'Cognition and motivation in early infancy', *Human Development* 23, 17–32.

Wachs, T. (1987) 'Specificity of environmental action as manifest in environmental correlates of infant's mastery motivation', *Developmental Psychology* 23, 782–90.

Watson, J. S. (1966) 'The development and generalization of "contingency awareness" in early infancy: some hypotheses', *Merrill-Palmer Quarterly* 12, 123–35.

Watson, J. S. (1972) 'Smiling, cooing and "The Game" ', *Merrill-Palmer Quarterly* 18, 323–9.

White, R. W. (1959) 'Motivation reconsidered: the concept of competence', *Psychological Review* 66, 297–333.

White, R. W. (1963) 'Ego and reality in psychoanalytic theory', *Psychological Issues* 3, 1–40.

Yarrow, L. J. and Messer, D. J. (1983) 'Motivation and cognition in infancy', in M. Lewis (ed.) *The Origins of Intelligence*, 2nd edition, New York, Plenum.

Yarrow, L. J. and Pedersen, F. A. (1976) 'The interplay between cognition and motivation in infancy', in M. Lewis (ed.) *Origins of Intelligence*, New York, Plenum.

Yarrow, L. J., Rubenstein, J. and Pedersen, F. A. (1975) *Infant and Environment: Early Cognitive and Motivational Development*, Washington, DC, Hemisphere, Halsted, Witney.

Yarrow, L. J., McQuiston, S., MacTurk, R. H., McCarthy, M. E., Klein, R. P. and Vietze, P. M. (1983) 'Assessment of mastery motivation during the first year of life: contemporaneous and cross-age relationships', *Developmental Psychology* 19, 159–71.

Part I

Developmental processes

Chapter 2

Mastery, attention, IQ and parent–infant social interaction

David J. Messer

In this chapter, two arguments are developed. One is that mastery motivation can be considered as part of the attentional system of infants. The other is that social interaction influences the development of both mastery and related attentional processes. In putting forward these arguments, emphasis is given to the way that attentional, cognitive and social behaviours fit together.

The model given in Figure 2.1 provides a framework for the structure of the review. A brief outline is now given to signpost the way through a more detailed examination of the evidence. At birth there appear to be congenital differences between infants in their ability to process information. During the first three months these early processing abilities appear unstable, and may be influenced by the characteristics of mother–infant interaction. From about 4 months, measures of mastery, habituation and novelty preference show stability and reliably predict later IQ. As infants reach 4–5 months of age, they become increasingly interested in objects rather than the body and interactive games of the first few months. The parents' ability to sustain their infants' interest in objects becomes a feature of social interaction, and this characteristic predicts later vocabulary achievement. Similarly, in the second year, maternal labelling which follows infant interest appears to contribute to vocabulary growth.

The chapter is divided into two sections: the first concerns the prediction of children's ability from attentional processes in infancy (mastery motivation, habituation and novelty preference) and the second concerns the influence of social interaction on these attentional processes.

ATTENTION AND THE PREDICTION OF LATER ABILITY

This section starts with a review of longitudinal studies which have found a relationship between mastery motivation in the first year and later ability. This is followed by a review of similar material for habituation and novelty preference. Lastly, the relationship between mastery and habituation/novelty preference is discussed. The aim is to show that these dimensions of attention are related to later abilities, and to raise questions about the relationship between the dimensions.

Mastery behaviour during the first year

The assessment of mastery motivation involves observing infants' inter-actions with their environment, in particular their exploration and persistence. It is supposed that infants who engage in these types of activity will aid their own cognitive development by practising skills, discovering new information and developing feelings of competence (Yarrow and Messer 1983). Mastery is often assessed by the amount of task-relevant behaviour. Indeed, it has been argued by Ruff (1990) that the measures of mastery motivation and of sustained attention during the manipulation of objects are assessing similar infant characteristics. It also should be noted that measures of mastery motivation are likely, to some extent, to assess competence (see Yarrow and Messer 1983; Barrett *et al.*, this volume, Chapter 5).

Part of the justification for the interest in mastery behaviour comes from its relation to later cognitive abilities, as indicated in Figure 2.1 by the arrows between exploration, sustained attention, goal directedness and later IQ. A small number of studies, involving observations of young infants' playing with objects, have investigated this relationship. The remainder of this section will outline the relevant findings.

Home observations of 4-month-old infants by Ruddy and Bornstein (1982: 184) revealed that more time spent in the active manipulation of objects during 'a typical half hour in the baby's home routine' was associated with higher abilities at 1 year (as assessed by the Bayley Mental Development Index score and measures of productive vocabulary; correlations of 0.41 and 0.53 respectively). In addition, at 4 months, longer active manipulation of objects was significantly and strongly correlated with faster concurrent habituation (0.60).

A study in which I was involved concerned the relation between mastery behaviour at 6 and 12 months, with scores on the McCarthy Scales of Children's Abilities at 30 months (Messer *et al.* 1986). At 6 months, the time spent in behaviour which involved simple manipulation and exploration of objects (e.g. shaking, hitting, banging, sucking, etc.) was significantly positively related to the later McCarthy scores (multiple R = 0.75). At 12 months, behaviours which involved task-directed behaviour and persistence were positively related to the McCarthy scores. At both ages there were more significant correlations for girls than for boys, and there were more significant correlations at 6 months than at 12 months. Neither success on the tasks nor Bayley scores predicted the later McCarthy scores. In other words, infants' attention to toys during

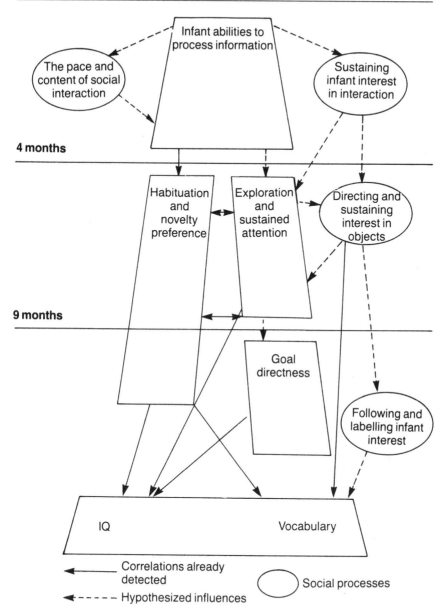

Figure 2.1 Proposals about the relation between infant attention, social interaction and ability

exploration and persistence gave a better indication of their future ability than success. This finding supports the idea that infants who persist in tasks and explore their environment will gain more information, which will in turn facilitate development.

Another interesting feature of these findings was that the behaviours predicting later competence changed with age. At 6 months infants who spent more time in general exploratory activities (banging, hitting, sucking, etc.) had *higher* scores on the McCarthy Scales. In contrast, 12-month infants who spent more time in this behaviour tended to have *lower* scores on the McCarthy scales; the 12-month-olds who engaged in persistent task-directed activities tended to have *higher* scores. We interpreted these findings as being, in part, due to the emergence of means–ends understanding towards the end of the first year; and supposed that when this capacity is present mastery behaviours become goal-directed (see also Barrett *et al.*, this volume, Chapter 5). This transition is indicated in Figure 2.1 with a line representing the general cognitive change which occurs at about 9 months.

The relation between exploratory activities and later competence has also been studied in a group of pre-term infants by Kopp and Vaughn (1982). Attention and exploration were assessed at 8 months by the amount of visual regard and of manipulation of cubes which were given to the infants by their mother. These measures were related to later scores on the Gesell Developmental Examination at 24 months. Similar findings are reported by Ruff *et al.* (1984), who found that object exploration and manipulation at 9 months was related to the Bayley MDI at 24 months ($r = 0.60$) and focused attention during the session was related to later Stanford-Binet scores at 3 and 4 years ($r = 0.55$; Ruff *et al.* 1984).

In older infants (13 months), Tamis-LeMonda and Bornstein (1990) have reported that the longest periods of sustained attention during unstructured free play was negatively (-0.3) related to concurrent language production (often a marker for later intellectual competence). Thus, it may be that by the second year simple attention is no longer associated with competence; more differentiated measures are needed by this age to identify attentional characteristics of more able infants. This echoes the findings of Messer *et al.* (1986) and supports the notion of a transformation in mastery behaviour.

These longitudinal studies indicate that measures of mastery motivation and sustained interest in objects predict later abilities. Infants who exhibit sustained attention during infancy tend to have higher scores on developmental tests at later ages.

Habituation and novelty preference during the first year

Studies of infant habituation and novelty preference have reawakened interest about the continuities in cognitive development from infancy to childhood. Following the recognition of the fallibility of infant tests to predict later intelligence, there has been a growing interest in the predictive power of attentional measures (e.g. Bornstein and Sigman 1986). A consistent finding is that faster habituation and greater preference for novelty in infants is associated with higher scores in IQ tests several years later. These findings will be outlined in the next section, concerned with measurement and predictability. The following section considers whether congenital abilities in habituation and novelty preference predict later intelligence. This leads on to a section that outlines hypotheses about why habituation and novelty preference predict later intelligence.

Measurement and predictability

Studies of habituation have for the most part involved either visual or auditory stimuli. In the past the main measures of attention involved decrement of attention to unchanging stimuli which are repeatedly presented (i.e. habituation), or the recovery of attention to novel stimuli (i.e. novelty preference or response to novelty). It has been proposed that both these behaviours are positively related to more efficient information processing. More recently, it has been reported that the longest fixation time and the total fixation time before reaching the habituation criterion have better psychometric properties than other measures.

Rose *et al.* (1986) have found that total fixation time has by far the best test-retest reliability of all the measures they employed, but it is worth noting there were also high intercorrelations between total fixation time, duration of first fixation, average fixation, and average trial duration. Furthermore, all these measures were correlated with measures of IQ at 4 years (the duration of first fixation had the highest correlations). Colombo *et al.* (1987), in a study of 3–9-month-olds, found that the longest fixation appeared to be the most stable measure. Thus, the infants' initial attention to a visual stimulus and the longest fixation appear to provide very useful measures of attention and cognition.

Bornstein and Sigman (1986) have shown in a review of eighteen longitudinal studies that there are consistent significant correlations of measures of infant habituation and novelty preference with later measures of IQ. The measures of habituation were obtained between 3 and 7 months and the IQ scores were obtained between 2 and 7 years, the correlations ranging from 0.28 to 0.66. Infants who had faster habituation and better recovery of attention at dishabituation tended to have higher IQ scores. The test-retest reliability of habituation measures is in the region of 0.4; given this figure, it is impressive that habituation correlates significantly with later IQ.

Habituation and novelty preference during the first three months

Most of the reports about habituation and novelty preference concern infants over 3 months of age. As a result, there is still uncertainty about whether measures from neonates predict later IQ. If such relationships could be established then this would strongly suggest that congenital characteristics predict later intelligence.

Some studies have found that neonates who are at risk for developmental delay have slower habituation. Kopp *et al.* (1975) found longer fixation to a stimulus in pre-term compared with full-term infants when both were assessed at 40 weeks' gestational age. Similar findings have been reported by Sigman (1983), who also found that differences in habituation rates between term and pre-term infants declined with age. A study by Zelazo *et al.* (1989) on neonates, using localized head-turning to sounds, detected differences in this ability which were related to the risk of delayed mental development.

Although measures of neonatal habituation appear to be related to the risk status of the infants, it is less clear whether habituation/novelty preference measures from non-delayed neonates will predict intellectual development. Visual attention in pre-term neonates has been reported to have low significant correlations (0.29) with IQ tests at 5 years (Cohen and Parmelee 1983), and 8 years (Sigman *et al.* 1986). In relation to these findings, it is worth remembering that in samples of infants with developmental delays there is greater predictability between scores from standardized infant tests and later IQ (Cohen and Parmelee 1983; Siegel 1983). As a result, we cannot be sure whether neonatal measures will predict IQ in all infants, or in only those infants who are at risk for developmental delay. For this reason no specific claim is made in Figure 2.1 about the congenital basis of habituation and novelty preference.

Habituation and mastery

In what ways are habituation and mastery behaviour related? As already mentioned, Ruddy and Bornstein (1982) report a correlation of 0.60 between habituation and exploration, with shorter habituation being associated with a longer time spent exploring objects. In addition, Riksen-Walraven (1978) found, at 9 months, that exploratory behaviour had a correlation of 0.4 with visual habituation (the possibility of a 'widening' gap is tentatively indicated in Figure 2.1). What is intriguing is that sustained attention to a stimulus during habituation is associated with *lower* scores of later IQ, while sustained involvement with an object during a mastery task is associated with *higher* IQ scores.

There are various ways in which this relationship might be explained. One obvious candidate is that habituation paradigms typically employ impoverished stimuli upon which infants cannot act or manipulate. In contrast, studies of mastery allow direct involvement with reasonably complex stimuli. Thus, competent infants may turn away from a visual stimulus in a habituation study after having assimilated its important characteristics. However, when presented with the possibility of manipulating a more complex toy in a mastery task, competent infants may activate a variety of procedures to explore and investigate the object.

Thus, habituation, novelty preference and mastery all predict later IQ. There is a paradox, however, as shorter attention during a habituation task and longer attention during a mastery task are related to later IQ. Even so, the two sets of measures appear to have moderate relations with one another. These findings suggest there could be a common characteristic or causal mechanism which produces shorter inspection in habituation tasks and longer attention in mastery tasks.

Why a relationship between attentional processes and later ability?

There is a complex set of possibilities that could account for the prediction of IQ from measures of attention. One possibility is that the measures of mastery simply reflect infant competence (see Messer, this volume, Chapter 1). However, the correlations between mastery and competence tend to be moderate rather than high; moreover, conceptually they are distinct entities. In a similar way, it has been proposed that habituation reflects one aspect of general intelligence, the speed of processing information (Colombo and Mitchell 1990). Children who are quicker at processing information would be expected to perform better on habituation tasks in infancy and on IQ tasks which involve a time limit. In addition, superior information-processing skills should mean more is gained from experiences (Rose *et al.* 1991). Findings congruent with the speed-of-processing hypothesis come from an investigation by Colombo *et al.* (1991).

Another reason for the connection could be that habituation and novelty preference involves mental representation skills, and later verbal ability may involve a similar capacity. Support for this position comes from a study by Slater *et al.* (1985), who have reported stronger relations of infant habituation with later verbal IQ scores than with performance IQ scores. However, Rose *et al.* (1991) have found that novelty preference in infancy predicts later intelligence when later language ability is used as a co-variate, although the power of prediction is considerably weakened.

The traditional explanation of the link between mastery and later ability is that, other things being equal, children who engage in mastery behaviour will develop cognitive abilities earlier because of their persistence in exploring and accomplishing tasks. In the same way, it has been suggested that measures of infant habituation reflect motivation and/or self-regulation, and that these in turn may be important in the development of intelligence (Bornstein and Sigman 1986). This provides a link between the processes of habituation and mastery. More recently, Bronson (1991: 53) has suggested that differences between infants in visual encoding are due to some infants being 'particularly disposed to continuously be engaged in acquiring new (visual) information', and this appears to suggest a cognitive-motivational characteristic.

Thus, there is considerable uncertainty about the reason why attentional processes in infancy are related to later intelligence. In the next section, I will consider another possibility, that social interaction effects these attentional processes. This could be used to explain the relationship between mastery and habituation/novelty preference, and also the relationship between attentional processes and later ability.

THE INFLUENCE OF SOCIAL INTERACTION ON ATTENTIONAL PROCESSES

In this part of the chapter, four forms of social interaction which could influence the development of attentional and cognitive processes are discussed. These four influences are represented by circles in Figure 2.1.

This part of the chapter is organized as follows. In the first section, it is proposed that the pace and content of social interaction influence habituation and novelty preference. In the second section, it is suggested that sustained periods of interaction may assist the development of mastery motivation. The third section reviews findings which indicate that directing and following infants' interest appears to facilitate vocabulary growth. The fourth section considers development in deprived circumstances, a topic which might be thought to pose difficulties for the views that I have put forward.

A proposal about social influences on habituation and novelty preference

The proposal

Social interaction in the first few months of life appears to be focused on the activities of the dyad (Kaye 1982; Schaffer 1984; Trevarthen 1982). Social interaction usually involves the adult using voice, facial expression, movement and contact to maintain infants' interest. This is accomplished by producing constant variation and change in these activities. It is not until 4–6 months that social interaction becomes routinely focused on external objects and events. In relation to this, it is worth remembering that habituation and novelty preference measures start to show predictability for IQ at about 3–4 months. Thus, if social interaction has a major early influence on such information-processing skills, this effect must be hypothesized as having to occur in the first few months.

What types of social experience could assist the development of the abilities present in habituation and novelty preference tasks? A first answer to this question might be that infants simply need a high rate of presentation of different stimuli. However, a little more thought suggests that a more appropriate experience would involve the repetition of behaviours with changes in content, pace or intensity when an infant's attention starts to decline; this would closely parallel the habituation tasks themselves.

Given this prediction, it is fascinating that social interaction in the first months of life is very repetitive, but that within the sequence of repetitions there is variation of pace, content and intensity (Stern et al. 1977). Parents do not produce the same social behaviour over and over again, which would result in infant habituation and boredom; nor do they produce startling changes of social behaviour, which would destroy the coherence of interaction. Thus, infants are provided with a constantly changing environment where they are challenged to absorb new social stimuli and relate these to previous displays.

Furthermore, the changes in the sequences of repetitions may well be governed by infant attention. It would appear that adults may organize early social interaction to obtain an optimal level of arousal in their infant partner (Stern et al. 1977; Stern 1979; Koester 1991). Stern suggested that with too much stimulation infants will become distressed or gaze away, while too little stimulation makes them become bored and gaze away. Adults achieve an optimal level of arousal by producing new variations on a theme. Thus, in response to infant inattention or over-arousal, adults change one or more aspects of their behaviour (tempo, content or intensity). The phenomenon may even be more general than this, as Bornstein and Ludemann (1989) have observed that habituation processes happen to faces and objects in naturally occurring situations.

It might be supposed that parents who are better at reading and responding to their infant's signals will provide an optimal level of stimulation and thereby increase their infant's ability to process new information. It might also be supposed that certain infants will be more easy to read and be more attentive, and that such characteristics may well facilitate social interaction (Lewis and Goldberg 1969). In addition, sensitive parents may not only be maintaining infant interest in the events during social interaction, but also be maintaining infant state at an optimal level for processing information.

Evidence in support of the proposal

In theory, it is possible to test whether parents respond to infant inattention by altering the pace or the form of behaviour. In practice, the subtle nature of cues about infant attention, the complexity of human social interaction, and the shared knowledge between parent and infant make this a very difficult enterprise. A study which has managed to overcome the problems has been conducted by DeBoer and Boxer (1979), who observed that, during interaction with 4–8-month infants, mothers responded to inattention and negative affect by changing content, pausing, or decreasing the pace of interaction. Thus, infant inattention and facial expression appear to lead mothers to modify their behaviour.

The investigation of gaze aversion has also provided some support for the description of social interaction that has been outlined. Gaze aversion appears to be involved in the infants' self-regulation of arousal levels during social interaction (Brazelton *et al.* 1974; Cohen and Tronick 1983; Stern 1974). Physiological measurements have revealed that infants' heart rates accelerate prior to gaze aversion and return to baseline during gaze aversion (Field 1981).

A recent quantitative analysis of the relation between arousal and gaze aversion during social interaction has been provided by Stifter and Moyer (1991). Moderately active mothers had infants who smiled with a higher intensity, who produced more gaze aversions after a smile, and had fewer gaze aversions which were not preceded by a smile. Stifter and Moyer interpret their findings as indicating that the low and highly active mothers may have been less attuned to the infants' interests.

An experimental study conducted by Riksen-Walraven (1978) has revealed that social interaction can influence habituation. However, it should be noted that the children who took part in the study were aged 9–12 months, and therefore older than the group that is being discussed here. In addition, the intervention programme advised about methods of stimulation rather than the organization of social behaviour. Riksen-Walraven's study was designed to test whether habituation, mastery and exploratory behaviour are related to parental behaviour. Four groups were studied, in three, the mothers were encouraged to develop different behaviours (the infants' attention to their environment in one, infant initiative and interest in the second, and both of these in the third), and a control group.

The assessment at 12 months revealed that maternal behaviour was different according to treatment group, and in ways which would be expected from their group membership. The stimulation programme had a significant effect on infant habituation, while the responsiveness programme was significantly related to infant exploratory behaviour, response to novelty, and learning a contingent relation (see Riksen-

Walraven *et al.*, this volume, Chapter 10). Thus, the study provides support for the idea that both habituation and mastery-related behaviours can be influenced by social experience.

Sustained interest and mastery

Can processes occurring during social interaction affect mastery motivation? Adults who are effective in sustaining infant interest by varying the form and pace of their behaviour will engage in longer bouts of social interaction. As a result, infant interest will be maintained in a complex set of individual social activities. Those infants who are exposed to longer periods of interaction should develop a greater attention span, and should engage in longer bouts of sustained exploration and persistence during mastery tasks (see Breznitz and Friedman 1988 for a version of this argument applied to older children).

Studies of early social interaction have described periods of sustained interest in a variety of ways. Stern *et al.* (1977) have used the term 'episode of maintained engagement' for periods when mothers produce a series of behaviours which are similar in content and patterning. More recently, Schaffer (1992) has used the term 'joint interaction episode'. The importance of these descriptions is the way that they suggest that social interaction is not only a stream of changing stimulus events, but also a stream of events that has coherence by being part of a framework of related behaviours.

It is well established that social activities can focus infant attention during play. Parrinello and Ruff (1988) manipulated the amount of attention-directing activities produced by an experimenter with 10-month infants. Moderate levels of attention direction were found to produce more manipulation of objects. Similarly, Lawson *et al.* (1992) found that infants' social interaction with their mothers usually increases infant attention to toys. Interestingly, Jacobvitz and Sroufe (1987) report that high rates of parental intrusiveness (not integrating activities with infant attention) occurred in a sample which was later identified as having attention deficit disorder with hyperactivity. A study of social activities in the home by Yarrow *et al.* (1984) revealed a complex set of relationships between social behaviour and mastery motivation. Unfortunately, global variables were used in the analysis, so it is difficult to know whether the findings support the proposal being put forward about the relationship between social interaction and mastery motivation.

Directing interest and cognitive-verbal development

Interaction during the first few months seems to be concerned with *sustaining* infant interest in social process. However, with increasing age, infants become interested in objects and events beyond the dyad. This seems to bring a change in social behaviour, with the adults' role being to *direct* or *maintain* infant attention in the world about them, thereby extending infants' attentional capacities and arousing their interest in the world. Both processes would be predicted to increase mastery motivation, and thereby general cognitive abilities.

There is a growing body of evidence about the relation of maternal attention-directing behaviour with later vocabulary and IQ. Ruddy and Bornstein (1982) found relations between maternal encouragement of attention to objects at 4 months and vocabulary size at 12 months (correlation = 0.55, but no significant correlation with later Bayley score). Similarly, Tamis-LeMonda and Bornstein (1989) have reported that at 5 months, measures of habituation and maternal encouragement of infant attention predict both language comprehension and the quality of pretence play at 13 months. These relations still occurred when a statistical control was instituted for the effect of each variable on the other. This has lead the authors to conclude that, by 4–5 months, habituation and maternal encouragement of attention have separate effects on development.

It is noteworthy that Riksen-Walraven (1978) found that maternal encouragement of infant interest and initiative in the environment resulted in more exploration and persistence. Similarly, another intervention study by Belsky *et al.* (1980) indicates the beneficial effects of directing attention. They report that reinforcing maternal attention-focusing behaviour with 1-year-olds resulted in higher levels of competence during play and more focused play at a later age.

Directing attention in young infants is associated with later vocabulary acquisition. This may be partly a result of increases in mastery motivation, which lead to discoveries about objects and speech. A more obvious explanation is that these patterns of social interaction provide the basic information necessary for vocabulary acquisition. It is highly unlikely that this interaction at 4 or 5 months has any concurrent effect on the acquisition of vocabulary. However, early styles of interaction may provide vital procedures for the better co-ordination of activities and establishment of mutually understood formats for conversations (Ninio and Bruner 1978). In addition, certain styles of interaction will continue until infants are of an age when such an interactive process assists vocabulary development. Thus, there may be a complex set of relations between mastery, social interaction and vocabulary development. These possibilities are indicated in the model given in Figure 2.1.

The importance of attentional processes during social interaction appears to continue into the second year. Hunter *et al.* (1987) found a relation between joint attention at 12 months (but not 6 months) and the McCarthy scores at 30 months (correlations ranging from 0.2 to 0.5).

Furthermore, joint attention, during the second year, is associated with vocabulary growth in both observational (Harris 1992; Harris *et al.* 1988; Tomasello and Todd 1983) and experimental studies (Tomasello and Farrar 1986).

Development in deprived circumstances

This chapter has mostly concerned parent–infant interaction which is typical of Western middle-class families. In other cultures, the intense interaction which I have described may not always occur outside of care-giving activities. Such infants develop within the normal range of IQ. For example, one may doubt whether the Guatemalan infants described by Kagan and Klein (1975) receive prolonged interaction of the sort I have described, yet they are reported ultimately to achieve scores within the normal range on standardized tests. Furthermore, children from severely deprived backgrounds can attain normal levels of cognitive functioning when given adequate care (Clarke and Clarke 1976).

However, we should be cautious before dismissing the role of social interaction based on this type of evidence. Recently, arguments have been put forward that there may be universal prosodic features of speech to infants (Fernald *et al.* 1989), and it may be there are universal pro-sodic patterns which adults use as a basis for providing variation in a habituation-dishabituation paradigm. In addition, it should be remembered that given the needs of the young baby for feeding, cleaning and sleeping, the possibility of a complete absence of social interaction is remote. Indeed, Kaye (1977) has described the way that social interaction and turn-taking are an implicit part of feeding a young baby, and the way that mothers adapt their behaviour to that of their baby during the early weeks of life. There is also evidence that minimal quantities of certain social experiences can have a profound effect on development; the exposure to an additional language for only an hour a day has been reported as sufficient for the development of bilingualism (Friedlander *et al.* 1972), and it would appear that only comparatively short conversations are needed for the development of language in children of deaf parents (Schiff-Myers 1988).

Thus, my review should not be taken to imply that infants' intelligence is established by 3–4 months of age or that social interaction is the sole contributing influence. It needs to be accepted that there are many influences on children's intellectual development and that these may increase or decrease a child's scores relative to others. For example, maternal education and socio-economic status correlate with IQ and may partly account for the styles of interaction seen in infancy. However, it should also be remembered that the characteristics of the infant, mother and the dyad which are established in the first three to four months could provide the basis for the child's intellectual profile. Once set up, the social system may have a degree of inertia which makes change less likely.

SUMMARY

Attentional processes are basic to mastery behaviour, habituation and social interaction. Furthermore, all three are related to later competence. The aim of this chapter has been to highlight the possible interrelations between these dimensions. Even with our limited knowledge, there are fascinating pointers to the way social interaction could influence mastery and habituation, but there is also the possibility that influences will flow the other way, with social interaction being affected by infant characteristics.

What are the implications of these proposals for the study of mastery motivation? The first is that we should see mastery as associated with other attentional-cognitive processes, such as habituation and novelty preference. More research is needed to discover the extent to which these dimensions can be considered as separate or related. The second is that we should directly investigate the impact of attentional processes in social interaction, on mastery motivation and habituation/novelty preference. To date, most interest has concentrated on the relation between contingent social behaviours and mastery (see Heckhausen, this volume, Chapter 4). It is possible that adults' extension of infant attention may be an equally important process. Lastly, it is worth noting that, although attentional processes may be a central characteristic of infant mastery motivation, it is not at all clear that this continues to be the case in older children. Although little is known about the relation between early and later forms of mastery, we can be more confident that the early attentional-cognitive processes, of which mastery motivation is one part, play an important part in children's development.

NOTE

I would like to thank the following for their very helpful comments: Ann Clarke, Alan Clarke, Robert MacTurk, Lynne Murray and Martin Richards.

REFERENCES

Belsky, J., Goode, M. K. and Most, R. K. (1980) 'Maternal stimulation and infant exploratory competence', *Child Development* 51, 1163–78.
Bornstein, M. H. (1985) 'How infant and mother jointly contribute to developing cognitive competence in the child', *Proceedings of the National Academy of Sciences* 82, 7470–3.

Bornstein, M. H. and Ludemann, P. M. (1989) 'Habituation at home', *Infant Behavior and Development* 12, 525–9.

Bornstein, M. H. and Sigman, M. D. (1986) 'Continuity in mental development from infancy', *Child Development* 57, 251–74.

Brazelton, T. B., Koslowski, B. and Main, M. (1974) 'The origins of reciprocity: the early mother-infant interaction', in M. Lewis and L. Rosenblum (eds) *The Effect of the Infant on its Caregiver*, New York, Wiley.

Breznitz, Z. and Friedman, S. L. (1988) 'Toddlers' concentration: does maternal depression make a difference?', *Journal of Child Psychology and Psychiatry* 29, 267–80.

Bronson, G. W. (1991) 'Infant difference in rate of visual encoding', *Child Development* 62, 44–54.

Clarke, A. M. and Clarke, A. D. B. (1976) *Early Experience: Myth and Evidence*, London, Open Books.

Cohen, J. F. and Tronick, E. Z. (1983) 'Three-month-old infants' reaction to simulated maternal depression', *Child Development* 54, 185–93.

Cohen, S. E. and Parmelee, A. H. (1983) 'Prediction of five-year Stanford-Binet scores in preterm infants', *Child Development* 54, 1242–53.

Colombo, J. and Mitchell, D. W. (1990) 'Individual differences in early visual attention: fixation time and information processing', in J. Colombo and J. Fagan (eds) *Individual Differences in Infancy*, Hillsdale, NJ, Erlbaum.

Colombo, J., Mitchell, D. W., Coldren, J. T. and Freeseman, L. J. (1991) 'Individual differences in infant visual attention: are short lookers faster processors or feature processors?', *Child Development* 62, 1247–57.

Colombo, J., Mitchell, D. W., O'Brien, M. and Horowitz, F. D. (1987) 'The stability of visual habituation during the first year of life', *Child Development* 58, 474–87.

De Boer, M. M. and Boxer, A. M. (1979) 'Signal function of infant facial expression and gaze direction during mother-infant face-to-face play', *Child Development* 50, 1215–18.

Fernald, A., Taeschner, T., Dunn, J., Papousek, M., de Boysson-Bardies, B. and Fukui, I. (1989) 'A cross-language study of prosodic modifications in mothers' and fathers' speech to preverbal infants', *Journal of Child Language* 16, 477–501.

Field, T. (1981) 'Infant arousal, attention and affect during early interactions', in L. P. Lipsitt and C. Roree-Collier (eds) *Advances in Infancy Research. Vol. 1*, Norwood, NJ, Ablex.

Friedlander, B., Jacob, A., Davis, B. and Wetstone, H. (1972) 'Time sampling analysis of infants' natural language environments in the home', *Child Development* 43, 730–40.

Harris, M. (1992) 'The relationship of maternal speech to children's first words', in D. Messer and G. Turner (eds) *Critical Influences on Language Acquisition and Development*, London, Macmillan.

Harris, M., Barrett, M., Jones, D. and Brookes, S. (1988) 'Linguistic input and early word meaning', *Journal of Child Language* 15, 77–94.

Hunter, F. T., McCarthy, M. E., MacTurk, R. H. and Vietze, P. M. (1987) 'Infants' social-constructive interactions with mothers and fathers', *Developmental Psychology* 23, 249–54.

Jacobvitz, D. and Sroufe, L. A. (1987) 'The early caregiver-child relationship and attention-deficit disorder with hyperactivity in kindergarten: a prospective study', *Child Development* 58, 1488–95.

Kagan, J. and Klein, R. E. (1975) 'Cross-cultural perspectives on early development', *American Psychologist* 28, 947–61.

Kaye, K. (1977) 'Toward the origin of dialogue', in H. R. Schaffer (ed.) *Studies in Mother-Infant Interaction*, London, Academic Press.

Kaye, K. (1982) *The Mental and Social Life of Babies*, Brighton, Harvester.

Koester, L. (1991) 'Intuitive parenting as a model for understanding parent-infant interaction when one partner is deaf', *American Annals of the Deaf* 137, 362–9.

Kopp, C. B. and Vaughn, B. E. (1982) 'Sustained attention during exploratory manipulation as a predictor of cognitive competence in preterm infants', *Child Development* 53, 174–82.

Kopp, C. B., Sigman, M., Parmelee, A. H. and Jeffrey, W. E. (1975) 'Neurological organisation and visual fixation in infants at 40 weeks conceptional age', *Developmental Psychobiology* 8, 165–70.

Lawson, K. R., Parrinello, R. and Ruff, H. (1992) 'Maternal behaviour and infant attention', *Infant Behaviour and Development* 15, 209–29.

Lewis, M. and Goldberg, S. (1969) 'Perceptual-cognitive development in infancy: a generalized expectancy model as a function of the mother-infant interaction', *Merrill-Palmer Quarterly* 15, 81–100.

Messer, D. J., McCarthy, M. E., McQuiston, S., MacTurk, R. H., Yarrow, L. J. and Vietze, P. M. (1986) 'Relation between mastery behaviour in infancy and competence in early childhood', *Developmental Psychology* 22, 366–72.

Ninio, A. and Bruner, J. S. (1978) 'The achievement and antecedents of labelling', *Journal of Child Language* 5, 1–15.

Parrinello, R. M. and Ruff, H. A. (1988) 'The influence of adult intervention on infants' level of attention', *Child Development* 59, 1125–35.

Riksen-Walraven, J. M. (1978) 'Effects of caregiver behaviour on habituation rate and self-efficacy in infants', *International Journal of Behavioural Development* 1, 105–30.

Rose, D. H., Slater, A. and Perry, H. (1986) 'Prediction of childhood intelligence from habituation in early infancy', *Intelligence* 10, 252–63.

Rose, S. A., Feldman, J. F., Wallace, I. F. and Cohen, P. (1991) 'Language: a partial link between infant attention and later intelligence', *Developmental Psychology* 27, 798–805.

Ruddy, M. G. and Bornstein, M. H. (1982) 'Cognitive correlates of infants' attention and maternal stimulation over the first year of life', *Child Development* 53, 183–8.

Ruff, H. (1990) 'Individual difference in sustained attention during infancy', in J. Colombo and J. Fagan (eds) *Individual Differences in Infancy*, Hillsdale, NJ, Erlbaum.

Ruff, H. A. (1984) 'Infants' manipulative exploration of objects: effects of age and object characteristics', *Developmental Psychology* 20, 9–20.

Ruff, H. A., McCaton, C., Kurtzberg, D. and Vaughan, H. G. (1984) 'Preterm infants' manipulative exploration of objects', *Child Development* 55, 1166–73.

Schaffer, H. R. (1984) *The Child's Entry into a Social World*, London, Academic Press.

Schaffer, H. R. (1992) 'Joint involvement episodes as context for development', in H. McGurk (ed.) *Childhood Social Development*, Hove, Erlbaum.

Schiff-Myers, N. (1988) 'Hearing children of deaf parents', in D. Bishop and K. Mogford (eds) *Language Development in Exceptional Circumstances*, Edinburgh, Churchill Livingstone.

Siegel, L. S. (1983) 'Correction for prematurity and its consequences for the assessment of the very low birth weight infant', *Child Development* 54, 1176–88.

Sigman, M. D. (1983) 'Individual differences in infant attention: relations to birth status and intelligence at five years', in T. Field (ed.) *Infant Born at Risk: Physiological, Perceptual and Cognitive Processes*, New York, Grune Stratton.

Sigman, M., Cohen, S. E., Beckwith, L. and Parmelee, A. H. (1986) 'Infant attention in relation to intellectual abilities in childhood', *Developmental Psychology* 22, 788–92.

Slater, A., Cooper, R., Rose, D. and Perry, H. (1985) 'The relationship between infant attention and learning, and linguistic and cognitive abilities at 18 months and 4.5 years', paper presented at the ISSBD meeting, Tours, France.

Stern, D. N. (1974) 'Mother and infant at play', in M. Lewis and R. Rosenblum (eds) *Effect of the Infant on its Caregiver*, New York, Wiley.

Stern, D. (1979) *The First Relationship*, London, Fontana.

Stern, D. N., Beebe, B., Jaffe, J. and Bennett, S. L. (1977) 'The infant's stimulus world during social interaction', in H. R. Schaffer (ed.) *Studies in Mother-Infant Interaction*, London, Academic Press.

Stifter, C. A. and Moyer, D. (1991) 'The regulation of positive affect: gaze aversion activity during mother-infant interaction', *Infant Behavior and Development* 14, 111–23.

Tamis-LeMonda, C. S. and Bornstein, M. H. (1989) 'Habituation and maternal encouragement of attention in infancy as predictors of toddler language, play, and representational competence', *Child Development* 60, 738–51.

Tamis-LeMonda, C. S. and Bornstein, M. H. (1990) 'Language, play, and attention at one year', *Infant Behavior and Development* 13, 85–98.

Tomasello, M. and Todd, J. (1983) 'Joint attention and lexical acquisition style', *First Language* 4, 197–212.

Tomasello, M. and Farrar, M. J. (1986) 'Joint attention and early language', *Child Development* 57, 1454–63.

Trevarthen, C. (1982) 'The primary motives for cooperative understanding', in G. Butterworth and P. Light (eds) *Social Cognition*, Brighton, Harvester.

Yarrow, L. J. and Messer, D. J. (1983) 'Motivation and cognition in infancy', in M. Lewis (ed.) *Origins of Intelligence*, 2nd edition, New York, Plenum.

Yarrow, L. J., MacTurk, R. H., Vietze, P. M., McCarthy, M. E., Klein, R. P. and McQuiston, S. (1984) 'Development course of parental stimulation and its relationship to mastery motivation during infancy', *Development Psychology* 20, 492–503.

Zelazo, P. R., Weiss, M. J., Papageorgiou, A. N. and Laplante, D. P. (1989) 'Recovery and dishabituation of sound localisation among normal-, moderate- and high-risk newborns: discriminant validity', *Infant Behavior and Development* 12, 321–40.

Chapter 3

Mastery motivation and the formation of self-concept from infancy through early childhood

Kay Donahue Jennings

Mastery motivation is a major impetus in the formation of children's early self-concept. In the self-concept literature, a fundamental distinction is made between the self as actor and the self as an object to be known by others and evaluated. This distinction is frequently referred to as 'the I' and 'the me' (Harter 1983; James 1890; Lewis and Brooks-Gunn 1979). It is through acting upon the environment that the infant becomes aware of the self as agent, which is one of the first steps in self-concept formation (the self as 'I'); this begins in the first year of life. The self as 'me' develops later – beginning in the second year of life.

Mastery motivation is concerned with infants' active attempts to interact with the world. This chapter examines how infants' experiences prompted by mastery motivation affect the construction of self-concept, and, conversely, how the development of self-concept affects the expression of mastery motivation.

The chapter places mastery motivation in a broader theoretical context than is usually considered. It begins with brief overviews of the constructs of self-concept and mastery motivation. These constructs are usually viewed in isolation; instead, the focus here is on the overlap and relationship between the two. Models are presented that graphically illustrate the interplay of self-concept and mastery motivation in development. These models change with age, and possible mechanisms of change are presented.

OVERVIEW OF SELF-CONCEPT

The self as actor or subject – the 'I'

This aspect of self has been described as the existential self (Lewis and Brooks-Gunn 1979) or executive self (e.g. Kagan 1981) because the 'I' directly perceives and acts upon the environment and directly experiences the results of interaction. It is the 'I' that knows, feels, wants and does. As Epstein (1991) describes, scientific study of the 'I' has been problematic. Indeed, James (1890) felt that the 'I' should be left to the study of philosophy and that only the 'me' could be scientifically studied. It has been difficult to conceptualize the 'I' without postulating some form of homunculus.

Recent cognitive theories suggest a more satisfactory way of studying the 'I'. The two major theoretical approaches can be described as information-processing and structural (Connell and Wellborn 1991). In the information-processing approach, the 'I' is conceptualized as the executive or operating system. The executive system organizes mental activities and behaviour in a hierarchical fashion with lower-order concepts or systems under the control of higher-order ones. Consciousness, or the sense of 'I', then can be defined as one's awareness of one's own executive system (Bretherton 1991; Johnson-Laird 1983). In the structural approach, emphasis is placed on the theories themselves rather than the organizing process. As an example of the structural approach, Epstein (1991) defines the 'I' (the 'self as agent') as the individual's meta-theory, which contains more specific theories, or beliefs, about the relations of self-initiated actions to outcomes. These cognitive approaches have a variety of roots including Heider's naive psychology, attribution theory, and scripts and schemata (Cranach *et al.* 1985; Eiser 1985; Heider 1958).

The self as object – the 'me'

This aspect of the self can be conceptualized as a set of ideas about the self as an *object* of one's knowledge, or people's view of themselves (Harter 1983). It is sometimes referred to as the categorical self because the child must develop categories to define the self (Lewis and Brooks-Gunn 1979). The self as object includes more objective knowledge of the self, such as facial recognition, categorization of one's gender and race, as well as self-evaluation of one's abilities, goodness and general worth. This aspect of self cannot develop until the child is aware of the self as an object, that is, as a separate entity that can be observed and evaluated by others.

OVERVIEW OF MASTERY MOTIVATION

Mastery motivation is the motivation to master the environment. This motivation is inferred when the apparent intent of an action or activity is to explore (gain knowledge), influence (cause an auditory or visual display) or control the physical environment (achieve a desired goal or outcome). Adopting the constructionist view of Piaget, White and others, we view mastery motivation as intrinsic, that is, part of the inborn 'wiring'. Accordingly, mastery behaviours are viewed as inherently pleasurable and, thus, engaged in for their own sake without immediate biological or social reward. These mastery behaviours play a central role in the child's constructing a view of his or her world.

The construct of mastery motivation has been based primarily upon theoretical work by White (1959), Hunt (1965) and Harter (1981). Action theory is a related conceptual framework that focuses upon understanding actions (i.e. behaviour) in terms of their intentions or goals (Frese and Sabini 1985). Action theory has received relatively little attention in the field of mastery motivation, probably because it has focused on older children and adults, whereas the field of mastery motivation has focused on infants and very young children.

RELATIONSHIP BETWEEN MASTERY MOTIVATION AND SELF-CONCEPT: TWO DEVELOPMENTAL MODELS

Recent work on the development of the construct of self may provide a framework on which to pin down the construct of mastery motivation. One attractive possibility is conceptualizing mastery motivation as part of the executive function, that is, as part of the 'I', the self as actor. Mastery motivation would be that part of the executive function that decides how much effort and resources to allocate to actions or tasks in which the goal is to master the environment.

Mastery motivation and self-concept are thus partially overlapping theoretical constructs. Two general developmental models of the relations among self-concept, mastery motivation, perceived outcome and emotions are presented in Figure 3.1. Model A represents these relationships in infancy prior to about 18 months of age. Model B is more complex and represents these relationships after 18 months, when the toddler has developed an awareness of self as object and is able to use standards. In both models, motivation is conceptualized as part of the 'I', that is, as part of the executive system.

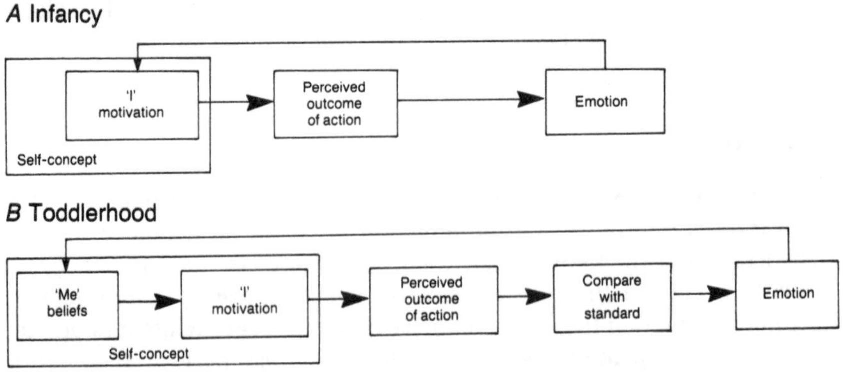

A Infancy

B Toddlerhood

Figure 3.1 Model of mastery motivation and self-concept during infancy (3–18 months) and toddlerhood (after 18 months)

Looking first at Model A, mastery motivation, experienced as the 'I' part of self-concept, leads to an action and a perceived outcome. This outcome, in turn, produces an emotion, which feeds back to the self-concept and either increases or decreases the motivation to engage in similar mastery behaviours in the future.

In Model B, a more complex feedback loop is indicated. Furthermore, the self-concept now consists of both the 'I' and the 'me'. Mastery motivation continues to be part of the 'I'. The 'me' contains various beliefs about the self; the relevant beliefs for mastery motivation include (eventually) beliefs about ability and control of outcome. The other change is the child's new-found ability to compare with a standard. The child can now compare the outcome obtained with the outcome expected, and this comparison determines the emotion experienced in mastery situations. This emotion then feeds back to the self-concept but no longer directly affects the motivation to engage in similar mastery behaviours. Instead, this emotion (and the results of comparisons with a standard) influences relevant beliefs about the self. These beliefs then either increase or decrease the motivation to engage in similar mastery behaviours in the future.

The above two models are very general, and developmental changes occur within each. Changes in the simpler model eventually result in the paradigm switch to the second, more complex model. The right-hand side of these models contain the traditional concerns of the field of mastery motivation: the investment of effort into producing an outcome, the comparison to a standard, and accompanying emotion. The left-hand side of these models contain the self-concept.

DEVELOPMENT OF MASTERY MOTIVATION AND SELF-CONCEPT

The aspects of the environment that elicit mastery behaviours change with development. This occurs because the intent of mastery behaviours changes as the infant focuses on different types of outcome. Cognitive changes and increasing motor capacities underlie this development. These developmental steps were originally outlined in Jennings (1991); they are based upon earlier empirical work that sought to differentiate facets of mastery motivation (Jennings *et al.* 1984, 1988; Messer *et al.* 1986; Morgan and Harmon 1984; Yarrow *et al.* 1982). Although these developmental steps are presented as a sequence, earlier steps are retained as the infant matures, leading to an increasingly differentiated system of mastery motivation with multiple components.

Only those aspects of self-concept that are most relevant to mastery motivation are discussed. For the development of the 'I', discussion focuses on volition, one of three avenues of experience cited by James

(1890). For the development of the 'me', discussion focuses on what Damon and Hart (1982) call the active aspect of self (that is, views of one's capabilities and typical activities).

The age demarcations given below are somewhat arbitrary but provide an order of skill development. The emergence of specific abilities has been pegged at different ages from study to study. In part, this is because children sometimes reveal an understanding in one domain of behaviour before they show it in another. Depending upon whether the researcher is attending to task engagement (or avoidance), emotional expression or verbal statements, different conclusions can be reached.

From birth to about 9 months

Mastery motivation – attend to the novel

Almost from birth, infants find novel objects visually attractive, and later they also explore them orally and manually (Frantz et al. 1975; Keller et al. 1987). The consequence of these activities is to make the novel familiar. The accompanying affect while exploring the novel is interest, which is marked by specific facial features (Izard et al. 1980; Sullivan and Lewis 1989).

Mastery motivation – influence the environment

By about 2 months of age, many infants are aware of contingency relations between their actions and environmental events. At first infants are aware of contingency only when the environmental effect is produced by a single action or repetitions of a single action. Later they can detect contingency produced by more complex actions. Infants show increased excitement and enjoyment when an interesting display is made contingent upon their own movements. They do not show the same increase when the display is not contingent on their own movements (Sullivan and Lewis 1989; Watson and Ramey 1972). Shaking and banging toys are the predominant form of action at 6 months, decreasing in frequency by 12 months (Yarrow et al. 1983). The accompanying affect is often joy, as indicated by broad smiles and laughter (Sullivan and Lewis 1989; Watson and Ramey 1972).

Self-concept ('I') – rudimentary sense of agency

Sense of agency refers to the infant's awareness of the self as an actor. As stated by Harter (1983: 284), the infant's task is to 'learn that it is an active causal bodily agent, separate from others, who are also active causal bodily agents'.

By 3 months of age, infants' emerging abilities to recognize their own agency are readily apparent in their reactions to contingent feedback from people and objects (Lewis and Michalson 1983; Stern 1977). Since the emotional reaction occurs only when the display is contingent upon the infant's own movement, the inference of some sense of agency and pleasure in exercising agency is readily made.

Self-concept ('me') – precursors of self as object

Visual self-recognition has been the traditional means of assessing whether infants have developed a notion of the self as object (see Harter 1983 for a review of these studies). These studies indicate that visual self-recognition begins only near the end of the first year of life.

Development from about 9 months to 18 months

Mastery motivation – control the environment (achieve a simple goal)

By about 9 months, many infants become capable of separating means from ends and thus of a higher level of intentionality. That is, infants can maintain a salient goal or simple outcome, and engage in an action different from the goal to obtain the goal (see Barrett et al., this volume, Chapter 5; Messer et al. 1986; Piaget 1954). At first, this new ability is demonstrated mainly in detour problems, when infants must use indirect means to obtain an attractive object (or goal) that cannot be accessed by a direct reach. Later, infants are able to maintain a simple conceptual goal (when the goal may be suggested by the materials but is imposed by the infant), for example, combining two objects (Fenson et al. 1976; McCall et al. 1977). These goals are process-oriented, in that they are temporary end points in a brief chain of actions that can be endlessly repeated. For example, putting blocks in a bucket involves the repetitive action of picking up a block and putting it in the bucket. The fact that the infant's goal is simply to put each block in the bucket (rather than to fill the bucket) becomes clear when the infant runs out of blocks and dumps out the bucket so that he or she can continue the activity of putting blocks in the bucket. The accompanying affect is frequently a serious expression of interest with occasional smiles (Kagan 1981).

Self-concept ('I') – self as agent

Towards the end of the first year of life, intentionality becomes a major component of sense of agency. Sander (1976) describes the period of 14–18 months as the 'self-assertion' stage, when infants begin to determine goals and activities independent of the mother and at times in opposition to her. For Spitz (1957), toddlers' heightened awareness of their own intentionality initiates the emergence of the 'I' experience. Autonomy, as shown by resisting the mother's help by pushing her hand away or saying 'no', can be seen by at least 14 months (Stipek *et al.* 1990).

At this same time, the infant begins to show some awareness of others' intentions and mental states. As summarized by Bretherton (1991), by 9 months infants easily follow their mother's line of regard and pointing gestures. Infants also become increasingly aware that people are animated objects capable of producing their own movements (Premack 1990). A primitive understanding of other people's intentions and desires is indicated by the 'give-and-take game' that occurs at about 12 months of age. The infant reaches an object out to the mother and then retracts it as the mother reaches for it, while laughing and looking at the mother's face (Wellman in press). However, the infant does not yet perceive the intentions of others as a threat to her or his own intentions and sense of agency.

Self-concept ('me') – beginning awareness of self as object

Visual recognition studies suggest beginning recognition of the self at about 9 months of age. At this age, infants begin to use a mirror to locate objects; i.e. when a toy is placed behind them while they are looking in a mirror, they will turn around to reach for the toy, suggesting they are able to recognize the image in the mirror as themselves. At first infants are able to do this only if the toy is made to move contingently upon their movements (for example, by attaching the toy to a wire clamped to a special vest the infant wears) (Bertenthal and Fischer 1978; Lewis and Brooks-Gunn 1979). Thus, younger infants apparently need more cues in order to recognize themselves. The saliency of contingency experiences for infants is also suggested.

By about 18 months, toddlers have developed an awareness of the self as object (the 'me') (Harter 1983); this is shown in several ways. Most toddlers now recognize their facial features: they can point to themselves in a photograph and will touch a mark that has been surreptitiously put on their nose when viewing themselves in a mirror (Bullock and Lutkenhaus 1990; Lewis and Brooks-Gunn 1979). Furthermore, by this age most toddlers know they must get off a blanket before they can pick it up, thus showing an awareness of themselves as physical objects (Bullock and Lutkenhaus 1990; Piaget 1954). A major cognitive advance occurring at the end of the first year is the development of object and person permanence (Piaget 1954). At about 18 months, a sense of 'self-permanence' begins to emerge; that is, infants begin to understand the self as independent of action and context and with some permanence over time. Thus, toddlers become able to 'represent the self as an independent entity, unbound by context-specific behavioral routines, and therefore distinct from the objects or events that were defined by those routines' (Brownell 1986: 38).

Development from about 18 months to 3 years

Mastery motivation – focus on outcome of action chains

As just discussed, by about 18 months, toddlers are able to form some constructs that are relatively independent of action and context and can thus be maintained in awareness over time. One consequence of this new ability is that toddlers can now conceptualize goals that are end points to their activities. Chains of actions to reach these end points can be longer, and the end points complete the activity for the toddler. Accordingly, activities are no longer repeated in an endless loop until the toddler loses interest. Thus, to return to the toddler playing with a bucket and blocks, the toddler can now maintain the goal of *filling* the bucket with all the blocks. This is indicated by a pause or termination of the activity once all the blocks are in. Bullock and Lutkenhaus (1988) document the increasing salience of the end point or goal for directing toddlers' task activities between the ages of 15 and 35 months.

The use of an end point or goal can also be described as the use of a standard to evaluate the outcome of actions (Kagan 1981; Stipek *et al.* 1992). In order to decide whether they have reached the end point in their activity, toddlers must compare the outcome obtained with the outcome (or goal) desired. Prior to this age, toddlers' ability to represent goals, and thus use a standard, has been quite limited; they have been unable to represent any goal beyond a single-step means–end goal for more than a fleeting moment (Stipek *et al.* 1992). The increasing use of standards can be seen in several ways. First, toddlers begin to construct objects (Heckhausen 1987; Smilansky 1968), as shown by their pausing to regard an object they have made, such as a block tower. Second, toddlers show an increase in mastery smiles (smiles that accompany a goal-directed activity) (Kagan 1981; Morgan *et al.* 1990). In addition, they sometimes show distress when an examiner models a mastery task the toddler may lack the ability to do (Kagan 1981). Finally, they begin to use standards to monitor and regulate their mastery behaviour; for example, they begin to build better and taller block towers by straightening misaligned blocks as they build (Bullock and Lutkenhaus 1988).

Comparison with a standard means that toddlers can now experience success or failure at a task. After successfully completing a task, they begin to exhibit pride (Heckhausen 1981, 1987; Kagan 1981; Stipek *et al.* 1992). Under certain circumstances, they also react to potential or actual failure with the emotions of shame or embarrassment (Kagan 1981; Lewis *et al.* 1989; Stipek *et al.* 1992). Generally, however, observers of young toddlers' task behaviour have been struck by the lack of emotional reaction to failure and their tendency to change goal when faced with failure and avoid the experimenter (e.g. Geppert and Kuster 1983; Stipek *et al.* 1992). Pride, embarrassment and shame are newly developed emotions that indicate self-evaluation (see discussion below) (Lewis *et al.* 1989). Self-evaluation thus becomes a major component of the toddler's affective reaction in mastery situations.

Self-concept ('I') – increased investment in sense of agency

At about 18 months of age, infants develop a heightened sense of their own agency, as evidenced by an increase in temper tantrums and greater insistence on doing things themselves. This heightened sense is probably due in part to the increased salience of outcome as the toddler is more able to organize his or her activities as goal-oriented actions (Heckhausen 1987). Also important is the increased awareness of others as active, independent agents and, consequently, a threat to one's own autonomy (Harter 1983). Wellman (in press: 13) summarizes available evidence and concludes that by 18–24 months, 'infants construe others as intentional in the sense of having internal mental experiences of external objects (situations, actions)'.

The heightened importance of agency (or self-efficacy) for older toddlers is shown in several ways. Older toddlers protest unneeded help in doing tasks (Geppert and Kuster 1983; Jennings 1992). They also prefer to do a play task independently, whereas younger toddlers prefer to do the same play task in a social context even when this gives control of the play task to the mother (Roggman 1989). In addition, focus on self-produced outcomes first appears at about 18 months; that is, toddlers focus on whether a task outcome was attained by themselves (Heckhausen 1982). For example, in building a ring tower with an adult, toddlers insist on putting on the final ring themselves, whereas they allow the adult to put on intermediate rings without protest (Geppert and Kuster 1983; Jennings 1992).

Self-concept ('me') – rudimentary view of self as competent or incompetent using absolute (pass/fail) standards

Soon after toddlers develop a sense of self as object (the 'me') that can have recognizable characteristics, they become aware that they can be evaluated by others. This increased self-awareness occurs during the latter half of the second year – at the same time that toddlers are showing an increased sensitivity to standards. Toddlers soon begin to evaluate themselves.

Beginning self-evaluation is shown in a variety of ways. The self-evaluative emotions of pride, shame and embarrassment emerge (Heckhausen 1987; Kagan 1981; Lewis *et al.* 1989; Stipek *et al.* 1992). These self-evaluative emotions emerge as the toddler becomes aware of the self as an object that can be evaluated according to standards. Toddlers show pride at success (Bullock and Lutkenhaus 1988), distress at potential failure (Kagan 1981), and embarrassment or shame at actual failure (Heckhausen 1982; Stipek 1983). Toddlers' spontaneous speech also suggests beginning self-evaluation; these statements usually reflect the ongoing activity but contain evaluative remarks about temporary capacities (e.g. 'I cannot swim'; 'I sing very well') (van der Meulen 1991). Another indication of beginning self-evaluation is that toddlers look up at the adult or call attention to their play after achieving a goal (Stipek *et al.* 1992). Although this attention seeking may simply reflect toddlers having learned to associate a positive response from an adult with achieving a goal, it is more likely to be a reflection of toddlers' awareness of themselves as an object that can be evaluated by others.

These early self-evaluations suggest that toddlers are beginning to evaluate themselves as competent or incompetent. There is some evidence that children may develop positive evaluations of their own competence before they develop negative self-evaluations (Bullock and Lutkenhaus 1988; Heckhausen 1987; Heckhausen 1988); however, Stipek *et al.* (1992) and Kagan (1981) report both positive and negative self-evaluations at 2 years.

These early self-evaluations are limited in many ways. Two-year-olds use absolute standards only: 'Did I achieve the outcome I wanted?' Comparisons with the accomplishments of others are not yet carried out. Thus, 2-year-olds tend to smile just as frequently upon completing a task whether or not they have won a race to see who could finish first (Stipek *et al.* 1992). They seem to use an absolute (task-intrinsic) standard of completing v. not completing the task. In addition, toddlers' self-evaluations tend to be global (a particularly salient dimension for them is 'good' v. 'bad') with little stability from situation to situation or over time (Harter 1983; Heyman *et al.* 1992; Stipek *et al.* 1992).

Development from about 3 years to 5 years

Mastery motivation – focus on difficulty level and challenge

By age 3, children understand more task-relevant information and are able to integrate this information into their actions on tasks. Prior to this age, children have focused only on (1) whether the action or activity was done by themselves (agency), and (2) whether the desired outcome was obtained (e.g. whether the task was completed or the standard met).

Now children begin to focus also on whether a task is challenging and requires some skill. For example, at age 3½, children begin to show more interest in a game that requires some ability to produce an interesting visual effect than a game that produces the same interesting effect with a simple, self-produced action (Schneider 1987). There is also some evidence that by age 3, children show greater motivation when carrying out moderately difficult tasks (with the greatest uncertainty of outcome) than when carrying out very easy or very difficult tasks. Schneider *et al.* (1989) found that children walked faster to middle-sized boxes in order to lift them than to either small-sized or large-sized boxes. Redding *et al.* (1988) found that 3-year-olds, but not 2-year-olds, persisted more on moderately difficult tasks. Barrett *et al.* (this volume, Chapter 5) found that even 2-year-olds may show greater motivation for moderately difficult tasks under certain conditions. They report that 25-month-olds persisted longer at difficult tasks, compared to two levels of easier tasks.

By age 3, children demonstrate their understanding of and attention to task difficulty in a variety of ways. They hesitate, look carefully, and make remarks, such as 'That won't work' (Heckhausen 1981). By age 3½, most children are able to use the words 'easy' and 'hard' with some discrimination across tasks and are consistent in describing tasks they judge 'easy' as 'something I can do' and tasks they judge 'hard' as 'something I can't do' (Bird and Thompson 1986). In a simple, familiar task (lifting boxes of various sizes), 3-year-olds are even able to make realistic verbal predictions of their ability to carry out the task (Schneider *et al.* 1989).

By age 3, children also begin to be able to compare their performance to that of others. Specifically, they are able to engage in a simple competition to determine who can finish a task first. They smile more when they complete a task faster than another person than when they simply complete the task (but lose the competition) (Heckhausen 1982; Stipek *et al.* 1992). Not until age 3½, however, do children appear to focus on the competition as their main goal; only then do they pause, slow down or stop working when the winner finishes (Stipek *et al.* 1992).

Children also develop more differentiated responses to success and failure. Three-year-olds show more pride when succeeding on difficult rather than easy tasks, and more shame when failing easy tasks than difficult tasks (Lewis *et al.* 1991). At about age 3, children begin to persist in their mastery attempts after failure (Geppert and Kuster 1983; Stipek *et al.* 1992); they also begin to frown at failed attempts, suggesting greater self-evaluation (Stipek *et al.* 1992). However, it is not until age 4½ that children smile more during a game that requires ability to produce an interesting effect than during a game in which a simple, self-produced action produces the same effect; this suggests that self-evaluation gradually becomes more firmly linked to competence (ability) rather than simply to efficacy (self-produced) (Schneider 1987).

Self-concept ('I') – greater understanding of self-efficacy

At about age 3, children's view of their own efficacy begins to become more differentiated, as they become more aware of task difficulty and other aspects of the environment that affect the probability of their obtaining desired outcomes. Prior to this, children's all-or-none thinking has led to a global perception of self-efficacy (i.e. the world has been either controllable or not). Although little studied, at about age 3 children appear to begin to distinguish between their own actions and the controllability of the environment, or, in other terms, between personal competence and degree of task difficulty (Heckhausen 1982). Eventually, children develop a highly differentiated system of beliefs about the extent to which the environment is controllable (and desired outcomes can be obtained) and about whether they personally have the means to obtain the desired outcomes (e.g. ability, luck, power; Abramson *et al.* 1978; Bandura 1977; Skinner 1992). Pre-school children are just beginning to understand that their self-efficacy depends upon both qualities of the environment or task and qualities of the self.

Self-concept ('me') – rudimentary view of self as competent or incompetent using relative standards

Increasing cognitive differentiation in self-concept occurs during the pre-school years. Children become more consistent and accurate over time in describing themselves in categorical terms such as gender, age and race (Harter 1983). When pre-school children spontaneously describe themselves, the most salient categories are action categories as opposed to body image, gender, or other possible descriptive categories (Keller *et al.* 1978). That is, children tend to describe themselves in terms of their usual activities (e.g. 'I watch TV', 'I go to school'), acts of competence (e.g. 'I can pick up things', 'I wash my hair myself'), or helpful actions (e.g. 'I help Mommy') rather than in terms of relationships (e.g. 'I have a baby brother'), body image, gender or age (e.g. 'I have two eyes', 'I'm a girl', 'I'm 3'). This finding suggests the importance of action and mastery motivation in the early stages of defining the self.

Although pre-school children show some evidence of being able to think in terms of a continuum in some areas (e.g. task difficulty), they continue to use all-or-none thinking across a variety of concrete situations in both self-descriptions and descriptions of others (Harter 1983). For example, if they describe themselves or someone else as good at doing puzzles, then they also describe them as also good at counting, climbing and singing. If faced with conflicting information at another time or in another situation, the child endorses the opposite label with no attempt to reconcile the contradiction. It is not until early school age that children exhibit even a rudimentary understanding of traits as dimensions (Harter 1983).

Thus, during the pre-school years, children's understanding of their competence or incompetence is still quite limited. They have not yet mastered the concept of 'normative difficulty', that tasks are more difficult and demand more ability if fewer individuals succeed at them (Schneider *et al.* 1989). They cannot compare themselves with others in terms of enduring and general characteristics such as ability (Harter and Pike 1984; Ruble *et al.* 1980), but they have some limited understanding of relative performance, such as who is first to finish in a race. Social comparison information appears not to be salient to children in evaluating their own performance until age 7 (Ruble *et al.* 1980), although under certain circumstances they can use this information even at age 3 (Yee and Brown 1992).

POSSIBLE MECHANISMS

There have been many suggestions on how the environment can effect the development of mastery motivation and related aspects of self-concept development. Socialization experiences by primary caretakers certainly play a role; some evidence is already available about their import (see Heckhausen, this volume, Chapter 4). Characteristics of the physical environment also play a role (Wachs 1987; Yarrow *et al.* 1984).

In addition to environmental influences, it is also clear that infants' experiences prompted by mastery motivation affect the construction of self-concept, and, conversely, that development of self-concept affects the expression of mastery motivation. From early infancy, mastery motivation seems to provide an important impetus for the development of self-concept. Initially, young infants' motivation to influence the environment (by causing audio-visual effects contingent on their movements) evokes a rudimentary sense of agency (and joy in agency) that is central to the 'I' experience. Later in the first year, infants' attention to contingency and joy in agency helps them to recognize themselves in a mirror (Bertenthal and Fischer 1978). Other evidence also suggests the importance of action and mastery motivation in the early stages of defining the self. Young children tend to describe themselves in terms of action (i.e. their usual activities, acts of competence and helpful actions) rather than gender, age or other descriptive categories (Keller *et al.* 1978). Furthermore, children are able to demonstrate an understanding of the self as agent before they are able to demonstrate an understanding of the other as agent (Pipp *et al.* 1987). Thus various lines of evidence suggest the importance of early mastery motivation for toddlers developing a sense of self as actor (the 'I').

In turn, the development of the self-concept greatly affects the expression of mastery motivation. Beginning at about 18 months, toddlers develop an awareness of the self as object and almost immediately begin evaluation of the outcome of their actions and evaluation of the self. These evaluations and the accompanying emotions of pride or shame moderate the toddlers' feelings of self-efficacy. Soon children's attempts to master the environment are accompanied by a focus on difficulty level and challenge. Children's mastery motivation then becomes tempered by their beliefs about themselves (the 'me'), including whether they believe they have the ability to succeed on this task.

CONCLUSIONS

In summary, mastery motivation and the formation of self-concept become increasingly intertwined as the infant develops. Figure 3.2 presents a time line of the behavioural manifestations in the development of mastery motivation and self-concept during infancy and toddlerhood. Between birth and 15 months of age, infants develop awareness that they are active, independent, causal agents; this is the beginning of a sense of

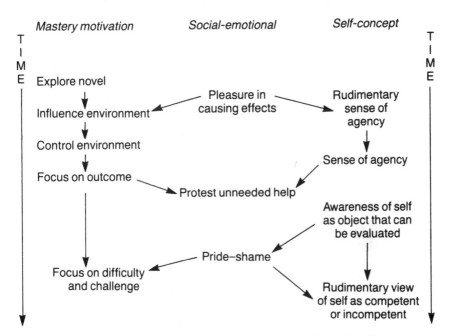

Figure 3.2 Time line of development of mastery motivation and self-concept during infancy and early childhood

agency. By 15 months of age, toddlers generally understand that they cause their own movements in space and have specific effects on the environment. After 15 months, they become increasingly aware of the self as object, that is, as a physical object with specific recognizable characteristics. Toddlers then begin to evaluate the self on various dimensions, including success and failure and eventually general competence. Children's evaluations of their abilities and their chances of success at a task then become an important part of their motivation.

Mastery motivation must be viewed in a broader theoretical context that includes children's self-concept. This broader view makes it clear that children's motivation to do a particular task is influenced by their conception of themselves at different ages. For example, the types of motives that are evident at particular ages vary in part because of children's conceptualization of themselves at that age. Furthermore, the evaluation of outcome varies depending upon children's conceptualization of themselves. These are important issues that require greater attention in the study of mastery motivation both in research studies and in elaborating more complete theoretical models.

REFERENCES

Abramson, L. Y., Seligman, M. E. P. and Teasdale, J. D. (1978) 'Learned helplessness in humans: critique and reformulation', *Journal of Abnormal Psychology* 87, 49–74.

Bandura, A. (1977) 'Self-efficacy: toward a unified theory of behavioral change', *Psychological Review* 84, 191–215.

Bertenthal, B. I. and Fischer, K. W. (1978) 'Development of self-recognition in the infant', *Developmental Psychology* 14, 44–50.

Bird, J. E. and Thompson, G. B. (1986) 'Understanding of the dimensional terms "easy" and "hard" in the self-evaluation of competence', *International Journal of Behavioral Development* 9, 343–57.

Bretherton, I. (1991) 'Pouring new wine into old bottles: the social self as internal working model', in M. R. Gunner and L. A. Sroufe (eds) *The Minnesota Symposia on Child Development. Vol. 23: Self Processes and Development*, Hillsdale, NJ, Erlbaum.

Brownell, C. A. (1986) 'Cognitive correlates of early social development', in G. Whitehurst (ed.) *Annals of Child Development. Vol. 3*, Greenwich, CN, JAI Press.

Bullock, M. and Lutkenhaus, P. (1988) 'The development of volitional behavior in the toddler years', *Child Development* 59, 664–74.

Bullock, M. and Lutkenhaus, P. (1990) 'Who am I? Self-understanding in toddlers', *Merrill-Palmer Quarterly* 36, 217–38.

Connell, J. P. and Wellborn, J. G. (1991) 'Competence, autonomy, and relatedness: a motivational analysis of self-system processes', in M. R. Gunnar and L. A. Sroufe (eds) *The Minnesota Symposia on Child Development. Vol. 23: Self Processes and Development*, Hillsdale, NJ, Erlbaum.

Cranach, M. von, Machler, E. and Steiner, V. (1985) 'The organization of goal-directed action: a research report', in G. P. Ginsburg, M. Brenner and M. von

Cranach (eds) *European Monographs in Social Psychology. Vol. 35: Discovery Strategies in the Psychology of Action*, London, Academic Press.

Damon, W. and Hart, D. (1982) 'The development of self-understanding from infancy through adolescence', *Child Development* 53, 841–64.

Eiser, J. R. (1985) 'Social cognition and social action', in G. P. Ginsburg, M. Brenner and M. von Cranach (eds) *European Monographs in Social Psychology. Vol. 35: Discovery Strategies in the Psychology of Action*, London, Academic Press.

Epstein, S. (1991) 'Cognitive-experiential self theory: implications for developmental psychology', in M. R. Gunnar and L. A. Sroufe (eds) *The Minnesota Symposia on Child Development. Vol. 23: Self Processes and Development*, Hillsdale, NJ, Erlbaum.

Fantz, R. L., Fagan, J. F. and Miranda, S. B. (1975) 'Early visual selection', in L. B. Cohen and P. Salapatek (eds) *Infant Perception: From Sensation to Cognition. Vol. 1*, New York, Academic Press.

Fenson, L., Kagan, J., Kearsley, R. B. and Zelazo, P. R. (1976) 'The developmental progression of manipulative play in the first two years', *Child Development* 47, 232–6.

Frese, M. and Sabini, J. (1985) *Goal Directed Behavior: The Concept of Action in Psychology*, Hillsdale, NJ, Erlbaum.

Geppert, U. and Kuster, U. (1983) 'The emergence of "wanting to do it oneself": a precursor of achievement motivation', *International Journal of Behavioral Development* 6, 355–69.

Harter, S. (1981) 'A model of mastery motivation in children: individual differences and developmental change', in W. A. Collins (ed.) *The Minnesota Symposia on Child Psychology. Vol. 14: Aspects of the Development of Competence*, Hillsdale, NJ, Erlbaum.

Harter, S. (1983) 'Developmental perspectives on the self-system', in M. Hetherington (ed.) *Carmichael's Manual of Child Psychology: Social and Personality Development*, New York: Wiley.

Harter, S. and Pike, R. (1984) 'The pictorial scale of perceived competence and social acceptance for young children', *Child Development* 55, 1969–82.

Heckhausen, H. (1981) 'Developmental precursors of success and failure experience', in G. d'Ydewalle and W. Lens (eds) *Cognition in Human Motivation and Learning*, Hillsdale, NJ, Erlbaum.

Heckhausen, H. (1982) 'The development of achievement motivation', in W. W. Hartup (ed.) *Review of Child Development Research. Vol. 6*, Chicago, University of Chicago Press.

Heckhausen, H. (1987) 'Emotional components of action: their ontogeny as reflected in achievement behavior', in D. Gorlitz and J. F. Wohlwill (eds) *Curiosity, Imagination, and Play: On the Development of Spontaneous Cognitive and Motivational Processes*, Hillsdale, NJ, Erlbaum.

Heckhausen, J. (1988) 'Becoming aware of one's competence in the second year: development progression within the mother-child dyad', *International Journal of Behavioral Development* 11, 305–26.

Heider, R. (1958) *The Psychology of Interpersonal Relationships*, New York, Wiley.

Heyman, G. D., Dweck, C. S. and Cain, K. M. (1992) 'Young children's vulnerability to self-blame and helplessness: relationship to beliefs about goodness', *Child Development* 63, 401–15.

Hunt, J. McV. (1965) 'Intrinsic motivation and its role in psychological development', in D. Levine (ed.) *Nebraska Symposium on Motivation. Vol. 13*, Lincoln, NE, University of Nebraska Press.

Izard, C. E., Huebner, R. R., Risser, D., McGinnes, G. C. and Dougherty, L. M. (1980) 'The young infant's ability to produce discrete emotion expressions', *Developmental Psychology* 16, 132–40.

James, W. (1890) *The Principles of Psychology*, New York, Holt.

Jennings, K. D. (1991) 'Early development of mastery motivation and its relation to the self-concept', in M. Bullock (ed.) *The Development of Intentional Action: Cognitive, Motivational, and Interactive Processes. Contributions to Human Development*, Basel, Karger.

Jennings, K. D. (1992) 'Development of mastery motivation and sense of agency in toddlers', presented at the International Conference on Infant Studies, Miami Beach, FL.

Jennings, K. D., Connors, R. E. and Stegman, C. E. (1988) 'Does a physical handicap alter the development of mastery motivation during the preschool years?', *Journal of the American Academy of Child and Adolescent Psychiatry* 27, 312–17.

Jennings, K. D., Yarrow, L. J. and Martin, P. P. (1984) 'Mastery motivation and cognitive development: a longitudinal study from infancy to 3½ years of age', *International Journal of Behavioral Development* 7, 441–61.

Johnson-Laird, P. N. (1983) *Mental Models*, Cambridge, MA, Harvard University Press.

Kagan, J. (1981) *The Second Year: The Emergence of Self-awareness*, Cambridge, MA, Harvard University Press.

Keller, A., Ford, L. H. and Meacham, J. A. (1978) 'Dimensions of self-concept in preschool children', *Developmental Psychology* 14, 483–9.

Keller, H., Scholmerich, A., Miranda, K. and Gauda, G. (1987) 'The development of exploratory behavior in the first four years of life', in D. Gorlitz and J. F. Wohlwill (eds) *Curiosity, Imagination, and Play: On the Development of Spontaneous Cognitive and Motivational Processes*, Hillsdale, NJ, Erlbaum.

Lewis, M. and Brooks-Gunn, J. (1979) *Social Cognition and the Acquisition of Self*, London, Plenum.

Lewis, M. and Michalson, L. (1983) *Children's Emotions and Moods: Developmental Theory and Measurement*, New York, Wiley.

Lewis, M., Alessandri, S. M. and Sullivan, M. W. (1991) 'Individual differences in shame and pride as a function of children's gender, task difficulty, and parental attribution', presented at the biennial meeting of the Society for Research in Child Development, Seattle, WA.

Lewis, M., Sullivan, S. W., Stanger, C. and Weiss, M. (1989) 'Self development and self-conscious emotions', *Child Development* 60, 146–56.

McCall, R. B., Eichorn, D. H. and Hogarty, P. S. (1977) 'Transitions in early mental development', *Monographs of the Society for Research in Child Development* 42 (3, Serial No. 171).

Messer, D. J., McCarthy, M. E., McQuiston, S., MacTurk, R. H., Yarrow, L. J. and Vietze, P. M. (1986) 'Relation between mastery behavior in infancy and competence in early childhood', *Developmental Psychology* 22, 366–72.

Morgan, G. A. and Harmon, R. J. (1984) 'Developmental transformations in mastery motivation: measurement and validation', in R. Emde and R. Harmon (eds) *Continuities and Discontinuities in Development*, New York, Plenum.

Morgan, G. A., Harmon, R. J. and Maslin-Cole, C. A. (1990) 'Mastery motivation: definition and measurement', *Early Education and Development* 1, 318–39.

Piaget, J. (1952) *The Origins of Intelligence in Children*, New York, International Universities Press.

Piaget, J. (1954) *Construction of Reality in the Child*, New York, Basic Books.

Pipp, S., Fischer, K. and Jennings, S. (1987) 'Acquisition of self- and mother-knowledge in infancy', *Developmental Psychology* 23, 86–96.

Premack, D. (1990) 'The infant's theory of self-propelled objects', *Cognition* 36, 1–16.

Redding, R. E., Morgan, G. A. and Harmon, R. J. (1988) 'Mastery motivation in infants and toddlers: is it greatest when tasks are moderately challenging?' *Infant Behavior and Development* 11, 419–30.

Roggman, L. A. (1989) 'Age difference in the goals of toddler play', presented at the Society for Research in Child Development, Kansas City, MO.

Ruble, D. N., Boggiano, A., Feldman, N. and Loebl, J. (1980) 'A developmental analysis of the role of social comparison in self-evaluation', *Developmental Psychology* 12, 192–7.

Sander, L. W. (1976) 'Issues in early mother-child interaction', in E. N. Rexford, L. W. Sander and T. Shapiro (eds) *Infant Psychiatry: A New Synthesis*, New Haven, CN, Yale Press.

Schneider, K. (1987) 'The development of emotions in preschool children during achievement-oriented striving', paper presented at the China Satellite International Society for the Study of Behavioral Development Conference, Beijing, China.

Schneider, K., Hanne, K. and Lehmann, B. (1989) 'The development of children's achievement-related expectancies and subjective uncertainty', *Journal of Experimental Child Psychology* 47, 160–74.

Skinner, E. A. (1992) 'Development and perceived control: a dynamic model of action in context', in M. R. Gunnar and L. A. Sroufe (eds) *The Minnesota Symposia on Child Development. Vol. 23: Self Processes and Development*, Hillsdale, NJ, Erlbaum.

Smilansky, S. (1968) *The Effects of Sociodramatic Play on Disadvantaged Preschool Children*, New York, Wiley.

Spitz, R. A. (1957) *No and Yes – On the Genesis of Human Communication*, New York, International Universities Press.

Stern, D. (1977) *The First Relationship*, Cambridge, MA, Harvard University Press.

Stipek, D. J. (1983) 'A developmental analysis of pride and shame', *Human Development* 26, 42–54.

Stipek, D. J., Gralinski, J. H. and Kopp, C. B. (1990) 'Self-concept development in the toddler years', *Developmental Psychology* 26, 972–7.

Stipek, D., Recchia, S. and McClintic, S. (1992) 'Self-evaluation in young children', *Monographs of the Society for Research in Child Development* 57 (1, Serial No. 226).

Sullivan, M. W. and Lewis, M. (1989) 'Emotion and cognition in infancy: facial expressions during contingency learning', *International Journal of Behavioral Development* 12, 221–37.

van der Meulen, M. (1991) 'Toddlers' self-concept in the light of early action theory', in M. Bullock (ed.) *The Development of Intentional Action: Cognitive, Motivational, and Interactive Processes. Contributions to Human Development*, Basel, Karger.

Wachs, T. D. (1987) 'Specificity of environmental action as manifest in environmental correlates of infant's mastery motivation', *Developmental Psychology* 23, 782–90.

Watson, J. S. and Ramey, C. T. (1972) 'Reactions to response contingent stimulation early in infancy', *Merrill-Palmer Quarterly* 18, 219–27.

Wellman, H. M. (in press) 'Early understanding of mind: the normal case', in S.
Baron-Cohen, H. Tager-Flusberg and D. Cohen (eds) *Understanding Other
Minds: Perspectives from Autism*, Oxford, Oxford University Press.

White, R. W. (1959) 'Motivation reconsidered: the concept of competence',
Psychological Review 66, 297–333.

Yarrow, L. J., Morgan, G. A., Jennings, K. D., Harmon, R. J. and Gaiter, L.
J. (1982) 'Infants' persistence at tasks: relationships to cognitive functioning
and early experience', *Infant Behavior and Development* 5, 131–41.

Yarrow, L. J., McQuiston, S., MacTurk, R. H., McCarthy, M. E., Klein, R. P.
and Vietze, P. M. (1983) 'Assessment of mastery motivation during the first
year of life: contemporaneous and cross-age relationships', *Developmental Psychology* 19, 159–71.

Yarrow, L. J., MacTurk, R. H., Vietze, P. M., McCarthy, M. E., Klein, R. P.
and McQuiston, S. (1984) 'The developmental course of parental stimulation
and its relationship to mastery motivation during infancy', *Developmental Psychology* 20, 492–503.

Yee, M. D. and Brown, R. (1992) 'Self-evaluation and intergroup attitudes in
children aged three to nine', *Child Development* 63, 619–29.

Chapter 4

The development of mastery and its perception within caretaker–child dyads

Jutta Heckhausen

This chapter discusses the early development of mastery in infancy in the light of a new life-span model of primary and secondary control. Mastery of behaviour–event contingencies, that is primary control, is conceived as a fundamental concern in human functioning. The striving for and development of primary control are promoted by self-evaluative aspects of mastery motivation. However, self-evaluation in case of repeated failure can also endanger basic motivational and emotional resources, and thus jeopardize primary control. In order to buffer such detrimental effects of failure, the individual needs self-protective strategies of secondary control, which probably start evolving in childhood.

Within this conceptual framework, the chapter is focused on three issues. First, the functional significance of mastery motivation for effective action regulation is discussed from a phylogenetic and ontogenetic viewpoint. Second, the role of social interactions with caretakers in the early development of action and mastery motivation is examined. Relevant findings from a longitudinal study on task-centred interactions of 1–2-year-old infants and their caretakers are reported and discussed. Third, research perspectives for the evolution of strategies to cope with failure are presented in view of the concept of secondary control.

FUNCTIONAL SIGNIFICANCE OF MASTERY MOTIVATION

To strive for mastery is a fundamental human predisposition. Its phylogenetic roots lie in the need for competence, comprising non-consummatory drives for exploration, activity and particularly manipulation, which have been identified in various mammal and even submammal species (White 1959). An abundance of studies employing operant conditioning paradigms demonstrated that various mammal species prefer behaviour–event contingencies to event–event contingencies, even when consummatory responses are prevented or not involved (see review by White 1959). Chimpanzees will spend more time with objects that can be moved, changed and made to emit sounds and light than with other unfamiliar objects (Welker 1956). Rhesus monkeys keep returning to mechanical puzzles which offer no reward except the sheer solution (raising of a clasp; Harlow 1953). And most significantly, responding to produce rewards is preferred to receiving the same rewards without responding by both rats and children (Singh 1970).

In human ontogenesis, striving for non-consummatory behaviour–event contingencies can be identified as early as in the first days of life. Neonates have been shown to detect behaviour–event contingencies, acquire operant responses and display anticipatory enjoyment of such contingencies (e.g. Janos and Papoušek 1977; Papoušek 1967). Very young infants can learn to turn their heads after specific acoustic signals when provided with milk as a reinforcement. Significantly, neonates who had learned the operant behaviour kept responding even after they were completely satisfied, and the milk had thus lost its reinforcing potential to reduce hunger. Head movements were elicited by the conditioned acoustic signal, and the infants displayed pleasure upon the occurrence of the expected contingent presentation of the milk bottle. Thus, it appears that the confirmation of an expected contingency was the primary reinforcer.

Watson (1966, 1972) observed a similar motivational potential of behaviour–event contingencies in experimental studies of operant conditioning of visual fixation. He concluded: 'Contingency awareness refers to an organism's readiness to react adaptively in a contingency situation and to an organism's sensitivity in the perception of contingency situations when they occur' (Watson 1966: 123–4). Watson's proposition of 'generalized expectancies' was supported by an abundance of studies, demonstrating inter-task transfer in operant conditioning, learning interference by non-contingent stimulus presentation (DeCaspar et al. 1976; Finkelstein and Ramey 1977; Ramey and Finkelstein 1978; Rovee and Fagan 1976; Watson and Ramey 1972), negative infant affect to non-contingent stimulation that had previously been contingent on their own behaviour (DeCasper and Carstens 1981), and the phenomenon of 'task pleasure' (see Barrett et al. this volume, Chapter 5).

Curiously enough, Watson was concerned about the potential long-term effects of the 'natural deprivation period' during the first months of life, when the infant is incapable of producing contingent outcomes by his or her own directed movements and manipulations of objects (Watson 1966). He proposed that contingency experiences should be artificially provided by suitable technical equipment or expert intervention, so that the ontogenesis of mastery in infants could be promoted to unheard-of optima, never previously attained in the history of humanity. This turned out to be quite naive. In fact, several studies reveal that not only are human infants prepared to detect behaviour–event contingencies, but also human care-givers are 'pre-programmed' to provide them (e.g. Kaye 1982; Lewis and Goldberg 1969; Papoušek and Papoušek 1975, 1980,

1983). Such care-giver facilitation of mastery learning will be discussed further below.

The functional significance of early onset preferences for behaviour–event contingencies lies in their potential to activate the organism, enhance the salience and direct attention towards potentially effective behaviour, and thus promote the acquisition of mastery. Even B. F. Skinner concluded that such phenomena would be difficult to attribute to a history of conditioning (Skinner 1953). Instead, they indicate a basic capacity to be reinforced by the environment, which can be assumed to be biologically advantageous to the organism because it promotes manipulation of the environment rather than passivity.

Human action motivation or mastery, however, involves not only striving for behaviour–event contingencies, but also reflective self-evaluation. Attaining the action goal appears desirable not only because of the intrinsic goal value, but also because successful action implies positive feedback about the capacities of the self (see Jennings, this volume, Chapter 3). In fact, anticipatory self-reinforcement, a fundamental concept in achievement motivation research (H. Heckhausen 1991), sets human motivation apart from animal motivation. Anticipatory self-reinforcement renders human action independent from external control and sets it free for self-regulation. Only in this way can persistent effort be invested in the pursuit of action goals in spite of a delay in gratification, which, in turn, is the prerequisite for time-extended acquisitional processes.

Achievement motivation models have proved to be very useful for research on the development of self-evaluation. Heinz Heckhausen, setting out from an 'achievement-motivation theory designed for ageless individuals', proposed that a defining feature of action is not only its intentionality but also that the action is reflected back to the self of the actor (H. Heckhausen 1982). The extent to which the actor sees himself or herself as the cause of action outcomes is a central feature and even a stimulus to the development of achievement motivation. Two major cognitive advances are developmental prerequisites for self-evaluative emotions, such as pride and shame: first, the centring on a self-produced outcome of action ('self as originator'), and second, the processing of an action outcome as an indicator of one's own competence (H. Heckhausen 1984; see also Jennings, this volume, Chapter 3).

It should be emphasized that in the first stage, when the infant cannot yet reflect upon her or his own competence (or outcome control for that matter), the infant still perceives herself or himself as the originator of the action outcome. Thus, even before a differentiated account of action–outcome contingencies and personal efficacy is possible, the self can be perceived as in control of behaviour-outcome contingencies. During the second year of life, then, the two aspects of control, namely those related to action-outcome contingencies and to personal efficacy, become differentiated. It is then that children recruit focused help from adult partners, and also refuse help when they perceive it as superfluous and thus corrupting their experience of their own competence (Geppert and Küster 1983; Heckhausen 1988). This developmental gain in the second year goes hand-in-glove with an important progression in the infant's conception of self, from the 'self as a subject' to the 'self as an object' (Geppert and Küster 1983; Heckhausen 1988). At about 18 months of age, the child starts to conceive of himself or herself as an entity, which has descriptive attributes and can therefore be characterized in terms of categories ('categorical self', Lewis and Brooks-Gunn 1979). Converging models have recently been proposed regarding the development of self-concept (Bullock and Lütkenhaus 1990; Kagan 1981; Lewis 1991) and related self-conscious emotions, such as embarrassment (Lewis et al. 1989), concern about wrong-doing (Stipek et al. 1990), mishaps (Cole et al. 1992) and broken norms or scripts (Kagan 1981).

The child's ability to evaluate the self reflectively in the light of a given action outcome, however, bears not only positive implications but also dangers. In case of failure, the outcome might be perceived as an indicator of lack of ability. Because of this, self-esteem may be threatened, optimism reduced, future action discouraged, and long-term action potential thereby impaired. In order to maintain the potential to act, the organism needs mechanisms for buffering these dangers of self-evaluation after failure. Such buffering strategies are captured by the construct of 'secondary control' (Heckhausen and Schulz 1993; Rothbaum et al. 1982; Schulz et al. 1991), and will be discussed in the last section of this chapter.

There is, however, a very early mechanism which effectively functions as a buffer of negative emotional impact of failure. This is the developmental *décalage horizontale* (Inhelder and Piaget 1964) of shame reactions (after failure) compared to pride reactions. Self-evaluative reactions after failure, such as shame, do not emerge at the same age as self-evaluative reactions after success, such as pride. Instead, shame reactions are developmentally delayed by at least one year (Geppert and H. Heckhausen 1990; H. Heckhausen 1984). When confronted with failure, 2–3-year-olds who already show full-blown pride reactions express surprise, frustration or anger, but do not seem to relate the negative outcome back to their own self in terms of a negative self-evaluation. Such a developmental delay may serve a protective function. It appears particularly suitable for very young individuals, who encounter frequent failures but also rapid improvements. Under the conditions of rapid developmental growth it would appear beneficial developmentally to favour success reactions over failure reactions. Likewise, it has been argued that even gross overestimations of one's own competence in early childhood are more adaptive than underestimations (see also Heckhausen and Schulz 1992).

CARETAKER–CHILD INTERACTION AND EARLY MASTERY DEVELOPMENT

Social interactions with caretakers play a key role in the early development of human mastery. It is argued in this section that this holds not only with regard to the social facilitation of behaviour–event contingency experiences, but also with respect to the evolution of action regulation (e.g. goal-directedness, persistence) and self-evaluative reactions to success and failure. Findings from a longitudinal study supporting this position will be presented in this section.

Social facilitation of contingency learning

In early infancy, behaviour–event contingencies can be experienced only in interactions with social partners who provide contingent reactions (facial, vocal, etc.) to the infant's behaviour. Caretakers, but also other adults and even older children in general, have been shown to be able and willing to provide such reactions (Kaye 1982; Lewis and Goldberg 1969; Papoušek and Papoušek 1975, 1980, 1983). Papoušek found, for instance, that in spite of the experimenter's instruction not to react, mothers could not help but display a greeting response (i.e. raise eyebrows and open mouth) when their infants looked or even smiled at them. Interestingly, comparisons of care-giver–infant interactions in apes and humans suggest that contingency play and early instruction might be the critical difference in the superior ontogenetic potential of human as compared to ape individuals (Chevalier-Skolnikoff and Poirier 1977). In fact, 1–2 month-old chimpanzee infants reared by humans were found to display superior responsive behaviour to the care-giver's vocal and facial stimulation (Hallock *et al.* 1989).

It does not come as a surprise, then, that the adult care-giver's sensitivity in detecting and using opportunities for contingency games with infants became the key candidate for predicting inter-individual differences in contingency awareness, exploration, manipulative skills and intellectual development (e.g. Clarke-Stewart 1973; Clarke-Stewart *et al.* 1979; Riksen-Walraven 1978). Much of the research in this area is plagued by the confusion of amount and contingency of naturally occurring care-giver-generated stimulation. However, Riksen-Walraven undertook an experimental field study in which mothers were experimentally induced to be more stimulating, more contingently responsive, or both, towards their infant during a three-month period. As expected, increased stimulation affected only infants' rate of habituation to visual stimuli, whereas heightened care-giver's responsiveness promoted both infants' exploratory behaviour and their ability to analyse contingencies (Riksen-Walraven 1978). Analogous findings were obtained in micro-sequential studies on

the effect of infant–mother interaction on subsequent contingency learning (Dunham and Dunham 1990). The amount of time spent in vocal
turn-taking between mother and infant was positively related to improved
performance on a subsequent non-social contingency task.

Social facilitation of action regulation and self-evaluation

During the early months, intentionality is primarily constructed by the
caretaker, who thus scaffolds the directedness of the child's behaviour.
In the second half of the first year, children become more independent
in striving for behaviour–effect contingencies. During this period of pre-
occupation with object-centred play, which Trevarthen (Trevarthen 1987;
Trevarthen and Hubley 1978) has called the 'praxic mode', children have
been observed to avoid or even resent adult participation, as if no-one
else's intentions are to compete with the evolving intentional guidance of
action in the child.

During the second year, the adult caretaker and the child attain a new
level of co-ordination in pursuing joint intentions with objects. Mothers,
for instance, can now rely more on verbal and outcome-oriented controls
when trying to get their infants to perform specific acts (Schaffer *et al.*
1983). Various studies have targeted adult care-givers' scaffolding and
teaching strategies. Such studies have demonstrated an impressive
capacity in adult care-givers (both mothers and fathers) to generate
instructional behaviour well suited to promote the child's development,
and entail both micro-sequential and longitudinal retuning and adaptation
in response to the child's growing competence (e.g. Freund 1990; Kaye
1977; Lütkenhaus 1984; McNaughton and Leyland 1990; Pratt *et al.* 1988;
Radzisewska and Rogoff 1988, 1991; Rogoff and Wertsch 1984; Rogoff
et al. 1984; Wood and Middleton 1975; Wood *et al.* 1976). However,
these studies have usually been restricted to pre-school or school-aged
children older than 3 years, so that the actual transition period from
other- to self-regulated action during the second year remained largely
unstudied.

The study presented in this chapter traced the child's and adult caretaker's joint efforts in promoting the development of mastery (Heckhausen, 1987a, 1987b, 1988). It was expected that instructional efforts on
the part of the adult are effective in promoting the development of
mastery in so far as they take account of the child's current weaknesses
and challenge his or her developmental potential. This was done, for
instance, by giving the child tasks that matched his or her current zone
of proximal development (Rogoff and Wertsch 1984), by using challenging means of communication (verbal instead of non-verbal) when possible, and by providing needed but avoiding superfluous help. Moreover,
the emergence of affective, including self-evaluative, responses to success

and failure was investigated and potential social facilitation by maternal behaviour examined.

The research was conducted at the University of Strathclyde, Glasgow. The joint task-centred activities of twelve mother–infant pairs were video-recorded at bi-monthly intervals between 14 and 22 months of age. Sessions lasted about twenty minutes. Mothers were requested by the experimenter to try to get the child to do a certain task, and in doing this to behave as usual towards their children. The experimenter did not present the next task until either the previous task was completed, or it became clear that the mother did not see any point in making further efforts. Findings about two tasks are presented: tower building (tower task) and sorting forms into slots on a wooden board (sorter task). For further details about the tasks see Heckhausen (1987a).

The protocols of the video-recordings were segmented into alternating turns of the mother and infant. These were coded with respect to the motivational level of maternal instructional attempts, the child's behaviour, the level of task performance, and infant's and mother's reaction to success and failure. Table 4.1 provides an overview of the variables considered in this report. As can be seen in Table 4.1, variables for

Table 4.1 Categorization system used for behaviour of mother and child

Variables	Mother	Child
Motivation variables	Tries to get child to: Look at task objects Manipulate task objects Attend to her modelling Do the task	Looks at task material Manipulates task objects Attends to mother's modelling Does the task
Performance variables (sorter task)	Tries to get child to: Attempt task generally Choose the correct slot (a) Indicates correct slot (b) Criticizes child's slot choice Fit form into slot	Attempts task generally Chooses correct slot Fits form into slot
Reactions to success	Acknowledgement Enjoyment Praise	Acknowledgement Enjoyment Pride
Mode of instruction	Only non-verbal Only verbal Verbal and non-verbal	

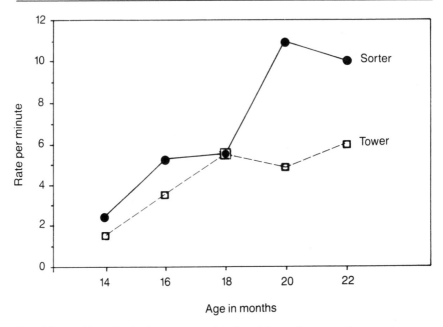

Note: Means of logarithmized rates were plotted and the antilog was subsequently imposed on the ordinate.

Figure 4.1 Children's task attempts: means of logarithmized rates per minute across ages (adapted from Heckhausen 1988)

maternal and infant's behaviour were coded to reflect corresponding levels of maternal instruction and child's task behaviour respectively.

Out of the larger set of findings obtained in this multi-task, multivariable and longitudinal study, only a subset can be presented here. Three aspects of the findings are considered: (1) the developmental progression in task-focused intention; (2) the complementary longitudinal and micro-sequential changes in children's acquisition of task competence and maternal instructions; and (3) the sequentially contingent changes in children's and mothers' reactions to success and failure.

The first aspect of development to be considered is the infants' task-centred intention. Figure 4.1 displays the per-minute rates of children's task attempts in the tower and the sorter tasks. For both, the rates of task attempts increased significantly across the longitudinal span, suggesting a developmental progression in the task-focused intentional guidance of the children.

Another indicator of intentional guidance of behaviour is the degree

Table 4.2 Child's persistence in task action

Month	14	16	18	20	22
Tower:					
1 turn	24	49	69	51	61
2 turns	6	14	19	29	24
3 turns	3	3	11	14	**6**
4 turns	0	1	1	8	**10**
5 and more turns	1	2	2	6	7
Sorter:					
1 turn	37	31	46	50	63
2 turns	19	17	22	34	43
3 turns	3	9	14	22	**28**
4 turns	1	6	5	14	**19**
5 and more turns	1	7	14	29	**23**

Note: Frequencies summed over subjects for five different lengths of task action episodes per age and task, and predicted developmental model (**bold figures**).

of persistence exerted in trying to solve the task. Table 4.2 gives the number of consecutive task attempts, which are an indicator of persistence in task activity. The bold numbers indicate a developmental model which assumes an increase in persistence across the longitudinal span. The model was tested and supported by prediction analysis of cross classification (von Eye and Brandtstädter 1988). Inspection of the table reveals that the number of consecutive task trials increased gradually with age. While during the first half of the second year all task attempts included only one interactive turn, multi-trial bouts became more common from 18 months onwards, until at 22 months a substantial number of task attempts with five and more trials were observed. Both indicators of task-focused intention – number of task attempts and degree of persistence – suggest a developmental progression.

The second aspect concerns the relation between children's performance and mothers' instruction. Figure 4.2 displays the per-minute rates of various levels of performance in the children's task attempts in the sorter task. *General* attempts to move the forms towards the slots, *choices* of the correct slot without correct fitting of the form, and completions of the task by correctly *fitting* the form significantly increased in rate across the longitudinal span. These age trends reflect the increasing overall rates of task attempts.

Figure 4.3 exhibits the longitudinal changes in per-minute rates of maternal instructions in the sorter task, which are defined in a manner matching the children's performance categories. *General* requests to move the forms towards the sorter board and instructions regarding the *fitting* of a form in a slot increased slightly but significantly in rate across the longitudinal span. Interestingly enough, instructions regarding the correct

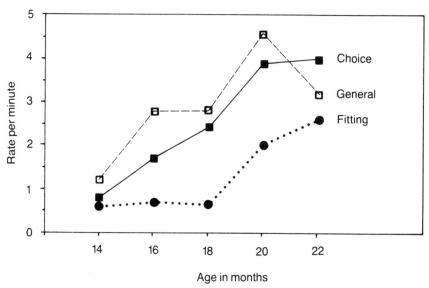

Figure 4.2 Children's performance in the sorter task: logarithmized rates (adapted from Heckhausen 1987a)

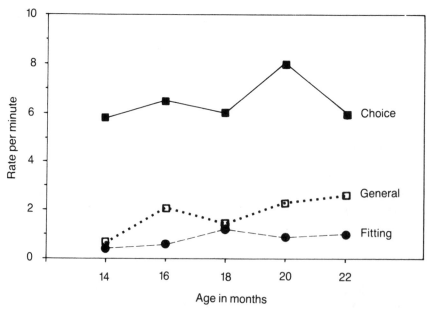

Figure 4.3 Mothers' instruction in the sorter task: logarithmized rates (adapted from Heckhausen 1987a)

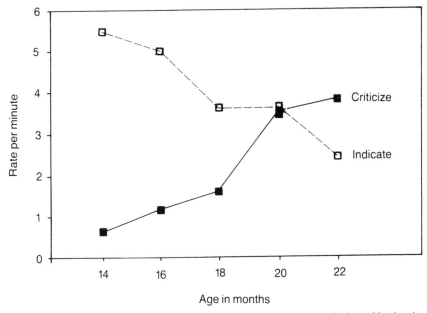

Figure 4.4 Mothers' choice-related instruction in the sorter task: logarithmized rates (adapted from Heckhausen 1987a)

choice of a slot remained stable in rate with age. This lack of increase in choice-related maternal instructions was surprising, because the increasing task attempts of the children should have enticed an increasingly greater focus of the mothers' interventions on this central aspect of the sorter task. However, when investigating the kinds of choice-related instructions in greater detail – as shown in Figure 4.4 – the issue is resolved. It becomes clear that the stable rate of choice-related instructions is composed of two counter-directional and thus complementary age trends. Figure 4.4 shows that the mothers directly *indicated* the correct slot less as the children became older, and instead increasingly *criticized* the child's choice when it was incorrect. Thus, overall the amount of maternal assistance offered to the child for selecting the correct slot decreased with the child's age. Given that the children exhibited increasing rates of correct choice (see Figure 4.2), it becomes clear that correct slot selection was achieved more and more self-reliantly and therefore indicates growing competency.

In order to investigate whether the mothers adapted their instructions by fine tuning on the basis of the child's immediate feedback, a microsequential model on the turn-to-turn contingencies between children's and mothers' behaviour was formulated and tested. According to this model, mothers are expected to address the level of performance which the children have just fallen short of. For instance, given that the child

A One-step-ahead model

B Attainment-of-request model

Child → *Mother*
Child

Mother → *Child*
Mother

Mother	Neutral	General	Choice	Fitting
Neutral				X
General	X			
Choice		X		
Fitting			X	

Child	Neutral	General	Choice	Fitting
Neutral	X			
General		X		
Choice			X	
Fitting				X

Figure 4.5 Pattern of contingencies between maternal and infant behaviour predicted by the one-step-ahead model and the attainment-of-request model (adapted from Heckhausen 1987a)

has just chosen the correct slot on the sorter board but failed in fitting the form in, the mother would be expected to instruct in form fitting rather than in choosing the correct slot. This is called the 'one-step-ahead model' and is displayed in Figure 4.5A.

Conversely, the attainment-of-request model, displayed in Figure 4.5B, captures whether the child has attained the level of performance aimed at by the mother's most recent instruction. For instance, given that the mother has just instructed the fitting of a form into the sorter slot, the child would be expected in his or her next turn to manage to fit the form in. Both micro-sequential models – the one-step-ahead and the attainment-of-request model – proved to fit the data: out of 60 Kappa-coefficients computed, 56 were positive for the one-step-ahead model and 55 for the attainment-of-request model. Thus, maternal instruction was tuned in to promote children's performance even on a micro-sequential level. And this one-step-ahead adaptation proved to be efficient in getting the child to attain the level of performance addressed in the instruction, as indicated by the fit of the attainment-of-request model.

Figure 4.6 illustrates the age-related changes in the mode of maternal instructions. As can be seen, non-verbal instructions significantly decreased while verbal instructions significantly increased in rate across the longitudinal span. Again, a decreasing rate of direct non-verbal hints

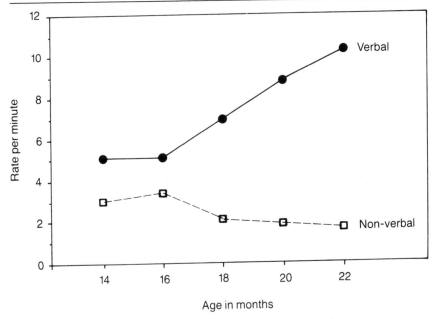

Figure 4.6 Verbal and non-verbal modes of mothers' instruction

(e.g. pointing) presents growing challenges to the children's task competence at increasing age levels.

The third aspect of the study was the emergence of affective responses to success and failure and the way mothers may have promoted this developmental advancement. Three types of behaviour were coded for maternal and child's reactions: acknowledgement of success (e.g. 'That's right'), enjoyment of success (e.g. 'What a nice tower') and self-evaluative reaction (praise/pride, blame/shame, e.g. 'What a clever girl'). In the case of mothers' reactions to success, rates were computed for each success of the child. These yielded a pattern of age-related changes, as shown in Figure 4.7. Each kind of of mother's reactions to the child's success was expressed at a decreasing rate (per success) across the longitudinal span. Thus, mothers emphasized successes less and less as children moved through the second year.

Table 4.3 provides information about the children's reactions to success, and mothers' and children's reactions to failure. For each category the absolute number of behaviour instances and the number of children/mothers expressing the respective behaviour is given. There were three types of infant's success reaction: noticing the success, enjoying the success, and pride about success. Merely noticing success and carrying on with the task was by far most frequent. Enjoying the successful outcome was first observed in more than one child at 16 months. Pride reactions to success did not become common until 20 months of age. Considering

Table 4.3 Number of child's success reactions, and child's and mother's reactions to failure

		14 months	16 months	18 months	20 months	22 months
Child's reactions to own success	**Tower:**					
	Notice	16 (6)	7 (4)	26 (10)	34 (8)	51 (12)
	Enjoy	1 (1)	9 (3)	3 (3)	4 (3)	9 (6)
	Pride	2 (2)	6 (2)	4 (3)	13 (5)	8 (4)
	Sorter:					
	Notice	17 (7)	15 (8)	19 (8)	69 (12)	110 (12)
	Enjoy	0 (0)	1 (1)	2 (1)	2 (2)	1 (1)
	Pride	0 (0)	1 (1)	2 (2)	4 (3)	1 (1)
Child's reactions to own failure	**Tower:**					
	Anger	**0 (0)**	**1 (1)**	4 (2)	7 (4)	7 (3)
	Refusal	0 (0)	0 (0)	**11 (2)**	**1 (1)**	1 (1)
	Help	0 (0)	1 (1)	1 (1)	1 (1)	**4 (1)**
	Sorter:					
	Anger	**1 (1)**	**6 (4)**	5 (2)	17 (4)	9 (4)
	Refusal	0 (0)	4 (1)	**6 (3)**	**6 (3)**	14 (5)
	Help	0 (0)	1 (1)	1 (1)	0 (0)	**3 (3)**
Mother's reactions to child's failure	**Tower:**					
	Outcome	5 (3)	12 (7)	35 (10)	33 (7)	20 (7)
	Competence	0 (0)	0 (0)	2 (1)	1 (1)	0 (0)
	Sorter:					
	Outcome	27 (9)	41 (10)	63 (11)	135 (12)	110 (12)
	Competence	1 (1)	0 (0)	1 (1)	1 (1)	2 (2)

Note: Number of subjects displaying behaviour is given in brackets. The developmental model is shown in **bold figures**.
Source: Adapted from Heckhausen (1988).

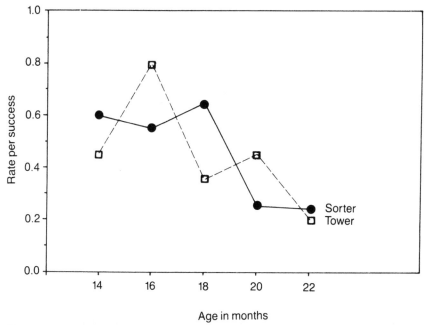

Figure 4.7 Mothers' reactions to children's success: logarithmized rates (adapted from Heckhausen 1988)

the age trends in the mothers' and the children's pride reactions together, the following conclusions can be drawn: mothers preceded children in expressing positive affect after success, and gradually withdrew reactions to success as their children became more competent and reacted positively to success themselves.

With regard to failure, no self-evaluative reactions (embarrassment) were observed in any of the children. For the other types of failure reaction (anger, refusal to continue the task activity, and seeking help), a developmental model was specified (indicated by bold figures in Table 4.3). Anger was predicted to predominate at 14 and 16 months. Refusal to continue task activity presumably required anticipatory avoidance of future failures, and thus was hypothesized to become more frequent at 18 and 20 months. Finally, seeking help implies the awareness of lacking competence and the notion that the mother's competence is superior to one's own, a cognitive challenge probably not mastered before 22 months. Prediction analysis revealed a significant model fit with the observed frequencies.

Mothers hardly ever reacted to failure by negatively evaluating their child's competence. Instead, negative comments were restricted to informational feedback on the child's trials (e.g. with regard to choosing the slot in the sorter), which gradually became more frequent when the children attempted the tasks more frequently and thus also produced more failures.

Table 4.4 gives the absolute numbers of help-seeking and help-rejection by the children, and help-offering and help-refusing by the mothers. Mothers offered help at all ages, and refusing to give help became fairly common at 20 months. Children did not start actively seeking help until 16 months. All early instances of rejecting maternal help by the child at 16 or 18 months turned out to be reactions to direct hand-tugging by the mother. Therefore, spontaneous help rejections were not expressed by the children before 20 months. It appears that help-related reactions were introduced by the mothers and then quickly acquired by the children.

In sum, the findings of this longitudinal study have demonstrated social facilitation provided by adult care-givers when interacting with infants during their second year. This age period appears to be particularly relevant for the acquisition of volitional action guidance (see also Bullock and Lütkenhaus 1988) and the emergence of self-evaluative reactions to successful action outcomes. During the second year of life, the child's development of mastery profits from a new level of adult-child cooperation in joint task-centred interactions. The adult can initiate goal intentions which are taken over by the child; the child learns how to recruit assistance from the adult in striving for the joint goal of action. The adult balances the child's weaknesses when the child's currently available skills appear insufficient; however, the adult instructor also avoids superfluous help and challenges the child's developmental potential whenever possible. As the child's competencies improve in the course of the second year, the adult instructor's scaffolding and developmental challenges are adapted gradually along a sliding developmental scale. This process of joint developmental progression is accompanied and propelled by the evolution of the child's growing awareness of his or her competence. The child comes to notice and appreciate the outcome of action as the attainment of an intended goal. Moreover, such goal attainment gives rise to self-evaluative reactions such as pride. Again, the adult caretaker fosters this developmental process towards motivational self-reliance, by initiating positive affect and praise after successful goal attainment. In contrast, negative evaluation of the child's competence after failure is avoided by the mothers and not shown by the children. The adult introduces the issue of self-reliance into the interaction by explicitly refusing help when it appears superfluous. Eventually, the child will reject help on his or her own account, so that at the end of the second year self-reliant task mastery becomes the primary objective of the instructional dyad between the elder and the young.

Table 4.4 Number of incidents of child's and mother's help-related behaviour

		14 months	16 months	18 months	20 months	22 months
Child's help-seeking and help-rejecting	Tower:					
	Seek help	0 (0)	2 (2)	0 (0)	16 (4)	25 (8)
	Reject help	0 (0)	0 (0)	3 (3)	1 (1)	7 (3)
	Sorter:					
	Seek help	0 (0)	5 (3)	11 (2)	23 (5)	44 (8)
	Reject help	0 (0)	1 (1)	1 (1)	1 (1)	1 (1)
Mother's help-offering and help-refusing	Tower:					
	Offer	0 (0)	8 (5)	10 (9)	18 (8)	29 (10)
	Refuse	0 (0)	1 (1)	0 (0)	11 (2)	12 (6)
	Sorter:					
	Offer	5 (3)	14 (15)	10 (4)	18 (7)	8 (4)
	Refuse	0 (0)	0 (0)	5 (3)	4 (4)	29 (8)

Note: Number of dyads with behaviour present is given in brackets.
Source: Adapted from Heckhausen (1988).

THE DEVELOPMENT OF STRATEGIES TO COPE WITH FAILURE

The developmental achievement of self-reflective representations and thus self-evaluation in response to action outcomes bears not only benefits but also costs. In case of failure, self-evaluation is likely to be negative, and thus potentially detrimental to action motivation and even to long-term self-esteem. In order to maintain a functional level of motivation and self-esteem, negative effects of failure need to be buffered. As demonstrated in the study and discussed above, self-evaluative reactions to failure in natural play are substantially delayed in comparison to pride reactions. Recent evidence reported by Stipek *et al.* (1992) suggests that this developmental delay seems to be considerably reduced when children are experimentally confronted with failure. Behavioural indicators in posture and gaze (i.e. aversion) suggested self-evaluative reactions to failure at as early as 24 months of age. It seems possible that primary caretakers contribute substantially to the developmental delay of failure reactions observed in natural play by avoiding confronting the child with activities which exceed her or his competence, or by providing help when necessary.

In any event, self-evaluative reactions to failure eventually occur in most children between 3 and 4 years of age (see review in Geppert and H. Heckhausen 1990). Such negative self-evaluations could have detrimental consequences unless buffered by specific strategies to cope with failure. In research about adults' coping with failure, losses and threat, the conceptual distinction between primary and secondary control has recently gained considerable attention (Heckhausen and Schulz 1993; Rothbaum *et al.* 1982). While 'primary control' refers to the individual's attempts to control the external world and to make the environment fit with one's own interests, 'secondary control' addresses strategies directed at internal representations of goals, expectancies and attributions, thereby aligning oneself with external conditions (Rothbaum *et al.* 1982). After failing in an achievement task, for instance, the individual might adjust his or her aspiration level by choosing less difficult tasks, adapt the goal priorities by downgrading the value of the achievement goal missed (the 'sour grape' phenomenon, Elster 1983), or resort to self-defensive attributions by blaming the failure on external obstacles.

Evidence for young children's secondary control behaviour following failure is as yet limited and merely anecdotal. In a study on competitive tower building with experimentally induced failure, episodical instances of failure denial ('It was me who has won'), excuses ('I was too tired') and reinterpretation ('Now, we have two towers') were observed in 3- and 4-year-olds who had shown negative self-evaluative reactions to failure (H. Heckhausen 1974).

Empirical studies addressing secondary control strategies in middle childhood and adolescence are still scarce, but the topic has recently received increased scientific interest (see review in Heckhausen and Schulz 1992). Initial evidence suggests that secondary control is increasingly used during middle childhood and reaches a – potentially intermediate – plateau during adolescence (Compas 1987; Compas *et al.* 1991). Altshuler and Ruble (1989), for instance, presented hypothetical scenarios about uncontrollable stressors (e.g. going to the dentist, having to wait patiently for a birthday party) to children between 5 and 12 years of age. Children's suggestions about what the main character should do can be classified as instantiations of primary or secondary control. In the case of primary control, the codes concerned approach (e.g. seeking information) and avoidance (e.g. running away). In the case of secondary control, the codes concerned behavioural strategies (do something else) or cognitive strategies (think something else). Even 5-year-olds suggested behavioural distraction techniques, and thus demonstrated awareness of secondary control strategies. For the negative stressors, the older children chose more cognitive distractors, while 5- and 6-year-olds favoured complete avoidance (e.g. run away from getting an injection).

Similarly, Band and Weisz (1988) demonstrated age differences in the availability of secondary control strategies (e.g. looking away, thinking of something else) when comparing 6-, 9- and 12-year-olds coping with everyday stressors in the medical domain. Other life domains, such as school or peer conflict, yielded a greater reliance on primary control strategies, and no age differences in the employment of secondary control.

Age differences in the use of secondary control were shown, however, by a study on recently encountered stressful situations with 7- and 10-year-olds (Wertlieb *et al.* 1987). The 10-year-olds more frequently reported having used 'emotional-management' ('I don't worry, because I am busy all day') and 'intra-psychic coping' ('I think about something fun') than the 7-year-olds.

The developmental precursors and gradual emergence of these secondary control techniques in mid-childhood are as yet unstudied. It seems likely that adult socialization agents play a prominent role in modelling and instructing children to use mental techniques to console themselves for the negative implications of failure and loss.

A most important set of relevant phenomena concerns the causal attribution of success and failure. A recurrent finding in studies comparing normal and depressed adults (Alloy and Abramson 1979), and adults whose achievement motivation is characterized by a strong 'hope for success' versus a strong 'fear of failure' (see review in Heckhausen 1991), is a contrasting pattern of causal attributions for success and failure. While normal adults and those high in 'hope for success' tend to exaggerate unrealistically the perceived influence of internal factors (their own ability) in the case of success, failure is blamed on external factors (task difficulty). In contrast, depressed adults and those high in 'fear of failure' blame failure on their own doing while attributing success to external facilitation.

The optimistic 'attributional bias' (e.g. Kelley and Michela 1980) can be conceived as a secondary control strategy which buffers the negative effect of failure by sparing the individual from self-blame. It is conducive to ambitious aspirations and prolonged persistence, and therefore promotes mastery in general. At least in adulthood, preferred causal attributional patterns are closely related to an achievement motivation characterized by 'hope of success' rather than 'fear of failure'. Inter-individual differences in hope for success versus fear of failure orientation, in turn, most probably evolve during early and mid-childhood, and appear to be related to parental independence and achievement demands (see review in Trudewind 1982). Developmentally inappropriate demands (i.e. ones made too early or too late) bring about low mastery motivation or a predominance of fear of failure, whereas appropriate demands foster high achievement motivation and hope for success. However, the question of how preferences for causal attributional patterns may be specifically socialized by primary care-givers is largely unexamined.

Another important dimension in causal attribution, besides the internal/external one, concerns the stability of causal factors. It makes an essential difference whether failure is ascribed to lack of competence or of effort. While perception of one's own ability is comparatively stable, effort is malleable. Thus, these two internal causal ascriptions may involve contrasting emotional and self-evaluative consequences, or, as John Nicholls put it (1975), 'effort is virtuous, but it's better to have ability'. Once older children can use compensatory causal schemata for ability and effort attribution (Nicholls 1978), such a maxim could prove to be quite debilitating, because children may choose to reduce their effort strategically, so that a failure can be attributed to insufficient effort rather than to lack of ability (Jagacinski and Nicholls 1990). However, such negative consequences would only ensue if the child perceived ability as a stable entity rather than as a 'learning goal' (Dweck and Leggett 1988). The latter approach could be promoted if major socialization agents modelled an emphasis on intra-individual improvement rather than inter-individual comparison. These phenomena of causal attribution in mastery contexts provide a glimpse of the potential role of adult care-givers in the socialization of secondary control strategies to cope with failure.

SUMMARY AND CONCLUSION

Striving to produce behaviour–event contingencies and thereby exert primary control is a powerful goal of behaviour in both human and subhuman species. While the latter mostly have to rely on their own manipulative powers when exploring non-instinct-driven contingencies, human care-givers provide their infants with salient and rich contingency experiences. Long before human infants can produce behaviour–event contingencies themselves, they are integrated in manifold contingencies with their caretakers' behaviour. This gives rise to an early evolution of generalized contingency awareness, the developmental precursor of mastery motivation. On the basis of generalized contingency expectation, the infant will strive for action-contingent outcomes, and in doing this is scaffolded by the adult caregiver. During the first half of the second year, the caretaker will extend the emotional appreciation of joint goal attainments from sheer enjoyment of action effects to a positive evaluation of the child's competence, thus adding a secondary motive to primary control. Becoming aware of one's own competence as a categorical feature is the source of autonomously motivated behaviour. The anticipation of a positive evaluation of oneself after success becomes a major motivator of mastery behaviour, and thereby sets the individual free from extrinsic gratifications or indeed social scaffolding. However, the evolution of a concept of one's own competence also has its costs. Repeated failure experiences at this stage may have long-term detrimental consequences for future mastery behaviour. Therefore, 'secondary control strategies' are required for buffering self-esteem against losses in primary control. These strategies are directed to the internal world (goals, attributions, evaluations) rather than the external one. They help the child, for instance, to find self-defensive attributions for failure, rearrange his or her goal hierarchy and level of aspiration, and make comparisons with similar or less fortunate others. Individual preferences for particular secondary control strategies may result from the different socialization of adult caretakers. Such preferences may have long-term consequences, in that they could promote or damage the development of primary control and mastery. The evolution of individual preferences for certain control strategies and their long-term impact on mastery across the life span should become a key interest of life-span developmental research.

REFERENCES

Alloy, L. B. and Abramson, L. Y. (1979) 'Judgement of contingency in depressed and non-depressed students: sadder but wiser?', *Journal of Experimental Psychology* 108, 441–85.

Altshuler, J. L. and Ruble, D. N. (1989) 'Developmental changes in children's awareness of strategies for coping with uncontrollable stress', *Child Development* 60, 1337–49.

Band, E. B. and Weisz, J. R. (1988) 'How to feel better when it feels bad: children's perspectives on coping with everyday stress', *Developmental Psychology* 24, 247–53.

Bullock, M. and Lütkenhaus, P. (1988) 'The development of volitional behavior in the toddler years', *Child Development* 59, 664–74.

Bullock, M. and Lütkenhaus, P. (1990) 'Who am I? Self-understanding in toddlers', *Merrill-Palmer Quarterly* 36, 217–38.

Chevalier-Skolnikoff, S. and Poirier, F. E. (eds) (1977) *Primate Bio-social Development: Biological, Social, and Ecological Determinants*, New York, Garland Publishing.

Clarke-Stewart, K. A. (1973) 'Interactions between mothers and their young children: characteristics and consequences', *Monographs of the Society for Research in Child Development* 153.

Clarke-Stewart, K. A., Vanderstoep, L. P. and Killian, G. A. (1979) 'Analysis and replication of mother–child relations at two years of age', *Child Development* 50, 777–93.

Cole, P. M., Barrett, K. C. and Zahn-Waxler, C. (1992) 'Emotion displays in two-year-olds during mishaps', *Child Development* 63, 314–424.

Compas, B. E. (1987) 'Coping with stress during childhood and adolescence', *Psychological Bulletin* 101, 393–403.

Compas, B. E., Banez, G. A., Malcarne, V. and Worsham, N. (1991) 'Perceived control and coping with stress: a developmental perspective', *Journal of Social Issues* 47, 23–34.

DeCasper, A. J. and Carstens, A. A. (1981) 'Contingencies of stimulation: effects on learning and emotion in neonates', *Infant Behavior and Development* 4, 19–35.

DeCasper, A. J., Butterfield, E. C. and Cairns, G. F. (1976) 'The role of contingency relations in speech discrimination by newborns', paper presented at the meeting of the Fourth Biennial Conference on Human Development, Nashville.

Dunham, P. and Dunham, F. (1990) 'Effects of mother–infant social interactions on infants' subsequent contingency task performance', *Child Development* 61, 785–93.

Dweck, C. S. and Leggett, E. L. (1988) 'A social-cognitive approach to motivation and personality', *Psychological Review* 95, 256–73.

Elster, J. (1983) *Sour Grapes: Studies in the Subversion of Rationality*, Cambridge, Cambridge University Press.

Finkelstein, N. W. and Ramey, C. T. (1977) 'Learning to control the environment in infancy', *Child Development* 48, 806–19.

Freund, L. S. (1990) 'Maternal regulation of children's problem-solving behavior and its impact on children's performance', *Child Development* 61, 113–26.

Geppert, U. and Heckhausen, H. (1990) 'Ontogenese der Emotion', in K. R. Scherer (ed.) *Enzyklopädie der Psychologie. Vol. C/IV/3: Psychologie der Emotionen*, Gottingen, Hogrefe.

Geppert, U. and Küster, U. (1983) 'The emergence of "wanting to do it oneself": a precursor of achievement motivation', *International Journal of Behavioral Development* 3, 355–69.

Hallock, M. B., Worobey, J. and Self, P. A. (1989) 'Behavioral development in chimpanzee (Pan troglodytes) and human newborns across the first month of life', *International Journal of Behavioral Development* 12, 527–40.

Harlow, H. F. (1953) 'Mice, monkeys, men, and motives', *Psychological Review* 60, 23–32.

Heckhausen, H. (1974) *Motivationsanalysen*, Berlin, Springer Verlag.

Heckhausen, H. (1982) 'The development of achievement motivation', in W. W.

Hartup (ed.) *Review of Child Development Research. Vol. 6*, Chicago, University of Chicago Press.

Heckhausen, H. (1984) 'Emergent achievement behavior: some early developments', in J. Nicholls (ed.) *The Development of Achievement Motivation. Vol. 3*, Greenwich, CT, JAI Press.

Heckhausen, H. (1991) *Motivation and Action*, New York, Springer.

Heckhausen, J. (1987a) 'Balancing for weaknesses and challenging developmental potential: a longitudinal study of mother–infant dyads in apprenticeship interactions', *Developmental Psychology* 23, 762–70.

Heckhausen, J. (1987b) 'How do mothers know? Infants' chronological age or infants' performance as determinants of adaptation in maternal instruction?', *Journal of Experimental Child Psychology* 43, 212–26.

Heckhausen, J. (1988) 'Becoming aware of one's competence in the second year: developmental progression within the mother–child dyad', *International Journal of Behavioral Development* 11, 305–26.

Heckhausen, J. and Schulz, R. (1992) *A life-span theory of control*. Manuscript submitted for publication, Max Planck Institute for Human Development and Education, Berlin, Germany.

Heckhausen, J and Schulz, R. (1993) 'Optimization by selection and compensation: balancing primary and secondary control in life-span development', *International Journal of Behavioral Development* 16.

Inhelder, B. and Piaget, J. (1964) *The Early Growth of Logic in the Child: Classification and Seriation*, London, Routledge & Kegan Paul.

Jagacinski, C. M. and Nicholls, J. G. (1990) 'Reducing effort to protect perceived ability: "They'd do it but I wouldn't" ', *Journal of Educational Psychology* 82, 15–21.

Janos, O. and Papoušek, H. (1977) 'Acquisition of appetitional and palpebral conditioned reflexes by the same infants', *Early Human Development* 1, 91–7.

Kagan, J. S. (1981) *The Second Year: The Emergence of Self-awareness*, Cambridge, MA, Harvard University Press.

Kaye, K. (1977) 'Toward the origin of dialogue', in H. R. Schaffer (ed.) *Studies in Mother–Infant Interaction*, London, Academic Press.

Kaye, K. (1982) *The Mental and Social Life of Babies: How Parents Create Persons*, Chicago, Harvester.

Kelley, H. H. and Michela, J. L. (1980) 'Attribution theory and research', *Annual Review of Psychology* 31, 457–501.

Lewis, M. (1991) 'Ways of knowing: objective self-awareness or consciousness', *Developmental Review* 11, 231–43.

Lewis, M. and Brooks-Gunn, J. (1979) *Social Cognition and the Acquisition of Self*, New York, Plenum.

Lewis, M. and Goldberg, S. (1969) 'Perceptual-cognitive development in infancy: a generalized expectancy model as a function of the mother–infant interaction', *Merrill-Palmer Quarterly* 15, 81–100.

Lewis, M., Sullivan, M. W., Stanger, C. and Weiss, M. (1989) 'Self development and self-conscious emotions', *Child Development* 60, 146–50.

Lütkenhaus, P. (1984) 'Pleasure derived from mastery in three-year-olds: its function for persistence and the influence of maternal behavior', *International Journal of Behavioral Development* 7, 343–58.

McNaughton, S. and Leyland, J. (1990) 'The shifting focus of maternal tutoring across different difficulty levels on a problem-solving task', *British Journal of Developmental Psychology* 8, 147–55.

Nicholls, J. G. (1975) 'Effort is virtuous, but it's better to have ability: evaluative responses to perceptions of effort and ability', *Journal in Personality Research* 10, 306–15.

Nicholls, J. G. (1978) 'The development of the concepts of effort and ability, perceptions of own attainment, and the understanding that difficult tasks demand more ability', *Child Development* 49, 800–14.

Papoušek, H. (1967) 'Experimental studies of appetitional behavior in human newborns and infants', in H. W. Stevenson, E. H. Hess and H. L. Rheingold (eds) *Early Behavior: Comparative Developmental Approaches*, New York, Wiley.

Papoušek, H. and Papoušek, M. (1975) 'Cognitive aspects of preverbal social interaction between human infants and adults', in *Parent–Infant Interaction*, Ciba Foundation Symposium 33, Amsterdam, ASP.

Papoušek, H. and Papoušek, M. (1980) 'Early ontogeny of human social interaction: its biological roots and social dimensions', in M. von Cranach, K. Foppa, W. Lepenies and D. Ploog (eds) *Human Ethology: Claims and Limits of a New Discipline*, Cambridge, Cambridge University Press.

Papoušek, H. and Papoušek, M. (1983) 'Biological bases of social interactions: implications of research for an understanding of behavioral deviance', *Journal of Child Psychology and Psychiatry* 24, 117–29.

Pratt, M. W., Kerig, P., Cowan, P. A. and Cowan, C. P. (1988) 'Mothers and fathers teaching 3-year olds: authoritative parenting and adult scaffolding of young children's learning', *Developmental Psychology* 24, 832–9.

Radziszewska, B. and Rogoff, B. (1988) 'Influence of adult and peer collaborators on children's planning skills', *Developmental Psychology* 24, 840–8.

Radziszewska, B. and Rogoff, B. (1991) 'Children's guided participation in planning imagery errands with skilled adult or peer partners', *Developmental Psychology* 27, 381–9.

Ramey, C. T. and Finkelstein, N. W. (1978) 'Contingent stimulation and infant competence', *Journal of Pediatric Psychology* 3, 89–96.

Riksen-Walraven, J. M. (1978) 'Effects of caregiving behavior on habituation rate and self-efficacy in infants', *International Journal of Behavioral Development* 1, 105–30.

Rogoff, B. and Wertsch, J. V. (eds) (1984) 'Children's learning in the "zone of proximal development" ', *New Directions for Child Development* 23.

Rogoff, B., Ellis, S. and Gardner, W. (1984) 'Adjustment of adult–child instruction according to child's age and task', *Developmental Psychology*, 20, 193–9.

Rothbaum, F., Weisz, J. R. and Snyder, S. S. (1982) 'Changing the world and changing the self: a two-process model of perceived control', *Journal of Personality and Social Psychology* 42, 5–37.

Rovee, C. K. and Fagan, J. W. (1976) 'Extended conditioning and 24-hour retention in infants', *Journal of Experimental Child Psychology* 21, 1–11.

Schaffer, H. R., Hepburn, A. and Collis, G. M. (1983) 'Verbal and nonverbal aspects of mothers' directives', *Journal of Child Language* 10, 337–55.

Schulz, R., Heckhausen, J. and Locher, J. (1991) 'Adult development, control, and adaptive functioning', *Journal of Social Issues* 47, 177–96.

Singh, D. (1970) 'Preference for bar-pressing to obtain reward over freeloading in rats and children', *Journal of Comparative and Physiological Psychology* 73, 320–7.

Skinner, B. F. (1953) *Science and Human Behavior*, New York, Macmillan.

Stipek, D. J., Gralinski, J. H. and C. B. Kopp (1990) 'Self-concept development in the toddler years', *Developmental Psychology* 26, 972–7.

Stipek, D., Recchia, S. and McClintic, S. (1992) 'Self-evaluation in young children', *Monographs of the Society for Research in Child Development* 57 (1, Serial No. 226).

Trevarthen, C. (1987) 'Sharing makes sense: intersubjectivity and the making of an infant's meaning', in R. Steele and T. Threadgold (eds) *Language Topics: Essays in Honour of Michael Halliday. Vol. 1*, Philadelphia, John Benjamin.

Trevarthen, C. and Hubley, P. (1978) 'Secondary intersubjectivity: confidence, confiding, and acts of meaning in the first year', in A. Lock (ed.) *Action, Gesture, and Symbol: The Emergence of Language*, London, Academic Press.

Trudewind, C. (1982) 'Ecological determinants in the development of the achievement motive and its individual differences', in W. W. Hartup (ed.) *Review of Child Development Research. Vol. 6*, Chicago, University of Chicago Press.

von Eye, A. and Brandtstädter, J. (1988) 'Evaluating developmental hypotheses using statement calculus and nonparametric statistics', in P. B. Baltes, D. J. Featherman and R. M. Lerner (eds) *Life-span Development and Behavior. Vol 8*, Hillsdale, NJ, Erlbaum.

Watson, J. S. (1966) 'The development and generalization of "contingency awareness" in early infancy: some hypotheses', *Merrill-Palmer Quarterly*, 12, 123–35.

Watson, J. S. (1972) 'Smiling, cooing, and "the Game" ', *Merrill-Palmer Quarterly* 18, 323–39.

Watson, J. S. and Ramey, C. T. (1972) 'Reaction to response-contingent stimulation in early infancy', *Merrill-Palmer Quarterly* 18, 219–27.

Welker, W. L. (1956) 'Some determinants of play and exploration in chimpanzees', *Journal of Comparative Physiological Psychology* 49, 84–9.

Wertlieb, D., Weigel, C. and Feldstein, M. (1987) 'Measuring children's coping', *American Journal of Orthopsychiatry* 57, 548–60.

White, R. W. (1959) 'Motivation reconsidered: the concept of competence', *Psychological Review* 66, 297–333.

Wood, D. J. and Middleton, D. (1975) 'A study of assisted problem-solving', *British Journal of Psychology* 66, 181–91.

Wood, D. J., Bruner, J. S. and Ross, G. (1976) 'The role of tutoring in problem solving', *Journal of Child Psychology and Psychiatry* 17, 89–100.

Part II

Conceptualization and measurement

Chapter 5

Three studies on the development of mastery motivation in infancy and toddlerhood

Karen Caplovitz Barrett, George A. Morgan and Christine Maslin-Cole

The purpose of this chapter is to describe three studies that shed light on (1) the validity of our conceptualization of mastery motivation and (2) developmental changes in such motivation during infancy and toddlerhood. For each study, we first examine the relation between task persistence and task pleasure, indices of two central aspects of mastery motivation. Second, we examine correlates of persistence and pleasure, to help provide construct validation for them as measures of mastery motivation. Third, we examine continuities and changes in behaviour, to provide evidence regarding the development of mastery motivation between 6 and 30 months of age.

The three studies also provide an opportunity to examine other themes. In Study 1, we explore one additional component of our view of mastery motivation – inclination to control events – and in Study 3, we explore another – the effects of difficulty level (challenge) on mastery motivation. In Study 2, we examine potential environmental influences on mastery motivation.

DEFINITION AND CONCEPTUALIZATION

Before discussing the specific studies, we will provide a brief synopsis of our conceptualization of mastery motivation. *Mastery motivation is viewed as a multifaceted, intrinsic, psychological force that stimulates an individual to attempt to master a skill or task that is at least moderately challenging for him or her* (cf. Morgan *et al.* 1990). We will focus on the features of this conceptualization that are most relevant to the three studies that are described.

A multifaceted force

Mastery motivation is multifaceted. Although most mastery motivation studies have focused on task persistence, and several have included task pleasure as an index of mastery motivation, there are other aspects of mastery motivation that deserve greater attention. This is especially true if we study mastery motivation across the infancy and toddler periods (see Barrett and Morgan, in press, for more details).

Indicators of mastery motivation may be categorized into two major types – instrumental and expressive. Instrumental aspects involve behaviours that are directed toward achieving an end state, such as controlling or mastering a task or outcome. Expressive aspects involve affective displays produced during or following attempts to control and/ or master tasks or outcomes. Task persistence has been the key indicator of instrumental aspects of mastery motivation, and task pleasure has been the key indicator of expressive aspects of mastery motivation. Other instrumental aspects of mastery motivation include preference for one's own physical and/or cognitive control over the environment and preference for moderate challenge or novelty (see Barrett and Morgan in press). Other expressive aspects of mastery motivation include responses pertaining to relevant emotions in addition to pleasure – e.g. interest, pride, frustration, anger, sadness, shame (see Heckhausen, this volume, Chapter 4; Jennings, this volume, Chapter 3). The various aspects of mastery motivation are separable, in that they are not always correlated and they do not all need to be measured in order to investigate mastery motivation.

Some form of both instrumental and expressive features is characteristic of mastery motivation across infancy, toddlerhood and probably the life-span. However, the nature of each feature changes as the child gets older. Study 1 shows that the specific kinds of behaviour required to succeed at a task may determine whether such task-related behaviours accurately reflect mastery motivation at that age. For example, if success at a task requires only behaviours that are already in a 6-month-old's repertoire (and are displayed frequently), task-directed persistence may accurately reflect mastery motivation. However, other studies of 6-month-olds indicate that if a task requires schemes that are not yet common or under volitional control, babies may attempt to solve the task by applying familiar schemes. As a result, young infants who are high in mastery motivation might display more 'irrelevant' behaviours (that are common in their repertoire) than 'task-directed' behaviours, and they may appear low in the motivation to master the task (see Messer et al. 1986). The nature of affective responses in mastery situations will also change as the child's abilities develop. For example, effectance pleasure may be augmented by pride in meeting a standard, and sadness at not accomplishing a goal may be supplemented by shame at not meeting a standard (see Barrett and Morgan in press; Jennings, this volume, Chapter 3). These developmental changes alert us to the fact that an understanding of the capabilities of the child is crucial to understanding and measuring mastery motivation.

The need for a challenge

Mastery motivation should be assessed during tasks that, at least initially, are moderately challenging for the individual. Persistence towards a goal is considered mastery motivation only if the goal is not yet mastered, i.e. the task is moderately challenging. If the task is too easy, there is nothing to master. Furthermore, tasks used to assess mastery motivation should be challenging relative to a *child's own* developmental level, not just a level selected as generally appropriate for the child's age (see Morgan, Busch-Rossnagel *et al.* 1992). Investigating the relationship of difficulty level to mastery motivation is the focus of the third study reported in this chapter.

An attempt at mastery

Mastery motivation involves a psychological force that impels the individual to attempt to master – not the ability of the individual to master successfully. Morgan *et al.* (1990) emphasized the distinction between motivation and competence. Studies 2 and 3 examine the relationships between competence and persistence (see also Hauser-Cram, this volume, Chapter 12; Yarrow and Messer 1983).

DEVELOPMENTAL CHANGES AND CONTINUITIES

Another major purpose of this chapter is to examine evidence, from these three studies, about developmental continuities and changes in mastery motivation between 6 and 30 months of age. Morgan and Harmon (1984) and Morgan *et al.* (1991) proposed two developmental transformations in instrumental mastery motivation based on changes in infant's behaviours in mastery situations, and changes in appropriate types of mastery task. The first transformation was hypothesized to occur at around 9 months of age, and involved a change from 'exploratory activities' being prototypical of the child's mastery motivation before that age to simple, goal- or task-directed behaviours after 9 months or so (see also Messer *et al.* 1986).

Barrett and Morgan (in press) modified this position slightly, to highlight the possibility that behaviours typically categorized as exploratory may be used by infants in an attempt to effect a goal. Study 2 provides some evidence that the modified position is reasonable, since by the end of the first year (after the 9-month transition), the child has a better sense of which actions actuate an event, and thus appears goal-oriented when seeking to attain an end. However, it also suggests that exploration remains an important activity for helping the child develop new skills.

The second transition was assumed by Morgan *et al.* (1991) to take place in the middle of the second year. One important development that contributes to change in mastery motivation at this age involves the child's improved ability to focus on a longer-term goal and solve a task that requires a sequence of steps to complete, such as a puzzle (see also Jennings, this volume, Chapter 3).

Barrett and Morgan (in press) have elaborated on this transition by noting other relevant and important changes as well. First, during this age period, infants manifest increased self-awareness and self-consciousness. Although even very young infants have some sense of themselves and their behaviour, around the middle to the end of the second year of life children seem to become self-conscious about their appearance and behaviour (e.g. see Lewis and Brooks-Gunn 1979; Lewis *et al.* 1989). In addition, it seems likely that by about 15 to 17 months of age, toddlers have acquired some behaviour standards (see Barrett and Morgan in press; Lewis *et al.* 1989; Stipek *et al.* 1992).

Toddlers' increased self-consciousness and awareness of standards has important implications for both instrumental and expressive aspects of mastery motivation. First, instrumental aspects should be affected. Children's increased self-awareness and self-consciousness should enable them to anticipate whether or not they will succeed with a task before actually trying it. However, given that there is also an increase in awareness of others, the child may be just as motivated (or even more motivated) to engage in easy tasks as moderately difficult tasks. In addition, infants' increased self-awareness and awareness of others should also improve their understanding of just what they can and do control. During this period, children become increasingly motivated to 'do it themselves' (cf. Geppert and Kuster 1983; Jennings, this volume, Chapter 3).

Expressive aspects of mastery motivation should be affected as well. Pride at successfully meeting standards, as well as shame at unsuccessful attempts to do so, should become increasingly common. Moreover, increasing numbers of children should manifest 'helpless' styles (see Dweck 1991), as they become more capable of determining that they have not reached a standard. Studies 2 and 3 provide data relevant to this second transformation.

STUDY 1 (KAREN C. BARRETT AND GEORGE A. MORGAN)

This study examines the validity of task-directed persistence as an index of mastery motivation during infancy. The vast majority of studies operationalize degree of mastery motivation as *duration of task- and/or goal-directed behaviours*, i.e. task persistence. However, differences of opinion remain regarding whether task-related persistence is a valid index of mastery motivation.

One set of findings that has raised this question is that of Messer *et al.*

(1986). These researchers investigated the relationship between mastery behaviours at 6 months and 12 months of age, and scores on the McCarthy Scales of Children's Abilities at 30 months of age. The behaviours coded were ordered into five levels of task involvement, ranging from simple visual attention to successful, goal-directed behaviour. Then the investigators determined the percentage of time babies spent engaging in each of these classes of task involvement, and examined the relationship between each of these percentages at 6 and 12 months and McCarthy scores at 30 months. Task- and goal-directed behaviours (traditionally combined and labelled persistence – cf. Yarrow *et al.* 1983) were expected to be related positively to later McCarthy scores, because they would imply greater motivation to control/master the task effectively – motivation that should facilitate cognitive growth.

As predicted, there was a significant positive relationship between goal-directed persistence at 12 months and McCarthy scores at 30 months (although this relationship was found only for girls). However, contrary to prediction, task-related persistence at 6 months, in those same children, was *negatively* correlated with the 30-month McCarthy scores. Since scores were calculated as percentages, a factor affecting these negative correlations was the significant *positive* relationship between 'general exploration' (manipulating the toy, hitting or examining it, etc., without attempting to solve the task) and the McCarthy scores. Messer *et al.* (1986: 370–1) explained their results in the following fashion:

> The findings . . . suggest that there may be a transformation in the nature of mastery behavior between 6 and 12 months. Piaget's (1952) work indicates that at 6 months the infants are likely to be in Stage 3 of the sensorimotor period . . . They explore by using their established repertoire of actions on new objects; they will mouth, manipulate, shake, and bat objects. They do not have the ability to identify means–ends relations.

We agree with these authors' emphasis on 6-month-old infants' use of familiar schemes such as mouthing and banging, as well as their point that such infants seem not to have a good understanding of what means will accomplish particular ends. We do believe that these aspects of young infants' behaviour and cognition distinguish them from older infants. However, we wish to emphasize that these are differences in specific behaviours and cognitions in the midst of similarity in *function* – attempts to effect interesting results. We think that even 6-month-olds often *try* to achieve particular ends, and if the behaviours required to achieve those ends are familiar and common, 6-month-olds will display their mastery orientation.

The results of the Messer *et al.* (1986) study suggested that 6-month-olds' 'task-directed behaviour' on those tasks might not have been directed at mastering experimenter-defined goals. Instead, 6-month-olds may have attempted to effect those or other goals using familiar behaviours – ones that were incapable of actually effecting the experimenter-defined goals, and were thus classified as exploratory. However, one can devise tasks that permit 6-month-olds to utilize their repertoire of mouthing and banging in mastering a problem. Under such circumstances, task-directed behaviour might index mastery motivation in 6-month-olds as well as 12-month-olds.

The present study utilized such a task, at both 6 and 12 months of age, in order to determine whether task-directed behaviour could be considered an indicator of mastery motivation and, more specifically, of attempts to control the situation. For half the infants (*contingent* subjects), banging and/or mouthing a cylinder activated a jack-in-the-box. The other babies (*non-contingent* subjects) observed the same rate of emergence of the jack-in-the-box, and had access to the same cylinder; however, the emergence of the jack-in-the-box was independent of cylinder pressing. We reasoned that if cylinder pressing signified attempts to activate the jack-in-the-box (rather than perseveration of responding or simple exploration), then there should be a *different pattern of relationships* between cylinder pressing and other behaviours in the two conditions. Four hypotheses were made:

1 If, as suggested by White (1959) and others, success in effecting events produces pleasurable 'feelings of efficacy', cylinder pressing should be associated with smiling in the contingent condition, but not in the non-contingent condition.
2 The positive relationship between pressing and smiling should not be due simply to increased stimulation.
3 If cylinder pressing in the non-contingent condition reflects infants' (unsuccessful) attempts to control the jack-in-the-box, it should increase as the rate of jack-in-the-box emergence increases (at least for most of this short, four-minute session).
4 Non-contingent subjects should remain uncertain about how to influence the emergence of the jack-in-the-box. Thus, given recent evidence that infants look to their care-givers for information *under conditions of uncertainty* (cf. Klinnert *et al.* 1983), non-contingent subjects should fixate their care-givers more often than should contingent subjects.

xp

Twenty-four 6-month-olds, twenty-four 12-month-olds and their primary care-givers participated, each pair being assigned to one condition. One half of the children in each age group were female. Each infant was seated in a high-chair, with the primary care-giver seated to the left and just in front of him or her. Directly in front of the infant was a 36.2 cm × 27.9 cm, open-faced, lighted wooden box, which appeared empty. The light remained on throughout the experimental session, to attract the infant's attention to the box and remind him or her of the stimulus event.

Light pressure on the surface of a blue, vinyl-covered cylinder (the manipulandum) either succeeded or failed in triggering a one-second, moderately high-frequency tone and the abrupt popping up of a plain red sphere (the jack-in-the-box) under the two conditions described earlier.

Outcome measures and results

All data were coded by assistants who were blind to the experimental hypotheses and conditions. The following outcome measures were employed (the relevant inter-observer reliability correlation appears in parentheses following each measure):[1]

1 *Rate of smiling* (0.99): number of smiles an infant emits per minute.
2 *Rate of fixating care-giver* (0.90): number of fixations per minute that an infant directs at the care-giver while the infant is not smiling.
3 *Rate of cylinder pressing* (0.99): number of discrete presses (with hand or mouth) an infant makes per minute. Each contingent subject's rate of cylinder pressing determined the rate of jack-in-the-box emergence received by the yoked non-contingent subject. Therefore, each contingent subject's score on this measure also served as an indicator of *stimulation level* for the corresponding non-contingent subject.

Preliminary ANOVA (Analysis of Variance) analyses indicated that there were no significant age[2] or sex differences on any of these measures. Therefore, results reported here concern all subjects in the relevant condition(s). We will present the results in terms of the four hypotheses outlined earlier.

Hypothesis 1 was strongly supported: there was a significant positive correlation between pressing and smiling for contingent subjects ($r = 0.44$; $p < 0.033$), but a non-significant negative correlation between these variables for non-contingent subjects ($r = -0.18$). The difference between these two correlations was significant as well ($p < 0.04$).

Hypothesis 2 was tested with two analyses, and both results supported it. First, increased stimulation in the non-contingent condition was not associated with increased smiling. There was a non-significant negative correlation between stimulation level and non-contingent subjects' smiling ($r = -0.27$). Second, the difference between the contingent and non-contingent conditions in the relationship between pressing and smiling remained when stimulation level was controlled statistically. The partial correlation between non-contingent pressing and smiling, controlling for stimulation level, remained negative and nonsignificant ($r = -0.08$), and again was significantly different from that between pressing and smiling in the contingent condition ($p < 0.04$).

Hypothesis 3 was supported only weakly: there was a trend for cylinder pressing in the non-contingent condition to increase as stimulation level increased (r = 0.39; p < 0.06).

Hypothesis 4, however, was supported: non-contingent infants, who should have remained uncertain as to how to control the jack-in-the-box, fixated their care-givers more than did contingent subjects, who knew how to control it (F (1,44) = 5.04; p < 0.03).

The overall pattern of results suggests that cylinder pressing did reflect mastery-oriented behaviour (attempts to activate the jack-in-the-box). This provides an organizing explanation for all findings. Contingent subjects smiled more as they pressed more, suggesting that they experienced pleasurable 'feelings of efficacy'. The responses of non-contingent subjects, on the other hand, implied *unsuccessful* attempts to control the jack-in-the-box. These babies pressed the cylinder more frequently as the jack-in-the-box emerged more frequently, but they did not seem to derive pleasure from either this unsuccessful cylinder pressing or the jack-in-the-box stimulation. Moreover, non-contingent babies referred to their care-givers frequently, as if attempting to disambiguate the situation – to find out how to activate the jack-in-the-box.

We did not find age differences in this study, a fact that at first glance would seem to suggest that there are no developmental changes in mastery motivation from 6 to 12 months. We do not believe that this is true. Rather, we think that by choosing task-related behaviours that were common in the 6-month-old's repertoire we were able to demonstrate the continuity in function in the midst of developmental change. We think it highly likely that results would have been different if the task had required behaviours that were unfamiliar to 6-month-olds. Under such circumstances, 6-month-olds probably would have used familiar, 'exploratory' behaviours such as mouthing and banging to try to accomplish the task, rather than those behaviours that actually would promote success at it. As a result, 6-month-olds probably would have looked much less mastery-oriented that 12-month-olds.

STUDY 2 (GEORGE MORGAN, REX CULP, NANCY BUSCH-ROSSNAGEL AND RICHARD REDDING)

Persistence at challenging tasks has been the key measure of mastery motivation during infancy, and, as indicated in Study 1, it seems to be a valid indicator. Task pleasure has also been considered a measure of mastery motivation. However, task pleasure and persistence seem to be different (expressive versus instrumental) aspects of mastery motivation; these two measures are correlated only at low levels (at least when measured during tasks typically used in mastery motivation studies: see Morgan *et al.* 1990).

Furthermore, although competence and task persistence are correlated during infancy (Redding *et al.* 1988; Yarrow *et al.* 1982), they seem conceptually quite distinct (see Morgan *et al.* 1990). A child who is high in mastery motivation should become more competent than should one of equal ability who is less motivated. However, a competent individual might not be very motivated, and one who is low in competence might be highly motivated to master tasks (perhaps to become more competent).

One purpose of the present study was to examine the interrelationships among persistence, pleasure and competence on the same tasks, as well as their relationship to other relevant behaviours, in order to determine similarities and differences in the constructs they represent.

A second purpose was to examine continuity and change in mastery behaviours during the second year of life. As stated earlier, Barrett and Morgan (in press) have predicted transformations around the third quarter of the first year of life and around the middle to the end of the second year of life. Consequently, we predicted that there would be a negative correlation between task persistence and simple exploration at 12 months (given that the first transformation would be complete), as well as a lack of stability in task persistence between 12 and 25 months (given that these ages straddle the second transformation). No instability of task pleasure was predicted between 12 and 25 months, since the transformation in expressive mastery motivation involves increased evidence of other affective responses (shame and pride), rather than a change in mastery pleasure.

Finally, we were interested in the potential impact of play experience and other environmental factors at 12 months on both contemporaneous mastery behaviour and mastery behaviour at 25 months. We predicted that greater exposure to play experiences involving mastery at 12 months would predict greater mastery motivation at both 12 and 25 months. We also examined, more specifically, whether 12-month-olds' involvement in two types of goal-directed free play at 12 months (cause/effect and combinatorial) was differentially associated with mastery behaviour at 25 months.

In this longitudinal study, 32 white infants (14 boys and 18 girls) were tested at 12 months; 17 were retested at 25 months, and 18 new children were added to the sample at that age. The infants had no major medical or developmental problems and were from predominantly middle-class families.

Mastery tasks

At each age, infants were tested in a laboratory setting, using standard mastery motivation tasks. At 12 months, we used nine tasks: two cause–effect tasks (e.g. surprise box), three combinatorial tasks (e.g. shape sorter), two means–ends tasks (barriers) and two symbolic tasks (e.g. telephone).

At 25 months, four sets of tasks were utilized: two combinatorial sets, one multi-part cause-and-effect set, and one set of means–end, barrier problems. Each set included one easy task, one moderately difficult task, and one difficult task for the *typical* 2-year-old. The task presumed to be moderately difficult was always presented first. If the child completed half or more of this task, he or she was then given the more difficult task. If not, the relatively easy task was presented. Thus, each child received eight tasks, two from each set, based on her or his performance. This procedure adjusted the average difficulty level of the tasks to the competence of the child.

At both ages, after a demonstration of the toy, interaction of tester and mother with the child was minimized. Each task was presented individually for a specified period (2 or 3 minutes, unless the child was off-task for 30 seconds, in which case that task was terminated).

Outcome measures

The following measures of mastery motivation and competence were assessed:

1 *Task persistence*: number of 15-second intervals of task-directed behaviour (e.g. trying to put the block in the shape sorter).
2 *Task pleasure*: number of 15-second intervals of positive affect during task-directed behaviour.
3 *Task competence*: number of different parts of the task completed.

After the mastery tasks at 25 months, the tester rated several additional aspects of the child's behaviour during the tasks, using a modified version of the Infant Behavior Record (IBR) (Bayley 1969). Matheny's (1980) factor analyses of the IBR scales were used to compute five cluster scores: (1) task orientation (e.g. ratings of object orientation, attention span and goal-directedness); (2) task affect-extroversion (e.g. social to E, fearfulness, emotional tone); (3) activity level; (4) audio-visual awareness (e.g. listening, looking); and (5) motor skill (gross, fine).

Free play

At 12 months the infant's behaviour was also observed during 10 minutes of unstructured play with a standard set of toys. Mothers were present, but remained uninvolved. Scores included the number of 15-second intervals of simple exploration (shaking, etc.) and two types of goal-directed play – cause and effect (e.g. pushing a music-making roller) and combinatorial (e.g. trying to put rings on a stacker). Continuity of free play (duration of the two longest bouts of play) was also computed, to provide another indicator of persistence.

Potential environmental influences on mastery motivation

At 12 months, the mother was asked to indicate her five most frequent types of play with her infant when at home. Her responses were classified as non-cognitive (e.g. rough-housing) or as one of four types of cognitively enriching play: (1) combinatorial play, (2) pretend/adult-imitation activities, (3) verbal play and (4) cause-and-effect play. A 'variety of mastery-oriented play' score was computed, based on how many of these latter four types were represented (see Gaiter *et al.* 1982 for more details).

When toddlers were 25 months old, their mothers provided demographic information: mother's and father's age, education and occupation; hours mother worked outside of the home; hours of non-familial care; and number of siblings. Mothers also described their children's five favourite toys, and a rating was made of the degree of similarity between these toys and the mastery-task toys.

Inter-rater reliability, for all measures in this study, ranged from 0.67 to 0.97.

Results

Concurrent correlations

Correlations between task persistence, task pleasure and task competence, as well as between each of these three variables and other relevant ones, reveal that these constructs are non-redundant with one another (see Figure 5.1). Differences between task pleasure, persistence and competence are also evident in the first panel of Table 5.1. At 12 months, these three measures are correlated quite differently with behavioural and maternal report measures of play at home.

As predicted, task persistence on 12-month mastery tasks was negatively related to free-play exploration, but positively related to task-related play with combinatorial toys. These findings, like those of Jennings *et al.* (1979) and Morgan, Culp *et al.* (1992), suggest that children who are more task-directed on structured mastery tasks are also, at least by the end of the first year of life, more task-directed during free play. This provides some construct validation for persistence at structured tasks as a measure of infant mastery motivation. On the other hand, task-related behaviour with combinatorial toys was not significantly correlated with task pleasure, although the correlation between these measures was positive. Moreover, task competence was virtually uncorrelated with task-related combinatorial free play.

Table 5.1 Correlations of 12-month child free play and maternal variety of play with 12- and 25-month mastery task measures

	12-month mastery tasks			25-month mastery tasks		
	Persistence	Pleasure	Competence	Persistence	Pleasure	Competence
Child play at 12 months:						
General exploration	−0.41**	–	–	0.54**	0.39	0.51**
Goal-directed functional play:						
Cause-and-effect	0.27	–	0.31	−0.63**	−0.25	−0.55**
Combinational	0.41**	0.34	–	0.56**	–	–
Continuity of play	–	0.50**	0.32	0.31	0.57**	–
Variety of maternal play	–	0.46**	–	0.39	–	0.44*

Notes: N = 21 at 12 months. N = 17 for 12 to 25 months. Correlations less than 0.20 are indicated by –. * p≤ 0.05, one-tailed. ** p ≤ 0.025, one-tailed.

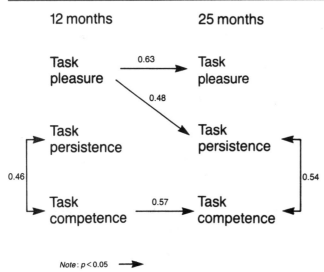

Note: p<0.05 ➡

Figure 5.1 Intercorrelations and stability of two measures of mastery motivation (task pleasure and persistence) and competence at 18 and 25 months

Interestingly, continuity of free play, which is a measure similar to persistence, was positively correlated with task pleasure at 12 months, but not with task persistence. Finally, as predicted, mothers engaging in a greater variety of cognitively oriented activities with their 12-month-olds were more likely to have infants high in task pleasure (r = 0.46, p < 0.05).

Table 5.2 shows concurrent correlations at 25 months involving the relations between the three mastery-task scores and clusters of IBR-type ratings made after the tasks. These ratings give us a profile of the 2-year-old child who has high scores on the measure of instrumental mastery motivation. The persistent child is somewhat extroverted or social during the session, attuned to the world including the experimenter's actions, and fairly well co-ordinated, and has a slight tendency to be less active

Table 5.2 Correlations of mastery-task scores with contemporaneous clusters of infant behaviour ratings at 25 months

Ratings after the tasks	Mastery task scores		
	Persistence	Pleasure	Competence
Task orientation	0.83**	0.26	0.57**
Extroversion	0.54**	0.20	0.44**
Activity level	−0.27	0.11	0.12
Audio-visual awareness	0.52**	0.02	0.21
Motor skill	0.38*	0.16	0.25

Notes: * p < 0.05. ** p < 0.01.

than average. On the other hand, the child who is high on task pleasure is not described well by any of these IBR clusters. Moreover, task competence was related only to the clusters of ratings labelled 'task orientation' and 'extroversion', and less strongly so than was task persistence.

In summary, these results provide evidence that the three mastery-related behaviours – task-directed persistence, task pleasure, and competence – do not measure a single construct. Task pleasure and task persistence are correlated only at low levels and are differentially correlated with other behaviours. Moreover, although persistence and competence are correlated at a higher level, they are by no means redundant and each is correlated with somewhat different measures. Nevertheless, task persistence and task pleasure are both significantly related to relevant other measures in predicted, meaningful ways, suggesting that it is reasonable to think of them as separate aspects of mastery motivation.

Continuity and change in mastery behaviours

As Figure 5.1 indicates, there was evidence of both continuity and change in mastery-task behaviours from 12 to 25 months. Although persistence was not stable from 12 to 25 months, pleasure and competence were relatively stable during this period. The lack of stability of persistence was predicted on the basis of the expected transformation in the second year of life, and the stability of task pleasure was consistent with the idea that *other* expressive aspects of mastery motivation (shame and pride) change during the second year transition, but that mastery pleasure does not.

Potential environmental influences on mastery motivation

Several aspects of 12-month-olds' play experiences were related to mastery-task measures at 25 months. The right side of Table 5.1 shows that there was a significant positive correlation between task-directed involvement in combinatorial play at 12 months and task persistence at 25 months. On the other hand, general exploration, which was *negatively* related to task persistence at 12 months, was *positively* related to persistence at 25 months. In addition, the functional use of simple cause-and-effect toys during free play at 12 months was *negatively* related to both persistence and competence at 25 months. Finally, continuity/persistence in free play at 12 months was *positively* related to task pleasure at 25 months.

Although not all of these findings were predicted, we believe that they can be readily interpreted *if* the tasks at 12 and 25 months, and the cognitive skills each involves, are carefully considered. Cause-and-effect toys at 12 months were straightforward, simple tasks that required a single behaviour for solution. Examples included a toy toaster that popped up and a toy that made music when pushed. In order to solve these tasks, a child did not need to plan a sequence of actions; not did she or he need to explore several possible strategies. The appropriate action was relatively obvious to a 12-month-old.

On the other hand, 12-month combinatorial toys, such as the ring stacker, could be solved completely only if the child engaged in considerable exploratory problem solving and/or planning. These latter skills would be much more useful in preparing children to solve the 25-month tasks, which required sequences of actions for solution.

Perhaps children who choose to focus on simple cause-effect toys during free play, rather than exploring and/or solving more complex toys, are less likely to acquire the requisite skills for the 25-month tasks. It could be that some children simply explore during free play, *without* engaging in much combinatorial problem solving. Such children might look less persistent on structured tasks at 12 months. However, exploration of more complex tasks, along with some attempts to solve them, may make possible greater competence and greater motivation to master similar, complex tasks at 25 months. This suggests complex developmental antecedents of the type of mastery behaviour characteristic of 2-year-olds – not simple relationships between persistence on any mastery tasks at one age and persistence on any mastery tasks at the other age.

As predicted, the variety of cognitively enriching activities mothers reported engaging in with their 12-month-olds was correlated with behaviours on the mastery tasks at 25 months, although only the relationship to competence was significant (see Table 5.1). This finding is similar to that of Gaiter et al. (1982), who found a strong correlation ($r = 0.61$) between a very similar measure of variety of maternal play at one year and the McCarthy General Cognitive Index at 3½ years. It is possible that the relationship between variety of play at 12 months and persistence at 25 months would reach conventional levels of significance in a study involving a larger n.

It will be recalled that there was a significant contemporaneous correlation between the variety of mother–infant play and task pleasure at 12 months. Moreover, Morgan, Culp et al. (1992) found positive relationships at 9 months and from 9 to 12 months between the amount and variety of mother–infant play and both task persistence and pleasure. This entire set of findings suggests a reciprocal relationship between mother–infant play and mastery motivation. Mothers whose children persist at mastery tasks and/or enjoy them may be more inclined to involve their children in such tasks, which, in turn, may cause the children to derive still more pleasure from mastery and to persist still more at such activities. Somewhat surprisingly, none of the nine family demographic variables, nor child gender, was related to any of the 25-month mastery-task scores. Likewise, similarity of mastery-task toys to the children's favourite toys was related to none of the three mastery-task scores.

The role of demographics in the development of mastery motivation is rarely mentioned in the literature, perhaps because others have found similarly non-significant effects. An absence of gender differences has been reported in several studies as well (e.g. Yarrow *et al.* 1982; Study 1, this chapter), but different patterns of relationships for boys and girls have been found in other studies (see Jennings *et al.* 1984; Messer *et al.* 1986). The lack of relationships between mastery-task variables, favourite toys and demographics may be due in part to the relative homogeneity of this sample. For example, all mothers had at least a high-school education, no mothers worked full time, and most families had one or two children. It could be that most or all homes were sufficiently stimulating to support mastery motivation, and that most children were exposed to sufficiently similar toys to wash out the effects of familiarity. In addition, it could be that the effects of similarity to favourite toys differ across children, with effects cancelling each other out.

Summary and implications

Data presented in this study suggest that task persistence and task pleasure can be thought of as different aspects of mastery motivation. In addition, the study provides some support for the hypothesized developmental transformations. The negative correlation between task persistence and free-play exploration is consistent with our view of the nature of mastery motivation following the 9-month transition, as well as with other findings in the literature. Morgan, Culp *et al.* (1992) found that, on structured mastery tasks, there was a significant decrease in simple exploration, accompanied by a significant increase in task persistence, between 9 and 12 months. In addition, they found that during free play, there was a significant increase between 9 and 12 months in goal-directed behaviour. Finally, they found that there was little stability in task persistence between 9 and 12 months. Together, these findings suggest a developmental transformation in mastery motivation at around 9 months of age.

A second transition seems to occur during the second half of the second year of life. In the current study, low stability of task persistence scores from 12 to 25 months is consistent with the existence of a transition during this period. This transition, which occurs at about 17–22 months of age, involves a number of changes. Toddlers become more able to maintain attention on a remote goal such as completion of a puzzle, and basic cause-and-effect behaviours become less central. In addition, there are significant changes in infants' self-awareness, which should be related to changes in both instrumental and expressive aspects of mastery motivation (see Barrett and Morgan in press; Jennings, this volume, Chapter 3). Some evidence for changes in expressive mastery motivation across this period will be found in Study 3.

Despite providing additional evidence for changes in mastery motivation during the second year of life, Study 2, like Study 1, highlights continuity in the face of change. Individual differences in the affective and more purely cognitive measures that were assessed in this study – task pleasure and competence – were relatively stable from 12 to 25 months. Moreover, there was evidence that exploratory activities are relevant to the development of mastery motivation even after the 9-month transition. Exploration, especially in conjunction with attempts to solve difficult problems, may help babies learn to solve the more complex, multi-step problems appropriate to 2-year-olds.

Study 2 also provided data indicating that task persistence and pleasure can be distinguished from task competence. We believe that *motivation* to master problems should be differentiated from *ability* to master problems, but this has proved difficult to accomplish. Study 3 provides a means of holding competence constant when assessing mastery motivation, and enabling researchers to study whether mastery motivation is greatest when tasks are moderately challenging.

STUDY 3 (GEORGE A. MORGAN AND CHRISTINE MASLIN-COLE)

The primary purpose of this study was to investigate whether toddlers are most motivated to master tasks which are moderately difficult. The hypothesis was that mastery motivation, as indexed by task persistence and task pleasure, would be lower during very easy or very difficult problems than during moderately difficult tasks – that an inverted U-shaped curve would best depict the relationship between these measures and task difficulty.

These predictions were based on the extensive literature regarding inverted U-shaped curves (see Berlyne 1960; Walker 1981), including two studies of mastery motivation. In one of these mastery studies, Harter (1977) found that school-aged children smile most to moderately challenging tasks. In the other, Redding *et al.* (1988) found that 1–3-year-old infants persisted less at the very difficult tasks than at moderately difficult ones, but only 36-month-olds persisted less at easy tasks than at moderate tasks. Another goal of the study was to determine the usefulness of a standard set of mastery tasks designed for 15–36-month-olds, and of an individualized method of assessing difficulty level.

This cross-sectional study included 24 children aged 15 to 20 months ($M = 17.5$) and 24 children aged 25 to 30 months of age ($M = 27.5$). Three relatively homogeneous sets of tasks were used (puzzles, shape sorters and cause-and-effect toys), each with six levels of difficulty.[3]

Children in each age group were tested using five of the six tasks from each of the three sets. Levels 1–5 were presented to the younger children, and levels 2–6 were presented to the older children. The order of tasks was randomized between and within sets, except that the first task of each set was always the easiest level, to ensure that the child understood the task and had an initial experience of success. Data from these first tasks were not included in analyses of the puzzles and shape sorters, because of order effects (persistence at the first task was higher than that on the other tasks, perhaps because novelty made it more appealing).

The tasks were presented to the child, one at a time, in the mother's presence. Two parts of the solution were demonstrated before the start of each task; then the child was prompted to try the task himself or herself. The task was ended when three minutes had passed or when the child manifested off-task behaviour for 30 seconds. If the child completed the task, it was suggested that he or she could do it again as many times as he or she liked.

Outcome measures and results

The following measures were obtained:

1 *Task persistence*: number of 15-second intervals of task-directed behaviour.
2 *Task pleasure*: number of intervals in which the child smiled during task-directed behaviour and/or immediately following a solution.
3 *Task competence*: a weighted proportion of different solutions performed correctly, divided by different solutions possible.
4 *Toy experience*: number of hours, during the last week, of play with toys similar to each mastery task (according to maternal report).

Inter-rater reliabilities of 0.80 or better were established for all behavioural measures before testing began, and reliability was checked periodically during the study. Behaviours were coded, live, by the tester.

Scalability of task sets

The predicted order of task difficulty within each sequence was supported; within an age group, the easiest tasks were solved more completely than the harder ones, and older children performed consistently better than younger children. From these data, we conclude that the sets of tasks did systematically increase in difficulty, as expected.

In order to see whether these group results also held for individual children, scalogram analyses were conducted for each of the three sets of tasks, using Green's (1956) Index of Consistency. The puzzles were found to meet the criterion for scalability best ($I = 0.83$), shapes were adequate (I = 0.52), while cause-and-effect tasks showed a number of reversals (mostly minor) from predicted difficulty and did not quite meet the criterion of 0.50 to be labelled scalable (I = 0.47).

The effect of difficulty on task persistence

Data regarding task persistence and task pleasure were first plotted as a function of the level of task difficulty (1–6). Plotted like this, the expected inverted U-shaped curves were not obvious. For each age group, repeated measures analyses of variance (MANOVAs) were used to test the effect of difficulty level on persistence at each type of task. Three of six average univariate Fs were significant, but no consistent linear or non-linear trends emerged.

Next, task persistence and pleasure were rescored based on each child's performance. We believe that this is the best approach because it takes into account individual differences in performance. Each task was rated as either 'too easy', 'too hard' or 'moderately difficult' *for a given child*. A task was judged to be 'too easy' if the child completed it quickly (e.g. got in all puzzle pieces in less than 60 seconds). Conversely, a task was judged to be 'too hard' if the child did not solve at least two parts of it in 60 seconds. The task was deemed 'moderately difficult' if it was neither too hard nor too easy.

Figure 5.2 shows the relationship between task difficulty, as determined by this individualized method, and persistence. For all three types of task, the hard tasks produced significantly less persistence than did the moderate ones: $F(1,39) = 32.53$, $F(1,41) = 84.01$, and $F(1,43)$ 5.38, for puzzles, shape sorters, and cause–effect toys. Note that the curves look similar to the expected inverted U, but persistence was significantly lower only for tasks that were too hard.

Figure 5.2 also indicates that there were significant age effects for puzzles and cause-and-effect toys, with 27.5-month-old children persisting more than the 17.5-month-olds: Fs $(1,46) = 6.47$ and 7.88, respectively. This indicates that there is a significant increase in persistence near the end of the second year of life, even when task difficulty is roughly equated.

Effect of difficulty on task pleasure

The curves shown in Figure 5.3 are, again, generally similar to the expected inverted U shape, but no significant effects of task difficulty on mastery pleasure were found. However, the older children showed significantly more pleasure on the puzzles and cause-and-effect tasks than did younger children: Fs $(2,46) = 2.88$ and 3.12, respectively.

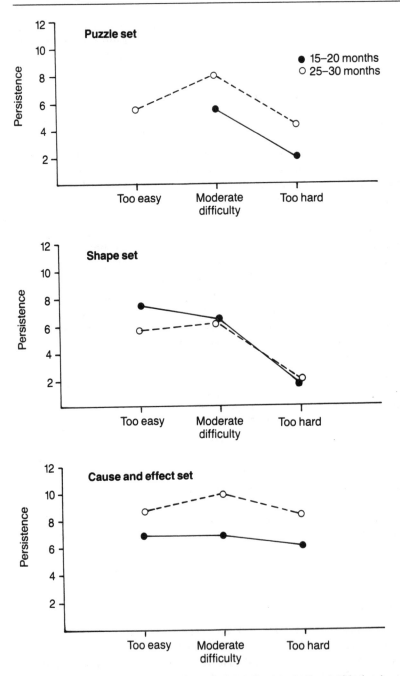

Figure 5.2 Number of intervals (out of sixteen) of task-directed behaviour (persistence) as a function of individualized difficulty level and age

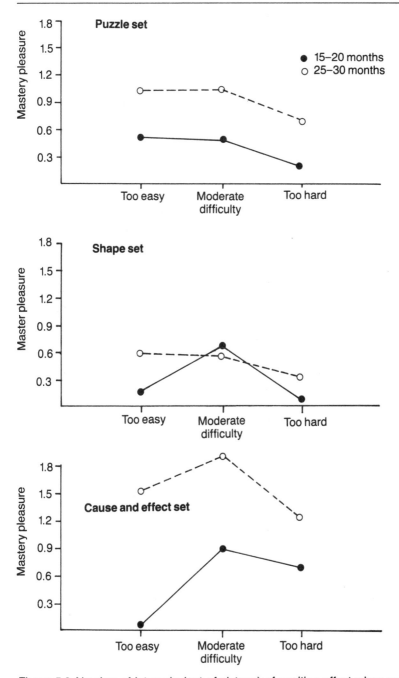

Figure 5.3 Number of intervals (out of sixteen) of positive affect when solving or while working at a task (mastery pleasure) as a function of individualized difficulty level and age

Summary and implications

The results of this study suggest that:

1 The puzzle and shape-sorter sets provide sequences of six tasks of increasing difficulty.
2 The individualized method of assessing task difficulty is more fruitful than is the normative approach.
3 Fifteen- to 30-month-olds persist significantly less at extremely difficult tasks than they do at moderately difficult tasks; and older toddlers show more persistence and pleasure than do younger toddlers.

Redding *et al.* (1988), using only the puzzle set, found similar results. For each of three age groups (12, 24 and 36 months), MANOVAs indicated a significant effect of task level on persistence. All three age groups persisted less at the most difficult puzzles than at the moderate ones, and the 36-month-old children also persisted less at the easiest puzzles. Redding *et al.* (1988) found little evidence of an inverted U-shaped relationship between task pleasure and task difficulty. There was, however, as in the current study, a significant age effect, with 36-month-old children showing more pleasure than either 12- or 24-month-old children.

Taken together, the findings of Study 3 and the Redding study provide some support for the hypothesis that instrumental mastery motivation, as measured by persistence, varies with the difficulty of the task. Toddlers do, in general, show less persistence at difficult tasks than at moderately challenging tasks.

It appeared, however, that 1- and 2-year-old children were as willing to persist at a relatively easy task as at a moderately challenging one. Perhaps this is because they derived intrinsic reward from completing even the easy tasks, or because they really had not yet mastered what we called easy tasks. We know that the youngest children had very few easy tasks and even those were not as quickly completed as the 'easy' tasks for the older children.

For task pleasure, graphic depiction suggested U-shaped curves; however, differences were not significant. This was unexpected, because task pleasure is a useful individual difference measure and because Harter (1977) found significant difficulty effects on smiling in older children. The relatively high variability in this measure, and the small proportion of children showing it on any given task in these studies (often less than 25 per cent) militated against finding significant group differences.

A direction for future research would be to use our individualized assessment method to study whether children who are highest on mastery motivation are those who will persist on very difficult as well as moderate tasks. There is some evidence from the present study that children's mastery experiences at home differentially affect their persistence on *moderate* versus *difficult* tasks. The total number of hours children reportedly played at home with toys that were similar to the mastery tasks was related positively to persistence on *difficult* cause and effect toys ($r = 0.32$, $p < 0.027$), but was not related to persistence on *easy or moderate* cause-and-effect toys. Similarly, the number of hours children reportedly played with puzzles at home was correlated positively with persistence on *hard* ($r = 0.33$, $p < 0.024$) but not *easy or moderate* puzzles.

More precise delineation of the apparent increase in both persistence and pleasure at around 2 years of age should also be investigated. It seems possible that the increase in persistence is due at least in part to an increased awareness of the societal standard that one should *complete* puzzles rather than just put in a few pieces – that success involves completion rather than putting in a piece. There is some evidence that the youngest children did not try to complete the puzzle, given that none of them completed even the easiest puzzle, despite the fact that they quickly put in the first piece and all pieces were the same size and shape (thus, if one could put one piece in, one could put any other piece in).

On the other hand, the increase in 'task pleasure' (primarily smiling) may be due to increased likelihood of pride responses during this period. This study did not provide data capable of distinguishing pride from pleasure responses. Further studies that more directly address the distinction between pride and pleasure in response to mastery tasks are needed (see Stipek *et al.* 1992 for relevant work).

OVERALL DISCUSSION AND CONCLUSIONS

The results of these three studies provide support for the conceptualization of mastery motivation outlined in the introduction and for the proposed transitions in mastery motivation during the latter part of the first and second years of life.

The first study offers support for the validity of task persistence as a measure of mastery motivation, even at six months of age, if the behaviours required of the child are well-learned schemes. The second and third studies suggest that task persistence and task pleasure are separate aspects of mastery motivation and that both can be distinguished from competence in the first two years of life. Task persistence and task pleasure at a particular age are not highly related and have different correlates. This suggests that they are not alternative indicators of the same aspect of mastery motivation. However, the fact that persistence and pleasure are correlated across ages and that both have appropriate and relevant correlates suggests that it is reasonable to think of them, as we stated in the introduction, as two different aspects of mastery motivation. Study 2, like most other existing studies, revealed that persistence and competence are moderately interrelated. However, Study 3 points to the value of defining and measuring mastery motivation as independently from competence as possible. The individualized assessment method suggested by this study provides a way of separating competence and persistence.

In regard to developmental continuities and transformations, the first study, in conjunction with the existing literature, suggests that the proposed transformation around 8 or 9 months involves the infant's capabilities and behavioural repertoire, rather than a change from less to more or a precursor to true mastery motivation. The results highlight how transformations in overt behaviour on particular tasks may coexist with continuity in the function of those behaviours. The second and third studies provide some evidence in support of the transformation in mastery motivation near the end of the second year of life. Much more research is needed regarding this transition, to document better the nature of the changes, as well as the sources of those changes (see Barrett and Morgan in press).

Although the findings of these three studies are consistent with our conceptualization, many parts of it remain untested. We hope that this chapter will help stimulate research aimed at better determining the nature and implications of individual differences in mastery motivation during the first three years of life.

NOTES

Studies reported in this chapter were supported in part by the Developmental Psychobiology Research Group, the John D. and Catherine T. MacArthur Foundation Research Network, and the W. T. Grant Foundation. Study 1 involved data collected for KCB's Master's thesis, and she would like to express her appreciation to Joseph J. Campos for his contributions to that study. The studies could not have been done without the assistance of the following students; Soosan Mardashti, Susan Williamson, Sue Jacobs Renner, and Annette Vance Dorey.

1 All measures were calculated as rates, because, for ethical reasons, the experiment was terminated early if an infant cried. Thus, some babies had shorter sessions than did others, and rate scores seemed most appropriate.
2 The correlational analyses described here were also conducted separately for 6-month-olds and 12-month-olds, given Messer et al.'s (1986) findings. In no case was a 6-month-old group correlation significantly different from the corresponding 12-month-old correlation.
3 For more information on these tasks, see Busch-Rossnagel et al., this volume, Chapter 7.

REFERENCES

Barrett, K. C. and Morgan, G. A. (in press) 'Continuities and discontinuities in mastery motivation during infancy and toddlerhood: a perspective and review', in R. MacTurk and G. Morgan (eds) *Mastery Motivation: Conceptual Origins and Applications*, Hillsdale, NJ, Ablex.

Bayley, N. (1969) *Bayley Scales of Infant Development*, New York, Psychological Corporation.

Berlyne, D. E. (1960) *Conflict, Arousal and Curiosity*, New York, McGraw-Hill.

Dweck, C. (1991) 'Self-theories and goals: their role in motivation, personality, and development', in R. Dienstbier (ed.) *Nebraska Symposium on Motivation, 1990. Vol. 38*, Lincoln, NE, University of Nebraska Press.

Gaiter, J. L., Morgan, G. A., Jennings, K. D., Harmon, R. J. and Yarrow, L. J. (1982) 'Variety of cognitively oriented caregiver activities: relationships to cognitive and motivational functioning at one and 3½ years of age', *Journal of Genetic Psychology* 141, 49–56.

Geppert, U. and Kuster, U. (1983) 'The emergence of "wanting to do it oneself": a precursor of achievement motivation', *International Journal of Behavioral Development* 6, 355–69.

Green, G. (1956) 'A method of scalogram analysis using summary statistics', *Psychometrika* 21, 79–88.

Harter, S. (1977) 'The effects of social reinforcement and task difficulty level on the pleasure derived by normal and retarded children from cognitive challenge and mastery', *Journal of Experimental Child Psychology* 24, 476–94.

Jennings, K., Yarrow, L. and Martin P. (1984) 'Mastery motivation and cognitive development: a longitudinal study from infancy to three and one half years', *International Journal of Behavioral Development* 7, 441–61.

Jennings, K., Harmon, R., Morgan, G., Gaiter, J. and Yarrow, L. (1979) 'Exploratory play as an index of mastery motivation: relationships to persistence, cognitive functioning and environmental measures', *Developmental Psychology* 15, 386–94.

Klinnert, M., Campos, J., Sorce, J., Emde, R. and Svejda, M. (1983) 'Emotions as behavior regulators: social referencing in infancy', in R. Plutchik and H. Kellerman (eds) *Emotions in Early Development. Vol. 2: The Emotions*, New York, Plenum.

Lewis, M. and Brooks-Gunn, J. (1979) *Social Cognition and the Acquisition of Self*, New York, Plenum.

Lewis, M., Sullivan, M., Stanger, C. and Weiss, M. (1989) 'Self development and self-conscious emotions', *Child Development* 60, 146–56.

Matheny, A. P. (1980) 'Bayley's infant behavior record: behavioral components and twins analysis', *Child Development* 51, 1157–67.

Messer, D., McCarthy, M., McQuiston, S., MacTurk, R., Yarrow, L. J. and Vietze, P. (1986) 'Relation between mastery behavior in infancy and competence in early childhood', *Developmental Psychology* 22, 366–72.

Morgan, G. A. and Harmon, R. J. (1984) 'Developmental transformations in mastery motivation: measurement and validation', in R. Emde and R. Harmon (eds) *Continuities and Discontinuities in Development*, New York, Plenum.

Morgan, G. A., Harmon, R. J. and Maslin-Cole, C. A. (1990) 'Mastery motivation: definition and measurement', *Early Education and Development* 1, 318–39.

Morgan, G. A., Busch-Rossnagel, N. A., Maslin-Cole, C. A. and Harmon, R. J. (1992) *Mastery Motivation Tasks: Manual for 15- to 36-month-old Children*, New York, Fordham University, Psychology Department.

Morgan, G. A., Maslin-Cole, C. A., Biringen, Z. and Harmon, R. J. (1991) 'Play assessment and mastery motivation in infants and young children', in C.

Schaefer, K. Gitlin and A. Sandgrund (eds) *Play Diagnosis and Assessment*, New York, Wiley.

Morgan, G. A., Culp, R. E., Busch-Rossnagel, N. A., Barrett, K. C. and Redding, R. E. (1992) 'A longitudinal study of mastery motivation in infants 9- to 25-months of age', presented as a poster at the Nebraska Symposium, Lincoln, NE.

Piaget, J. (1952) *The Origins of Intelligence in Children*, New York, International Universities Press.

Redding, R. E., Morgan, G. A. and Harmon, R. J. (1988) 'Mastery motivation in infants and toddlers: is it greatest when tasks are moderately challenging?', *Infant Behavior and Development* 11, 419–30.

Stipek, D., Recchia, S. and McClintic, S. (1992) 'Self-evaluation in young children', *Monographs of the Society for Research in Child Development* 57 (1, Serial No. 226).

Walker, E. L. (1981) 'The quest for the inverted-U', in H. I. Day (ed.) *Advances in Intrinsic Motivation and Aesthetics*, New York, Plenum.

White, R. W. (1959) 'Motivation reconsidered: the concept of competence', *Psychological Review* 66, 297–333.

Yarrow, L. J. and Messer, D. J. (1983) 'Motivation and cognition in infancy', in M. Lewis (ed.) *Origins of Intelligence*, 2nd edition, Hillsdale, NJ, Erlbaum.

Yarrow, L. J., Morgan, G. A., Jennings, K. D., Harmon, R. J. and Gaiter, J. L. (1982) 'Infant's persistence at tasks: relationships to cognitive functioning and early experience', *Infant Behavior and Development* 5, 131–41.

Yarrow, L. J., McQuiston, S., MacTurk, R. H., McCarthy, M. E., Klein, R. P. and Vietze, P. M. (1983) 'Assessment of mastery motivation during the first year of life: contemporaneous and cross-age relationships', *Developmental Psychology* 19, 159–71.

Chapter 6

Parent and teacher perceptions of young children's mastery motivation
Assessment and review of research

George A. Morgan, Christine Maslin-Cole, Robert J. Harmon, Nancy A. Busch-Rossnagel, Kay D. Jennings, Penny Hauser-Cram and Lois Brockman

This chapter reviews the published and unpublished research about parent and teacher ratings of young children's mastery motivation. The Dimensions of Mastery Questionnaire (DMQ), or its predecessor the Mother's Observation of Mastery Motivation (MOMM), has been used with over thirty samples of 1–5-year-olds, including normally developing, developmentally delayed and premature children.

These studies provide a different perspective on mastery motivation from the more typical mastery motivation study, which has utilized brief behavioural observations of infants working at mastery tasks or during semi-structured play. Thus, researchers have usually observed children for only a small amount of time in a single setting. Parents and teachers, on the other hand, have the opportunity to observe their child over a long period of time and in various settings. Therefore, a questionnaire completed by parents can augment laboratory measures of mastery motivation. In addition, the DMQ provides a quicker and easier measure of young children's mastery motivation than that gained from behavioural assessments.

If the DMQ produces valid measures – a topic to be discussed in a later section – this would be a significant advantage. We recognize that parents' perceptions may be influenced not only by the child's actual behaviour but also by characteristics of their own personalities and response biases. Yet, we view parent and teacher perceptions of mastery motivation as important in themselves because adult perceptions undoubtedly influence the nature of adults' interactions with the child. The purpose of this chapter is to introduce a useful questionnaire to readers and demonstrate its utility, especially what it can add to other research approaches to mastery motivation.

Barrett and Morgan (in press; Barrett, Morgan and Maslin-Cole, this volume, Chapter 5) have proposed that mastery motivation is a multifaceted, intrinsic psychological force that stimulates an individual to attempt to master a skill or task that is at least moderately challenging for him or her (see Morgan, Harmon *et al.* 1990). Facets of mastery motivation are subsumed under two major aspects: *instrumental* (e.g. persistence at challenging tasks and preference for moderate challenge and/or novelty) and *expressive* (e.g. facial, vocal and postural communication of pleasure, pride and shame). This view of mastery motivation evolved from research over the last two decades, including that on parent and teacher perceptions utilizing the MOMM and DMQ.

Historically, mastery motivation has been viewed as pertaining primarily to persistence at object-oriented tasks (e.g. Yarrow *et al.* 1982). However, recent years have seen an expansion of the construct to include social mastery motivation (e.g. Combs and Wachs, this volume, Chapter 9; MacTurk *et al.* 1985; Maslin and Morgan 1985; Wachs 1987). In this chapter, we use adult perception questionnaire data as a basis for proposing an expanded conceptualization of children's mastery motivation. This questionnaire measures three domains of the *instrumental aspect* of mastery motivation: persistence at object oriented, social/symbolic and gross motor play. There is also one measure of the *expressive aspect* of mastery motivation, mastery pleasure.

The remainder of this chapter is divided into the following sections: development of the questionnaires; their reliability; their validity; correlates of mastery motivation; and conclusions and recommendations.

DEVELOPMENT OF THE QUESTIONNAIRES

The MOMM: an early version of the DMQ

When development of the MOMM (Mother's Observation of Mastery Motivation) questionnaire began in the early 1980s, there were no parental report questionnaires designed to assess the motivation of infants and pre-school children. Infant temperament questionnaires did assess perceptions of some aspects of persistence (e.g. Carey and McDevitt 1978; Lerner *et al.* 1982; Rowe and Plomin 1977), but none of them provided adequate coverage of the motivational aspects of toddlers' or pre-schoolers' problem solving and play. Two questionnaires for school-aged children, Gottfried's (1986) Academic Intrinsic Motivation Inventory and Harter's (1981b) Intrinsic versus Extrinsic Orientation in the Classroom Scale, came closer conceptually to measuring the aspects of behaviour in which we were interested. However, those scales focused on intrinsic versus extrinsic motivation in school, which is only partially applicable to the play of infants and pre-school children. In developing items for the MOMM questionnaire, we drew upon several of Harter's scales and some themes from the persistence scales of infant temperament measures.

Busch-Rossnagel, Culp and Morgan wrote items to fit several a priori conceptual scales: (1) persistence at difficult tasks, (2) exploration in depth, (3) preference for novel/unfamiliar, (4) preference for challenge, (5) works to please adults, (6) dependent on adult help, and (7) reliance on adult feedback.

The first four scales were intended to assess high versus low mastery motivation as it had been measured behaviourally in other studies. (e.g. Jennings *et al*. 1984; Yarrow, *et al*. 1982). Scales four to seven were adapted from Harter's (1981b) Intrinsic versus Extrinsic Orientation in the Classroom scales.

Pilot work led to a 36-item questionnaire which was completed by approximately 200 mothers of normally developing children and 60 mothers of at-risk or handicapped children aged 9 months to 5 years, some of whom participated in intervention programmes. These data were collected as part of several different studies (see Table 6.1).

Table 6.1 lists sources of MOMM and DMQ data. They come from published and unpublished studies as well as samples for which the DMQ was the only instrument. The table provides basic descriptive information about the sample, grouped by the version of questionnaire used. These samples will be referred to by number in the sections discussing research results.

Two principal components factor analyses of the mothers' ratings from the pilot studies were conducted: for high-risk and for low-risk subjects. The factors produced were similar for the two analyses but differed considerably from the original a priori scales. The first factor accounted for about half the variance and contained most questions from the a priori scales of persistence and preference for challenge, as well as items from the exploration scale and selected items from several other scales. This factor was labelled 'general mastery motivation'. The second factor, labelled 'dependence in mastery situations', consisted of questions which dealt with the child's bids to adults for help in playing with toys, especially when the tasks are difficult. Other, smaller factors varied from sample to sample and usually accounted for relatively small percentages of the variance.

The factor analyses and details of results of studies using the MOMM are provided in Morgan *et al*. (1983), and the papers cited in Table 6.1. These results supported the usefulness of the MOMM questionnaire, but it was thought that the psychometric properties and the conceptualization of mastery motivation underlying the questionnaire could be improved without losing its strengths.

The Dimensions of Mastery Questionnaire general scales (DMQ-G)

Morgan, Pipp, Harmon and Maslin produced an extensive revision of the MOMM questionnaire. The twenty-one general scale items of the DMQ were written to be age-appropriate for toddlers and pre-school children.

Table 6.1 Characteristics of studies/samples utilizing the Mother's Observation of Mastery Motivation (MOMM) or the Dimensions of Mastery Questionnaire (DMQ)

Sample	Location plus	Types of sample(s)[a]	Respondent[b]	Age	N	Design[c]	DMQ references
MOMM:							
1	Fort Collins	N	M	2–5 y	53	C	Morgan et al. 1983[d]
2	Fort Collins	D, N	M	2–5 y	32	C	Flagle 1982; Morgan et al. 1983
3	Denver	P, N	M	1 y	41	C	Butterfield and Miller 1984;[e] Harmon et al. 1982,[d] 1984,[d] Morgan et al. 1983, 1988[d]
4	Pittsburgh	MI, N	M, T	3½, 4½ y	77	L	Jennings et al. 1985, 1988, 1989[d]
DMQ-G							
5	Fort Collins	N	M	18–25 m	38	L	Maslin-Cole et al. this vol., Ch. 11
6	Fort Collins	N	M	15–30 m	47	C	Barrett et al., this vol., Ch. 5[e]
7	Denver	N	M	1–3 y	60	C	Redding et al. 1988[e]
8	Manitoba	N	M	18 m	38	C	Fung 1984[d]
9	Unknown	N, DD	M	8–36 m	65	C	Hupp and Abbeduto, 1988,[d] 1992[d]
10	Minnesota	N, K	M	1 y	32	C	Hupp et al. in press[d]
11	Germany	DD	M	2–7 y	35	C	Sarimski and Warndorf 1991[d]
DMQ-E:							
12	Fort Collins	N	M	37 m	26	L	Bretherton and Ridgeway, 1986[f]
13	Boulder	N	M	18–, 24 m	76	L	Morgan et al. 1988[d]
14	Colorado	T	M	1–3 y	250	C	Morgan, Maslin-Cole et al. 1990[d]

No.	Location	(a)	(b)	Age	N	(c)	Citation
15	Colorado	T	M	3–5 y	332	C	Morgan, Maslin-Cole et al. 1990[d]
16	Manitoba	N	T	3–5 y	49	C	Brockman and Barnes 1986[f]
17	Manitoba	N	M	3–5 y	32	C	Brockman and Barnes 1986[f]
18	Manitoba	N	F	3–5 y	30	C	Brockman and Barnes 1986[f]
19	*Colorado	T	M	1 y	34	C	Robinson 1987[f]
20	*Fort Collins	N	M	3–5 y	39	L	Morgan et al. 1986[f]
21	*Massachusetts	N	M	2–5 y	28	C	Hauser-Cram 1987[f]
22	*Massachusetts	N	T	2–5 y	29	L	Hauser-Cram 1987[f]
23	*Fort Collins	N	M	4½ y	26	L	Bretherton and Ridgeway 1987[f]
24	*Boulder	N	M	39 m	48	C	Biringen 1987[f]
25	*Fort Collins	N	T	2–5 y	113	C	Morgan 1990[f]
26	*Fort Collins	N	M	2–5 y	87	C	Morgan 1990[f]
27	*Bronx	HL	M	1–5 y	85	C	Busch-Rossnagel et al. this vol., Ch. 7[d]
28	*Pittsburgh	N	M	15–35 m	57	C	Jennings 1992[e]
29	*Massachusetts	DD, D, MI	M	1–2 y	105	C	Hauser-Cram 1992[f]
30	Massachusetts	DD, D, MI	M	3 y	169	L	Hauser-Cram 1992[f]
31	*Hawaii	S	M, C	1–3 y	12	C	Stump 1992[f]

Notes: The raw MOMM or DMQ data from most of the studies were available to the authors and were used to do the composite analyses reported in this paper. Samples are listed in the approximate order in which they were collected.

[a] N = Normally developing, mostly European Americans; MI = Motor impaired; P = Premature; D = Down's syndrome; DD = Developmentally delayed; K = Korean; T = Twins; HL = Hispanic, mostly low socio-economic status; S = Parent Substance Abuse.

[b] M = Mother/parent; F = Father; T = Teacher; C = Care-giver.

[c] L = Longitudinal; C = Cross-sectional.

[d] These citations refer to entries in the reference list which include DMQ results, but the cited authors were not necessarily the principal investigators (see chapter acknowledgements).

[e] These citations refer to a publication during which the DMQ was collected, but not reported.

[f] These citations refer to data for which there is no publication or paper at this time. The data may have been collected specifically for inclusion in one of the composite samples. The year is when data collection was completed.

* Indicates samples from which the composite groups were formed. See text and Table 6.2 for groupings.

They have, however, been used successfully with children as young as 8 months (Hupp and Abbeduto 1988, 1992) and as old as 6 years. The questions were written in descriptive, behavioural language similar to that used by mothers. These general scales of the Dimensions of Mastery Questionnaire (DMQ-G) were designed to tap four dimensions of child behaviour that we have observed during the mastery tasks. These dimensions were: (1) general persistence at tasks, (2) mastery pleasure, (3) independent mastery attempts, and (4) general competence.

The first and third dimensions were based on the first two factors from the MOMM. The second and fourth dimensions were added to represent two important aspects of the young child's behaviour in mastery situations that had not been included in the MOMM.

The first dimension, *general persistence*, was based on items from the first MOMM factor, general mastery motivation. This scale was intended to correspond to the typical mastery motivation measure, observed persistence at challenging, structured tasks, and is one index of the *instrumental aspect* of mastery motivation.

The second dimension, *mastery pleasure*, was added because Harmon and Morgan (Harmon *et al.* 1984) realized its importance to a conceptually complete view of mastery motivation in early childhood. Mastery pleasure is defined as smiling, laughing or other behavioural indicators of positive affect *during* task-directed behaviour or *immediately following* the solution of a task. It is viewed as a measure of the child's developing sense of self efficacy and of a second aspect of mastery motivation, the *expressive aspect*.

The third dimension, *independent mastery attempts*, was derived by reversing some questions in the second factor of the MOMM questionnaire (dependence in mastery situations) and adding some additional items. Independent mastery attempts are necessary in the standard mastery motivation assessment situation because the child must work on his or her own in order to achieve a high persistence score.

The fourth dimension, *general competence*, is not considered to be a measure of mastery motivation, but it is an important aspect of mastery-related behaviour. Furthermore, there is usually a somewhat analogous score derived from the mastery tasks. The competence items provide an index of a mother's perceptions of her child's cognitive abilities, which should be related to standardized tests such as the Bayley Mental Development Index.

The items from these general scales of the DMQ were used in the studies listed under DMQ-G in Table 6.1, and they have, with minor modifications, continued to be used with all the other DMQ samples reported in this chapter. Findings from the general scales of the DMQ form the basis of most of the results we report in this chapter (except for those in the psychometrics section, which utilize the additional items and rescoring of the questionnaire as described in the next section).

The Dimensions of Mastery Questionnaire – Expanded (DMQ-E)

Results from the structured mastery tasks have shown that persistence is quite specific to the type of task (e.g. Yarrow *et al.* 1982, 1983). For example, even relatively similar mastery tasks such as those using puzzle-like tasks or cause-and-effect toys did not have very highly correlated persistence scores. In addition, mastery motivation researchers have shown a growing interest in the expression of persistence during social and symbolic play (Maslin-Cole *et al.*, this volume, Chapter 11) and in social behaviour during tasks (e.g. Combs and Wachs, this volume, Chapter 9; Maslin and Morgan 1985; Morgan *et al.* 1991). Thus, there seemed to be clear value in developing ways to assess aspects of mastery motivation not tapped by the four general scales of the DMQ.

In response to these results and concerns, the DMQ was expanded. Five new scales, of three items each, were added to the items of the DMQ-G in order to create a more differentiated assessment of the instrumental aspect of mastery motivation. These scales measure persistence during five specific types of play: gross motor, combinatorial, means–end, social and symbolic.[1]

The rescored, five-factor DMQ-E

Recently, for both psychometric and conceptual reasons, we deleted five of the thirty-six items and reanalysed the data. This resulted in five scales which are conceptually meaningful and psychometrically stronger than previous formulations. This new conceptualization includes an *expressive facet or component* of mastery motivation, mastery pleasure, and three *instrumental components* of mastery motivation, which are: persistence at object, social/symbolic and gross motor play. These instrumental components roughly parallel Harter's (1981a) three aspects of perceived competence (academic, social and athletic) in school-aged children. Our new conceptualization also includes an overall perceived competence factor, which is not viewed as an aspect of mastery motivation. Thus, the re-scored DMQ-E has five scales:

1 object-oriented persistence;
2 social/symbolic persistence;
3 gross motor persistence;
4 mastery pleasure;
5 general competence.

Psychometric data regarding this rescoring of the DMQ-E data are presented in the next sections.

As the conceptualization of mastery motivation evolved, we made minor modifications in items to improve the internal consistency of the scales and the readability and translatability of the items (see Busch-Rossnagel *et al.*, this volume, Chapter 7). The DMQ scales of mastery pleasure and general competence are considered to be essentially equivalent across versions because item wording and content differ at most moderately, and 'alternate forms' reliability was adequately high (see reliability section).

The new object-oriented persistence scale is highly related to the general persistence scale ($r = 0.91$), in part, because it includes the general persistence items plus ones from the independent mastery scale and the combinatorial and means–end persistence scales. The social/symbolic persistence and gross motor persistence scales were formed from items added for the expanded DMQ, so they have no equivalents in the four general scales.

In summary, as our conceptualization of mastery motivation evolved, the MOMM became the DMQ-G, which provided measures of both the expressive and instrumental aspects of mastery motivation. The DMQ-E was a further expansion to include other potential components of an instrumental aspect (i.e. persistence) of mastery motivation. The recent rescoring of the DMQ-E has produced a conceptually and psychometrically stronger questionnaire.

RELIABILITY OF THE DMQ

In order to examine the psychometric properties of the DMQ, three *composite groups* were formed, using the rescored DMQ-E from twelve samples. The first group included seven samples of mothers of normally developing 1–5-year-old children (N = 319). The second group was comprised of two samples of teachers of normally developing pre-schoolers (N = 142). The third composite group included 83 at-risk or delayed children drawn from three samples (27, 29 and 31). They included predominantly low SES (socio-economic status) Hispanic toddlers, developmentally delayed toddlers and children of in-patient maternal substance abusers. The samples that make up these three composite groups are identified by asterisks in Table 6.1.

The great majority of the 319 mothers in the first composite group were white and middle-class, and had at least some education beyond high school; however, two of the samples were from university pre-schools which had considerable cultural, if not educational, diversity. Geographically, Colorado was over-represented, with mostly small city and suburban families, but this composite group also included children

Table 6.2 Alphas for the five rescored scales of the Dimension of Mastery Questionnaire (DMQ-E)

Scales	Mothers of low-risk children[a] (N = 319)	Mothers of high-risk/ delayed children[b] (N = 83)	Teachers of pre-school children[c] (N = 142)
Object-oriented persistence	0.86	0.87	0.92
Social/symbolic persistence	0.78	0.73	0.83
Gross motor persistence	0.76	0.74	0.89
Mastery pleasure	0.78	0.70	0.78
General competence	0.69	0.80	0.87

Notes: [a]Composite of seven samples: 19, 20, 21, 23, 24, 26 and 28.
[b]Composite drawn from three samples: 27, 29 and 31.
[c]Composite of two samples: 22 and 25.

from the urban areas of Boston and Pittsburgh. The teachers of the 142, mostly 3–5-year-old pre-school children in the second composite group, were well educated and trained in observational and rating techniques. The results from these two composite groups would probably be representative of typical university research samples of predominately normally developing, low-risk children whose parents agree to participate in a study.

Internal consistency

In general, alphas for the five rescored DMQ-E scales are acceptable to good. Table 6.2 shows alphas for the three composite groups described above. As can be seen, teachers had the highest alphas (median alpha = 0.87); mothers of normally developing children (median alpha = 0.78) had somewhat higher alphas than mothers of the at-risk/delayed children (median alpha = 0.74). Perhaps the teachers were more aware or observant of the types of behaviour rated on the DMQ. Lower maternal reading levels or higher child behaviour variability could have produced the somewhat lower alphas for the composite at-risk/delayed group. Alphas for samples 27 and 29 treated separately were more variable. The mastery pleasure alpha was very low (0.36) for the Hispanic sample, as was the alpha for gross motor persistence (0.47) for the 1–2-year-old developmentally delayed children.

Test-retest reliability and stability

The mothers of sample 20 (N = 39) were asked to respond to two versions of the DMQ about three weeks apart. For the object-oriented persistence scale, alternate-forms reliability was quite high, 0.81. For the social/symbolic persistence, mastery pleasure and competence scales these reliabilities were 0.54, 0.57 and 0.52, respectively, despite modifications to several items. Busch-Rossnagel *et al.* (this volume, Chapter 7, sample 27) found similar results for test-retest reliabilities for a sub-sample (N = 10) of Hispanic children. However, the coefficient for gross motor mastery motivation was not sufficiently high to be reliable.

Moderately high stability over six months or more has been found for the DMQ scales. In the Boulder Longitudinal study (samples 13 and 24), the DMQ-E was administered at 18, 24 and 39 months. Stability correlations ranged from 0.32 to 0.80, with median coefficients for object-oriented, social/symbolic and gross motor persistence, mastery pleasure and competence of 0.63, 0.50, 0.37, 0.62 and 0.68, respectively. There was no indication that stability was lower if the interval was longer. Moderately high stability was, likewise, found in the Massachusetts Developmental Disabilities Study (samples 29 and 30) for ratings more than a year apart. Stability correlations ranged from 0.45 to 0.67, with a median of 0.60.

VALIDITY

Several approaches to testing validity have been used with the MOMM and DMQ questionnaires. The following sections summarize the results.

Factor analysis of items

To assess construct validity, principal components factor analyses with varimax rotation were computed separately for the two composite groups of 319 mothers and 142 teachers. The ratings by mothers yielded five factors, which provide construct validity for the five rescored DMQ-E scales (see Table 6.3). The first factor, object-oriented persistence, had twelve items with loadings 0.40 or above. These included all of the general persistence, means–end persistence and combinatorial persistence items, and the two positive independent mastery items. The second factor, social/symbolic persistence, included the six items designed to assess persistence at those two related types of play. The other three factors corresponded to the scales of mastery pleasure, gross motor persistence, and competence. As can be seen from Table 6.3, the five factors are distinct, with all items loading 0.40 or more on the appropriate factor and with no dual-loading items. For teachers, the results were similar, except that the object-oriented persistence and competence factors were somewhat overlapping.

High- versus low-risk comparisons

Support for the validity of the questionnaires was also obtained through comparisons of mothers' perceptions of normally developing versus risk children, who were matched for mental age. As would be expected, mothers of Down's syndrome, premature and physically handicapped children (samples 2, 3 and 4) rated their children significantly lower on the general mastery motivation factor of the MOMM than did mothers of low-risk children. Questions on preference for challenge were especially likely to show significant differences between mothers of high- and low-risk infants (see Morgan *et al.* 1983). Both teachers and mothers of 4½-year-old physically handicapped children, who used a short version of the MOMM, rated the handicapped children as significantly lower on general mastery motivation and lower on independence (see Appendix A in Morgan *et al.* 1983; Jennings *et al.* 1988, sample 4). Because the findings are meaningful and also in agreement with Jennings' behavioural results, they provide strong support for the validity of the ratings.

In addition, mothers' perceptions of the normally developing and at-risk/delayed *composite* groups were compared using the rescored DMQ-E. As expected, the mothers of the at-risk or delayed children rated them lower in all three instrumental mastery motivation domains and competence. However, there was no difference in the ratings of mastery pleasure. Hupp (sample 9) found that 24–36-month-old developmentally delayed children were rated lower on persistence and competence, but not mastery pleasure, than mental-aged equivalent 8–18-month-old normally developing children. These two sets of findings with delayed children are consistent, and indicate that parents of delayed children believe their toddlers are lower on the instrumental but not expressive aspects of mastery motivation.

The validity of the questionnaires was also supported by the findings from an intervention programme. Butterfield and Miller's (1984, sample 3) intervention, designed to teach parents how to 'read' and respond to their baby's cues, raised children's motivation on mastery tasks *and* raised mothers' perception of their children's mastery motivation (Harmon *et al.* 1984). Because the effect of the intervention on the task scores was as large as (or larger than) that on maternal perceptions, we conclude that the mothers' ratings were largely based on observed behaviour, not just increased expectations.

Correlations with behavioural assessments

Support for the criterion validity of the questionnaires has been obtained from significant correlations of maternal mastery ratings with behavioural mastery task scores. As predicted, general mastery motivation scores

Table 6.3 Factor analyses of mother ratings of their 1–5-year-old on the DMQ (five-factor solution with five items deleted)

	Object mastery motivation	Social/ symbolic motivation	Mastery pleasure	Gross motor motivation	General competence
Object-oriented persistence:					
23 Works to put things together	0.72	—	—	—	—
14 Attempts to complete	0.71	—	—	—	—
24 Attempts to use cause-and-effect toys	0.67	—	—	—	—
29 Tries to open things	0.67	—	—	—	—
31 Finishes puzzle-like toys	0.64	—	—	—	—
1 Repeats until can do it well	0.63	—	—	—	—
17 Explores all parts	0.62	—	—	—	—
9 Does not keep at challenging toy	0.58	—	—	—	—
34 Tries hard to make things work	0.58	—	—	—	—
8 Likes to do things on own	0.56	—	—	—	—
5 Gives up if difficult	0.49	—	—	—	—
19 Prefers to do hard things on own	0.47	—	—	—	—
Social/symbolic persistence:					
33 Likes make-believe	—	0.84	—	—	—
25 Engrossed in pretend play	—	0.83	—	—	—
32 Involved in games with others	—	0.59	—	—	—
28 Will wait for turn in social play	—	0.58	—	—	—
26 Tries to get others to play	—	0.56	—	—	—
30 Play house, etc.	—	0.49	—	—	—

Mastery pleasure:

Item		Loading
2	Smiles after making an effect	0.77
11	No smile after making an effect	0.76
21	Smiles while playing	0.72
18	Excited when figures things out	0.71
7	No smile when playing	0.63

Gross motor persistence:

Item		Loading
27	Involved in physical play	0.81
22	Repeats throwing, etc.	0.79
36	Repeats motor skills to do well	0.72

General competence:

Item		Loading
6	A little slow catching on	0.73
13	Has difficulty doing things well	0.71
4	Solves problem quickly	0.50
20	Does things that are advanced	0.50
10	Acts very competently	0.40

Notes: Principal components factor analysis with varimax rotation. Eigenvalues = 6.16, 3.71, 2.20, 1.93 and 1.44. These five factors account for 50 per cent of the variance. N = 319.
– Item loading less than 0.40.

were significantly correlated $(r = 0.37)^2$ with infants' actual persistence at tasks (Morgan *et al.* 1983, sample 3). In another study, pre-school teachers rated the usual behaviour of eighteen children who had also been tested at a different time with the mastery tasks (Morgan *et al.* 1983, sample 1). There was a significant correlation $(r = 0.41)$ between teacher ratings of the children's persistence and tester ratings of the children's task orientation (persistence).

Fung (1984, sample 8) asked thirty-eight mothers of 18-month-old infants to answer the general scales of the Dimensions of Mastery Questionnaire. Infants were also tested with the Bayley Scales of Infant Development and a version of the mastery tasks developed by Brockman (1984). Mothers' perceptions of the child's persistence and competence were significantly related to the child's behaviour on the Brockman tasks. That is, persistence across the three tasks was significantly correlated with the DMQ general persistence scale $(r = 0.33)$. The mother's ratings of the child's competence were correlated with the child's behavioural competence score summed across the three mastery tasks $(r = 0.34)$ and also with the Bayley Mental Development Index $(r = 0.49)$. As predicted, perceived competence did not correlate significantly with the Bayley Psychomotor Development Index $(r = 0.05, \text{n.s.})$.

The results of a longitudinal study of thirty-eight toddlers (Maslin-Cole *et al.*, this volume, Chapter 11, sample 5) also provide some evidence for the validity of the general scales of the DMQ. Three out of the four correlations between observed task pleasure and DMQ mastery pleasure were significant. This, in contrast to the Fung study, was good evidence for the validity of the mastery pleasure scale. Like the Fung study, there were significant relationships (three out of four correlations) between the Bayley Mental Development Index and the DMQ competence scale.

Sarimski and Warndorf (1991, sample 11) found a significant correlation between developmental quotient and DMQ ratings of competence in a sample of retarded German children. Similarly, in the Massachusetts developmental disability study (sample 29), a relatively high correlation $(r = 0.56)$ was found between DMQ competence ratings and measured IQ, suggesting that mothers accurately rated the degree of their child's disability. In that same study (samples 29 and 30), three out of four correlations of mothers' ratings of object-oriented persistence were significantly related to observed persistence at tasks. However, none of the ratings of mastery pleasure were related to the small amount of observed positive affect on the tasks.

Consistency across types of rater

Another approach to checking the validity of the ratings is to correlate ratings of the same group of children by two different persons. Teacher–

teacher, mother–teacher, father–teacher and mother–father correlations have been examined, with generally significant results.

In the study of Fort Collins teachers and mothers (samples 25 and 26), most children had more than one student-teacher who knew them relatively well. For these fifty-nine children, there were significant teacher–teacher correlations for four of the five rescored DMQ-E scales. Correlations ranged from 0.21 (n.s.) for mastery pleasure to 0.51 for competence, with the three instrumental aspects (i.e. persistence scales) of mastery motivation having significant teacher–teacher correlations of 0.32 to 0.43.

Mother–teacher correlations, for samples 21, 22, 25 and 26 combined, were somewhat lower, but four of the five correlations (the exception being object-oriented persistence) were significant. In the Manitoba pre-school study (samples 16, 17 and 18), there was also general agreement between teachers and parents, with four out of five mother–teacher and father–teacher correlations reaching significance. Mothers and fathers also agreed on their ratings of the child's competence ($r = 0.76$), social/ symbolic persistence ($r = 0.74$) and object-oriented persistence ($r = 0.53$), but the correlations for gross motor persistence and mastery pleasure were non-significant.

Summary of psychometric data

The rescored DMQ-E provides five scales with generally good reliability, shown by internal consistency and stability over time. We think these indicators underestimate the questionnaire's true reliability, since some items were modified as the DMQ evolved. Construct validity is supported by a clear-cut factor structure, especially for ratings from mothers of normally developing children. Other methods of assessing the validity of the questionnaire provide support, but not all are as strong as might be hoped. Parents' ratings of their children correlate moderately with teacher ratings and with behaviour on mastery tasks and standard assessments. Inter-rater agreement was generally best for competence and social/symbolic persistence and modest for gross motor persistence and mastery pleasure. Agreement between mother ratings and child behaviour has, likewise, been best for competence, and modest or variable for mastery pleasure and object-oriented persistence. Comparisons of at-risk or delayed children with normally developing, low-risk groups have shown the expected differences in general and object-oriented persistence, but no difference in mastery pleasure ratings.

One reason for modest correlations between parent and teacher ratings or parent ratings and behaviours observed in the laboratory is that parents see their child in settings which differ from the pre-school or a laboratory environment. Thus, high correlations would not be expected even if each type of assessment were highly valid.

CORRELATES OF MASTERY MOTIVATION

Gender differences

Few significant gender differences were found in the several samples in which this variable was examined. This is consistent with the infant and toddler behavioural literature, where few *mean* gender differences between the sexes in persistence at mastery tasks have been found. On the DMQ-E, however, boys were rated higher on gross motor persistence by both mothers and pre-school teachers, and girls were rated higher on symbolic (pretend) persistence by both mothers and pre-school teachers. For the Massachusetts developmentally disabled group (sample 30), only one out of eighteen gender comparisons was significant, with 3-year-old girls (but not 1–2-year olds) rated higher on symbolic persistence. Parents may, of course, provide different types of toys based on gender stereotypes, and the influence of gender stereotypes may increase as infants become pre-schoolers. These factors may have led to the above differences in gross motor and symbolic motivation.

Hupp *et al.* (in press, sample 10) found that 1-year-old girls were rated higher than boys on mastery pleasure. This finding is not consistent with the above studies or the behavioural results.

Age differences

Age-group comparisons were made for the first composite group using mothers' ratings of normally developing children from 1 to 5 years old. On six of nine DMQ-E scales, the 1–2-year-old children scored lower than at least one of the older groups. Several items on the gross motor, combinatorial and, especially, the symbolic and social persistence scales refer to behaviours that may be too advanced for children under 18 months, so these lower ratings make sense. There was also a linear increase in symbolic and social motivation over the 1 – 5-year age span. Aside from these findings, there were no meaningful patterns of age differences. That is, mothers' ratings of mastery behaviours do not vary much from 1½ to 5 years, perhaps because they are comparing their child to others of roughly the same age. Furthermore, Hupp and Abbeduto (1992, sample 9) found no significant age differences in DMQ-G ratings for normally developing children at 8, 12 and 18 months.

Thus, it appears that the general DMQ scales do not reflect well the developmental changes taking place during infancy and the pre-school years. However, the social/symbolic and gross motor persistence scales do reflect changes taking place in the last part of the second year of life, and social/symbolic persistence seems to increase throughout the 1–5-year age period.

Demographic variables

For the Pittsburgh cross-sectional study (sample 28), we were able to examine relationships of the DMQ scale scores with race (22 per cent minority), number of adults in the home, maternal employment, and socio-economic status. There were no significant correlations with race or maternal employment. The number of adults in the home, which averaged 1.93 with a standard deviation of 0.42, was negatively related to means–end persistence ($r = -0.31$). Thus, toddlers in single-parent homes are perceived to be more involved with or persistent at cause-and-effect and other problem-solving toys than toddlers from two-parent or extended family homes. Social class was positively related to general persistence ($r = 0.30$), and there was a trend in the same direction for means–end persistence. Thus, higher-income families seem to have toddlers who are perceived to be slightly more persistent, especially with toys. In the Massachusetts developmentally disabled study (sample 30), there were no differences between first-born and later-born children or between children of mothers of three education levels on any of the DMQ-E scales.

In general, we were struck by the modest number and size of the significant correlations with demographic variables. In both the Pittsburgh and Massachusetts samples, there were no more significant correlations with these demographic variables than expected by chance. These results are consistent with those based on mastery *task* data (see Barrett *et al.*, this volume, Chapter 5, Study 2).

Mother, father and teacher differences

The mean ratings of mothers and teachers were compared in three studies, one of which also compared mothers with fathers and fathers with teachers. For analyses combining the Massachusetts pre-school study (samples 21 and 22) and the Fort Collins study (samples 25 and 26), mothers rated their children higher than did teachers on seven of the nine DMQ-E scales. In the Manitoba pre-school study (samples 16, 17 and 18), mothers rated their child higher than did teachers on three scales and fathers rated higher than teachers on four scales. It was not surprising that mothers and fathers rated their children somewhat higher than teachers, but it was surprising that the scales on which such teacher–parent differences occurred were generally not the same for the US and Canadian groups. The only consistent differences across samples were on the combinatorial and symbolic persistence scales, where teachers made consistently lower ratings. Other parent–teacher differences were not consistent across samples, perhaps indicating that they are not of practical importance.

Comparing the findings from this and preceding sections, we note that gender, age and parent–teacher variables were differentially related to DMQ mastery ratings. For example, no gender, age or parent–teacher differences were found for independent mastery. On the other hand, mean differences for gender, age and parent–teacher comparisons were found for symbolic persistence.

Mother–child affect exchanges

Results of several studies suggest a relationship between mother–child interaction patterns and DMQ ratings. In the Boulder longitudinal study (Morgan *et al.* 1988, sample 13), observed positive mother–child exchanges at 18 months were related, as would be predicted, to mothers' perceptions of high mastery pleasure in their children. Negative mother–child interactions were related to low scores on the specific persistence items.

The longitudinal results indicate, as did the contemporaneous results, that frequent negative mother–child affective exchanges, in the 18-month play situation, were related to low DMQ persistence and competence ratings later when the child was 39 months (Morgan, Maslin-Cole *et al.* 1990). Mixed affective exchanges (for example, child smile followed by maternal frown or vice versa) at 18 months led to lower independent mastery on the DMQ at 39 months, and frequent positive exchanges at 18 months predicted high persistence, independence and competence on the DMQ at 39 months.

These results suggest that positive exchanges between mother and toddler lead to later child persistence, while earlier negative affective exchanges seem to inhibit both contemporaneous and later child persistence. These findings also suggest that 39-month child independence at mastery tasks, characterized by a tendency not to ask for adult help even when the task is hard, may be enhanced by earlier positive exchanges and reduced by exchanges that were affectively mixed. Pre-school child competence seems to be fostered by earlier positive exchanges with mother but hampered by earlier exchanges which were negative or mixed. Surprisingly, mastery pleasure at 39 months does not seem to be influenced by mother–child affect exchanges at 18 months, even though positive exchanges were contemporaneously related to pleasure.

Mother directiveness and teaching styles

Jennings and Connors (1989, sample 4) found a significant negative correlation ($r = -0.60$) between mothers' perceptions of their 3-year-olds'
mastery motivation and maternal directiveness. Jennings' results are
consistent with several based on mastery tasks. Harmon et al. (1984)
concluded that the mothers of very small premature infants may have
inhibited the development of their children's independent mastery motivation by being overly involved and directive in their attempts to help
their children develop. Fung (1984, sample 8) found some evidence that
if mothers attempted to interact while their child was working on the
mastery task (thus being overly directive), the child showed lower persistence and competence. On the other hand, if the mother only responded
when the child asked for help, the child was likely to be more competent.
Sarimski (1992) likewise found that higher task persistence correlated
with a less directive maternal interaction style. A similar relation was
reported by Hauser-Cram (this volume, chapter 12, sample 30) in a study
of 3-year-old children with Down's syndrome. She found that children
whose parents were highly involved in structuring play activities were less
persistent than other children when presented with a challenging,
problem-posing task.

Busch-Rossnagel et al. (this volume, Chapter 7, sample 27) found that
maternal modelling, which was perhaps too directive, was negatively
related to ratings of all three instrumental aspects of mastery motivation
and to mastery pleasure. Busch-Rossnagel et al. also report that maternal
praise was related to ratings of object-oriented persistence. This is similar
to the results on positive affect exchanges (above) by Morgan, Maslin-
Cole et al. (1990).

Temperament

Using data from the Boulder study (sample 13), Morgan et al. (1988)
examined contemporaneous correlations of the DMQ with ratings of child
temperament. The 18-month DMQ measure of mastery pleasure was
significantly related ($r = 0.45$) to the mothers' ratings of activity level on
the Colorado Child Temperament Inventory (CCTI) (Rowe and Plomin
1977), but mastery pleasure was not related to emotionality or sociability.
This provides evidence that mothers' perceptions of mastery pleasure are
clearly different from their perceptions of their child's emotionality or
sociability. DMQ ratings of the specific persistence items were, as
expected, related to CCTI attention span ($r = 0.46$). Similarly, Sarimski
and Warndorf (1991, sample 11) found DMQ persistence to be related
to temperament measures of approach, intensity and persistence in a
mentally retarded sample.

Behaviour Problems

Mothers' perceptions of mastery motivation have been found to predict certain behaviour problems. In a large group (N = 332) of pre-school-aged twins (sample 15), Morgan, Maslin-Cole *et al.* (1990) found relationships between the DMQ scale scores and mothers' reports of their children's behaviour problems, using the Achenbach and Edelbrock (1983) Child Behavior Checklist. The twins were treated as belonging to two samples; only correlations that were significant in both samples are discussed. As expected, low persistence was related to hyperactivity, and low mastery pleasure was related to depressed behaviour. Other significant correlations make sense, but the conceptual linkages are less clear. For example, low independent mastery was related to social withdrawal; low competence ratings were also rated to social withdrawal and to depressed behaviour, the internalizing clusters. Low persistence was related to aggression and social withdrawal, probably due in part to the fact that in these samples most of the behaviour problems were intercorrelated, forming a 'problem child' cluster.

CONCLUSIONS AND RECOMMENDATIONS

The DMQ has been shown across a number of studies to be a reliable and valid instrument for assessing aspects of young children's mastery motivation and competence. By using this brief assessment technique, investigators have been able to examine relationships between aspects of mastery motivation and other behaviours in studies in which the structured task assessments of mastery motivation would have been too costly and/or time-consuming. Thus, it seems that the Dimensions of Mastery Questionnaire is a useful tool for measuring several aspects of young children's mastery motivation and for differentiating high- and low-risk samples.

The DMQ also provides useful data about the multifaceted nature of young children's motivation to master various types of task. From the pattern of parent and teacher responses to the DMQ, we have found support for an *expressive component* of mastery motivation – mastery pleasure – and for three *instrumental components* of mastery motivation – persistence at object-oriented, social/symbolic and gross motor play. These instrumental components roughly parallel Harter's (1981a) three aspects of perceived competence (academic, social and athletic) in school-aged children.

This multifaceted conceptualization of mastery motivation is seen as a useful way of viewing not only the adult perception data but also what is needed for a more well-rounded behavioural assessment of mastery motivation than has yet been developed. We believe that investigators should not only focus on persistence at object-oriented tasks but should also develop appropriate behavioural methods for assessing social and gross motor domains of mastery motivation. In addition, more attention should be paid to the expressive aspects of mastery motivation, such as task pleasure. We recommend that investigators use the DMQ in conjunction with traditional mastery tasks in order to obtain familiar adults' perceptions and a well-rounded view of young children's mastery motivation.

NOTES

We wish to acknowledge the assistance of a number of colleagues at several points in the development and testing of the questionnaire. Special thanks go to Leola Schultz who conducted most of the statistical analyses. Data were provided by each of the authors and by: Zeynep Biringen (sample 24 in Table 1), Inge Bretherton (samples 12 and 23), Judy Flagle (2), David Fulker (14 and 15), Sandra Pipp (7), Doreen Ridgeway (12 and 23), JoAnn Robinson (13 and 19), and Jane Stump (31). We also acknowledge the advice and assistance of Janelle Carsten, Robin Connors, Anne Culp, Rex Culp, Kent Downing, Jikyeong Kang-Park, Sandra Pipp, Jacqueline Powers and Susan Spieker. Financial support was provided by the Developmental Psychobiology Research Group Endowment Fund provided by the W. T. Grant Foundation and the John D. and Catherine C. MacArthur Foundation Research Network on the Transition from Infancy to Early Childhood.

1 Extensive item and scale psychometric data about the expanded DMQ are provided in a manual by the authors (Morgan *et al.* 1992). This manual, including the questionnaire, is available from the first author (for $6 in the US, $10 abroad) at the Human Development and Family Studies Department, Colorado State University, Fort Collins, CO 80523.
2 Correlations reported in this chapter were significant at p = 0.05 or less, unless otherwise stated.

REFERENCES

Achenbach, T. M. and Edelbrock, C. S. (1983) *Manual for the Child Behavior Checklist and Revised Child Behavior Profile*, Burlington, VT, University of Vermont, Child Psychiatry.
Barrett, K. C. and Morgan, G. A. (in press) 'Continuities and discontinuities in mastery motivation in infancy and toddlerhood: a conceptualization and review', in R. H. MacTurk and G. A. Morgan (eds) *Mastery Motivation: Conceptual Origins and Applications*, Norwood, NJ, Ablex.
Brockman, L. (1984) 'Mastery motivation and competence in young children', paper presented at the NIH Workshop on Mastery Motivation, Bethesda, MD.
Butterfield, P. M. and Miller, L. (1984) 'Read your baby: a follow-up intervention program for parents with NICU infants', *Infant Mental Health 5*, 107–16.
Carey, W. B. and McDevitt, S. C. (1978) 'Revision of the infant temperament questionnaire', *Pediatrics 61*, 735–9.
Flagle, J. R. (1982) 'The effects of occupational therapy intervention on task

performance in Down's syndrome children', unpublished master's project, Colorado State University, Fort Collins, CO.

Fung, A. Y. (1984) 'The relationship of mother's perception to the child's competence and mastery motivation', unpublished master's thesis, University of Manitoba, Winnipeg.

Gottfried, A. E. (1986) *Children's Academic Intrinsic Motivation Inventory (CAIMI)*, Odessa, FL, Psychological Assessment Resources.

Harmon, R. J., Morgan, G. A. and Glicken, A. D. (1984) 'Continuities and discontinuities in affective and cognitive-motivational development', *International Journal of Child Abuse and Neglect* 8, 157–67.

Harmon, R. J., Morgan, G. A., Jacobs, S. E., Glicken, A. D., Culp, A. M., Busch, N. A. and Butterfield, P. M. (1982) 'Comparison of risk and low-risk infants' motivation on a maternal report questionnaire and mastery tasks (summary)', *Program and Proceedings of the Developmental Psychobiology Research Group Second Biennial Retreat* 2, 25.

Harter, S. (1981a) 'A model of intrinsic motivation in children: individual differences and developmental change', in W. A. Collins (ed.) *Minnesota Symposium on Child Psychology*. Vol. 14, Hillsdale, NJ, Erlbaum.

Harter, S. (1981b) 'A new self-report scale of intrinsic versus extrinsic orientation in the classroom: motivational and informational components', *Developmental Psychology* 17, 300–12.

Hupp, S. C. and Abbeduto, L. (1988) 'Comparison of the organization of play by young retarded children who exhibit high and low levels of mastery motivation', presented at the 21st Annual Gatlinburg Conference on Mental Retardation/Development Disabilities, Gatlinburg, TN.

Hupp, S. C. and Abbeduto, L. (1992) 'Comparison of the use of mastery behaviors by eight-, twelve-, and eighteen-month-old children', manuscript submitted for publication.

Hupp, S. C., Lam, S. F. and Jaeger, J. (in press) 'Differences in exploration of toys by one-year-old children: a Korean and American comparison', *Behavior Science Research* 26.

Jennings, K. D. (1992) 'Development of mastery motivation and sense of agency in toddlers', presented at the International Conference on Infant Studies, Miami Beach, FL.

Jennings, K. D. and Connors, R. E. (1989) 'Mother's interactional style and children's competence at 3 years', *International Journal of Behavioral Development* 12, 155–75.

Jennings, K. D., Connors, R. E. and Stegman, C. E. (1988) 'Does a physical handicap alter the development of mastery motivation during the preschool years?', *Journal of the American Academy of Child Psychiatry* 27, 312–17.

Jennings, K., Yarrow, L. and Martin, P. (1984) 'Mastery motivation and cognitive development: a longitudinal study from infancy to three and one half years', *International Journal of Behavior Development* 7, 441–61.

Jennings, K. D., Connors, R. E., Stegman, C. E., Sankaranarayan, P. and Mendelsohn, S. (1985) 'Mastery motivation in young preschoolers: effect of a physical handicap and implications for educational programming', *Journal of the Division for Early Childhood* 9, 162–9.

Lerner, R. M., Palermo, M., Spiro, A. and Nesselroade, J. R. (1982) 'Assessing the dimensions of temperamental individuality across the life-span: the Dimensions of Temperament Survey (DOTS)', *Child Development* 53, 149–59.

MacTurk, R. H., Hunter, F., McCarthy, M. E., Vietze, P. and McQuiston, S.

(1985) 'Social mastery motivation in Down syndrome and nondelayed infants', *Topics in Early Childhood Special Education* 4, 93–109.

Maslin, C. A. and Morgan, G. A. (1985) 'Measures of social competence: toddlers' social and object orientation during mastery tasks', presented at the Biennial Meeting of the Society for Research in Child Development, Toronto.

Morgan, G. A., Harmon, R. J. and Maslin-Cole, C. A., (1990) 'Mastery motivation: its definition and measurement', *Early Education and Development* 1, 318–39.

Morgan G. A., Harmon, R. J., Pipp, S. and Jennings, K. D. (1983) 'Assessing mothers' perceptions of mastery motivation: the utility of the MOMM questionnaire', unpublished manuscript, Colorado State University, Fort Collins, CO.

Morgan, G. A., Maslin-Cole, C. A., Biringen, Z. and Harmon, R. J. (1991) 'Play assessment of mastery motivation in infants and young children', in C. E. Shaefer, K. Gitlin and A. Sandgrund (eds) *Play Diagnosis and Assessment*, New York, Wiley.

Morgan, G. A., Maslin-Cole, C. A., Downing, K. and Harmon, R. J. (1990) 'Antecedents of mastery and prediction of behavior problems (summary)', *Program and Proceeding of the Developmental Psychobiology Research Group Retreat* 6, 31–2.

Morgan, G. A., Maslin-Cole, C. A., Ridgeway, D. and Kang-Park, J. (1988) 'Toddler mastery motivation and aspects of mother–child affect communication (summary)', *Program and Proceeding of the Developmental Psychobiology Research Group Retreat* 5, 15–16.

Morgan, G. A., Harmon, R. J., Maslin-Cole, C., Busch-Rossnagel, N. A., Jennings, K. D., Hauser-Cram, P. and Brockman, L. M. (1992) *Assessing Perceptions of Mastery Motivation: The Dimensions of Mastery Questionnaire, its Development, Psychometrics and Use.* Fort Collins, CO, Colorado State University, Human Development and Family Studies Department.

Redding, R. E., Morgan, G. A. and Harmon, R. J. (1988) 'Mastery motivation in infants and toddlers: is it greatest when tasks are moderately challenging?', *Infant Behavior and Development* 11, 419–30.

Rowe, D. C. and Plomin, R. (1977) 'Temperament in early childhood', *Journal of Personality Assessment* 41, 150–6.

Sarimski, K. (1992) 'Ausdauer bei zielgerichteten Tatigkeiten und mutterliche Strategien in der Interaktion mit behinderten Kindern' (Persistence of intentional actions and maternal intervention style in mentally retarded children), *Psychologie in Erziehung und Uterricht* 39, 170–8.

Sarimski, K. and Warndorf, P. K. (1991), 'Zur Beurteilung der Ausdauer bei zielgerichteten Tatigkeiten in der Psychodiagnostik geistigbehinderter Kinder' (Assessment of persistence in goal-directed activities and psycho-diagnostics of mentally handicapped children), *Sonder-Padagogik* 21, 210–16.

Wachs, T. D. (1987) 'Specificity of environmental action as manifested in environmental correlates of infant's mastery motivation', *Developmental Psychology* 23, 782–90

Yarrow, L. J., Morgan, G. A., Jennings, K. D., Harmon, R. J. and Gaiter, J. L. (1982) 'Infant's persistence at tasks: relationships to cognitive functioning and early experience', *Infant Behavior and Development* 5, 131–42.

Yarrow, L. J., McQuiston, S., MacTurk, R. H., McCarthy, M. E., Klein, R. P. and Vietze, P. M. (1983) 'Assessment of mastery motivation during the first year of life: contemporaneous and cross-age relationships', *Developmental Psychology* 19, 159–71.

Chapter 7

Mastery motivation in ethnic minority groups

The sample case of Hispanics

Nancy A. Busch-Rossnagel, Maribel Vargas, Diana E. Knauf and Ruth Planos

The purpose of this chapter is to examine mastery motivation in ethnic minority groups and to place this work in the context of cross-cultural endeavours in psychology. The concept of mastery motivation described in this chapter is consistent with the notion of effectance motivation proposed by White (1959) and the operationalization of mastery motivation by Yarrow and his colleagues (cf. Yarrow and Messer 1983). Most of this work focused on Euro-American samples; exploration of the validity of the mastery motivation concept for subcultural groups was absent in the literature. Thus, our research was undertaken to adapt two measures of mastery motivation for use with Hispanic populations. The aims of the research were to examine the psychometric properties of the measures (particularly inter-rater reliability, internal consistency and test-retest stability) and to gather initial evidence regarding the validity of the measures for the Hispanic population.

Why Hispanic? Hispanics represent the most rapidly increasing minority population in the United States, and are projected to become the largest ethnic minority group by the year 2000. Hispanic is simply a label that identifies Americans who trace their familial background to a Spanish-speaking country. Groups of Hispanics, such as Mexican-Americans, Cuban-Americans, Puerto Ricans or the more recent immigrants from Central and South America, have different demographic characteristics; what identifies them as a clear ethnic group is their cultural values. These include familism (Fitzpatrick 1987), collectivism and power distance (Hofstede 1980), and present-time orientation (Hall 1983). Because adherence to these cultural values cuts across ancestral background and is the key to self-identity as an Hispanic, Hispanics represent an opportunity to study subcultural influences in American society.

This chapter reports on our early work to explore mastery motivation in subcultural and cross-cultural samples of Hispanic Americans and Puerto Ricans. This research began with an etic or universal approach (Brislin 1976). That is, we took the construct of mastery motivation developed on Euro-American samples (Morgan, Harmon *et al.* 1990) and adapted two measures of the construct for Hispanic samples. The first section outlines the necessary adaptations to the standardized mastery motivation tasks (Morgan *et al.* 1991), and presents reliability and validity evidence for the adapted tasks. The second section includes studies with the Dimensions of Mastery Questionnaire (Morgan *et al.* this volume, Chapter 6). We conclude with questions concerning the psychological processes underlying mastery motivation which might be explored in future subcultural or cross-cultural work.

THE STANDARDIZED MASTERY MOTIVATION TASKS

The standardized mastery motivation tasks were developed by Morgan *et al.* (1987; Morgan *et al.* 1991) as an individualized assessment of mastery motivation. The tasks provide opportunities to observe the behaviour of young children aged 15–36 months when presented with moderately challenging activities. Their testing materials consisted of three sets of tasks (puzzles, shape sorters and cause–effect toys), each set containing six toys that were of increasing difficulty to complete.[1]

The puzzle set was the first to be presented to the child, and the task was to place the pieces correctly. The difficulty of the six puzzles ranged from one with pieces that are interchangeable circles through ones with varied, simple geometric shapes to ones with irregularly shaped, interlocking pieces. All puzzles were commercially available, although we did modify them by adding knobs to pieces or gluing down pieces to simplify the child's task.

The second task set, shape sorters, involved a custom-made shape box similar to those available commercially, except that only one hole was available at a time. The task was to put ten identical pieces into the box through the hole which matched the shape presented to the child. The pieces were three-dimensional shapes of increasing complexity: circles, squares, triangles, rectangles, pentagons and Z-shapes.

The third and last task set involved cause-and-effect toys. These were commercial toys which required the child to perform actions (e.g. push a button, pull a lever or wind a key) to produce an audio-visual effect. The behaviours required at the lowest levels of difficulty were simple motor acts that produced an effect by themselves. At the higher levels, the toys required increasingly long and complex sequences to complete all parts of the task. However, some feedback could be obtained by the operation of less complicated sequences.

The key to the individualized method was the selection of tasks which were moderately difficult for the child. Two criteria were used to define a moderately difficult task:

1 The child must be able to complete at least one part of the task

(e.g. insert one puzzle piece or perform one appropriate action with a cause–effect toy) in the first minute.[2] If the child cannot complete one part in one minute, the task is considered too difficult.

2 The child must not complete all of the solutions or parts of the task in the first minute. If the child does so, the task is considered too easy.

The level of difficulty chosen for the initial task was based on the child's chronological or developmental age. This task was demonstrated by the experimenter, and then the child was encouraged to work on it. Occasionally, the task level selected was too easy or too hard for the child. When this occurred, the original task was stopped, and the child was presented with a toy from the more appropriate level. When the task was moderately difficult for the child, the child's behaviour with the task was observed and coded for a four-minute period. This process was repeated for each of the three task sets, puzzles first, then shape sorters, then cause–effect toys.

According to Barrett and Morgan (in press), mastery motivation has two aspects: a psychological force that stimulates actions (the instrumental aspect) and a positive affect while mastering a task (the expressive aspect). Both aspects were measured with the individualized method. The instrumental aspect was operationalized by the number of fifteen-second intervals (out of sixteen in the four-minute observation) in which the child persisted at solving the problem or working at the task. The expressive aspect was indexed by the number of fifteen-second intervals in which the child smiled or showed other signs of pleasure while involved with the task. A competence score derived from the percentage of total solutions, weighted by the difficulty level of the task, was also obtained during the testing.

Adaptation of the tasks

When we began the research with Hispanics, the three most difficult puzzles used as testing materials by Morgan *et al.* (1991) were no longer commercially available. Thus, the first step in the adaptation process was to select replacement puzzles. The sequence of six puzzles had been tested for scalability, that is, there was evidence to support that puzzle level 6 was more difficult to complete than puzzle level 5, which was more difficult than level 4, and so on. To select new puzzles, we had to identify the parameters that provided this ordering. The difficulty of children's puzzles is determined by a combination of the number of pieces, the shape of the pieces (from simple geometric forms, e.g. a circle, to more complex, irregular forms), the relationship of the shape to the picture (the circle that represents a balloon versus the circle that is a part of a larger picture in a jig-saw puzzle) and the relationship of the pieces to each other (separate versus interlocking). By analysing these attributes in the previous puzzles, we were able to select new puzzles with similar characteristics, and thus lay a foundation for the scalability for the new sequence of puzzles.[3] Identifying the parameters of difficulty also facilitates replacing puzzles in the future, as toy manufacturers change their product lines once again.

The second step in the adaptation process was the translation of the instructions directed to the child during administration of the tasks from English to Spanish. Because the tester has limited interaction with the child, this translation was relatively straightforward.[4]

A third adaptation, namely a change in the testing order, was unantici-pated. Morgan et al. (1991) presented the three different types of task in a counterbalanced order. When we began training testers to administer the tasks, it was clear that our training subjects (who were middle-class Euro-American) were very reluctant stop playing with the cause–effect toys and turn their attention to the puzzles or shape sorters. We antici-pated that this reluctance might be exacerbated in children from families whose financial situations may not allow for the provision of novel, attractive and more engaging play materials, such as the cause–effect toys used in the study. Thus, the decision was made to control the order of the tasks, always administering the puzzles first, then the shape sorters, and finally the cause–effect toys. This change was incorporated in the revision of the manual as well (Morgan et al. 1992).

Assessment of mastery motivation

The adapted, translated tasks were used with Hispanic children to exam-ine the reliability of the scores on the tasks, to explore the hypothesized relationships of mastery motivation and difficulty, and to make prelimi-nary comparisons between the performance of the Hispanic children and children previously tested with the tasks.

The Hispanic sample consisted of 17 Hispanic children, ranging in age from 16 to 38 months ($M = 26.5$). There were 11 boys and 6 girls, and 71 per cent of the sample were of low socio-economic status. The obser-vation of mastery motivation behaviour occurred in a laboratory setting, following the procedures outlined by Morgan et al. (1991). Testing was done by an Hispanic examiner in the language used by the mother when talking with the child. A second observer also scored the child's behaviour and videotaped the test. Eleven of the children were retested after approximately two weeks.

We first examined the inter-observer reliabilities and retest stabilities of the persistence and mastery pleasure scores obtained during the actual testing (as opposed to scoring from the videotapes). The inter-rater reliabilities for the persistence, pleasure and competence scores were

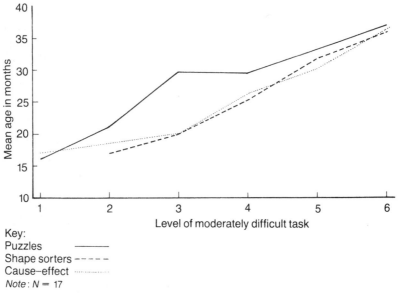

Key:
Puzzles ————
Shape sorters — — — —
Cause–effect ⋯⋯⋯⋯
Note: N = 17

Figure 7.1 Mean ages of children who met criteria for moderate difficulty at each level of task

0.88, 0.87 and 0.99, respectively. The retest stability of the persistence scores was $r = 0.46$, $r = 0.73$ for the pleasure scores, and $r = 0.97$ for the competence scores.

A basic premise of the approach to mastery motivation used by Morgan and his colleagues and adapted here is that persistence is greatest at moderately difficult tasks (Redding *et al.* 1988). While not designed to address this hypothesis, the data of these studies can be utilized to assess the premise indirectly. First, we examined the sequencing of the tasks to see whether the hypothesized ordering of difficulty held for new puzzles as well as for all tasks in the Hispanic sample. The correlations of child age with level of task meeting the criteria for moderate difficulty (i.e. that a child be able to complete at least one part of the task, but not all parts, within the first minute of observation) were significant for each type of task: *rho* (15) = 0.85 for puzzles, 0.86 for shape sorters and 0.91 for cause–effect toys.

Further evidence for the ordering of the tasks is found in Figure 7.1, which presents the mean ages of the children who met the criteria for characterizing a particular level of the task as being moderately difficult. With the exception of the transition from puzzle level 3 to 4, the mean ages ascended from level 1 to level 6 for each task. The aberration in puzzles was the result of two children (33 and 35 months old) who met the criteria for a level 3 puzzle, which was expected to be moderately difficult for 23–24-month-old children. These two children were in foster care, and there was a high probability of prenatal drug exposure.

Twelve of the children were also given more than one level of puzzle, which allowed examination of their performance on tasks of differing difficulty levels. Seven of these children were given puzzles which were too difficult for them (i.e. they did not place one piece of the puzzle within the first minute). Of these seven, six (86 per cent) showed more task persistence on the puzzle that was moderately difficult for them than on the puzzle that was too difficult for them. Eight children worked on puzzles which were too easy for them (i.e. they completed all parts of the puzzle within the first minute), and six children (75 per cent) showed equal or more task persistence on the moderately difficult puzzles than on the too-easy puzzle. Recognizing the small sample, these data are consistent with Redding et al. (1988), and suggest that the hypothesized relationship between task difficulty and task persistence would hold in Hispanic samples.

The effect of repeated testing on difficulty level was also explored by comparing the level of the tasks meeting the criteria for moderate difficulty at the two times of testing. Of the 33 tasks which were moderately difficult at the retesting (3 tasks for each of 11 children), 19 (58 per cent) were at the same level as at the first testing, while 12 (36 per cent) were at the next higher level of difficulty. Two children (6 per cent) failed to complete any part of a task which they had partially completed before; one task was a puzzle, the second a shape sorter.

After examining the difficulty level of the tasks, we compared the children's persistence scores at the two times of testing. The overall mean persistence scores across the three tasks and separate means for each type of task at the two times of testing are presented in Table 7.1. The overall means were significantly different at the two times of testing, $t(10)$ = 3.15, p < 0.01, with children showing more persistence at the first time of testing than at the second. Such a difference is consistent with the difficulty hypothesis, if we assume that a task is more difficult (but still moderately difficult) at first presentation than at later exposures. The significant difference in the overall scores between the two times of testing can be attributed to the mean difference in persistence at the shape-sorter task, although the means for the puzzle and cause–effect tasks for time 1 are higher than at time 2.

In addition to difficulty, there is a second interpretation of the difference in persistence at the two times of testing. Spontaneous comments by the mothers suggested that many of these children had not been exposed to puzzles or cause–effect toys before the administration of the standardized tasks. The shape sorters were constructed for the mastery motivation studies, so every child was unfamiliar with them. The behaviour termed effectance motivation by White (1959) is intimately tied to the child's search for novelty, and the shape sorters (which showed the greatest difference at the two testing times) were the most novel task.

Table 7.1 Mean persistence scores at first and second testing

Type of task	Time 1 testing	Time 2 testing	t-value
All tasks:			
Mean	10.58	7.21	3.15**
SD	2.52	3.93	
Puzzles:			
Mean	9.36	7.45	1.18
SD	3.20	4.85	
Shape sorter:			
Mean	10.55	4.45	4.97**
SD	3.80	4.97	
Cause–effect:			
Mean	11.82	9.72	1.76
SD	4.09	4.29	

Notes: $N = 10$. **$p < 0.01$.

The approach to mastery motivation developed by Morgan and his colleagues stresses difficulty (or complexity) of tasks, but difficulty and novelty are often intertwined. Morgan, Culp, Busch-Rossnagel and Redding (Study 2 in Barrett *et al.*, this volume, Chapter 5) did not find a relationship between familiarity of mastery motivation toys (defined as similarity to children's favourite toys) and mastery-task scores. However, they caution that the range of familiarity might be limited. Thus, research should explore further the relationship between novelty and difficulty in affecting the persistence of young children.

The final analysis of the scores from the standardized mastery motivation tasks involved comparing the pleasure and persistence scores of the Hispanic sample (at the first time of testing) to the currently available norms. Because the range of scores for mastery pleasure is usually very small (few children show mastery pleasure in more than one or two intervals), the norms for pleasure are presented as a dichotomous variable indexing any pleasure versus no pleasure. The Hispanic children showed little mastery pleasure: for both the puzzles and the shape-sorter tasks, four children (24 per cent) showed mastery pleasure (positive affect while task oriented), while two children (12 per cent) showed mastery pleasure on the cause–effect toys. Morgan *et al.* (1992) found that, depending on age, between 9 per cent and 42 per cent of the children working on puzzles, between 25 per cent and 50 per cent of the children working with the cause–effect toys, and between 10 per cent and 33 per cent of the children working on shape-sorter tasks showed some mastery pleasure. The comparison of the Hispanic samples to the earlier studies suggests that the incidence of mastery pleasure maybe lower in Hispanic samples. However, the heterogeneity of the sample and the small size limit any conclusions. Given the high level of non-verbal expression characteristic of Hispanic mothers, the limited affect on the part of the tester (as specified in the standardized procedure) was potentially very discrepant with the experience of these children. Thus, another variable besides their mastery motivation may have influenced their behaviour.

We used a clinical approach to evaluate each child's persistence scores. That is, we took the normative age group closest to the children's age and ascertained whether their persistence score was within a normative range (defined as plus or minus one standard deviation). These comparisons are shown in Table 7.2. On shape-sorter and cause–effect tasks, more than half (59–71 per cent) of the children were at or above the mean, with approximately one-quarter being greater than one standard deviation above the mean on each task. On the puzzles, 58 per cent of the Hispanic children were below the mean, with half of these (29 per cent of the total) being more than one standard deviation below the mean. Across the three tasks, the percentage of children above and below the normative range is approximately equal (18 per cent v. 16 per cent, respectively) and consistent with expectations for a normally distributed individual characteristic. These results suggest similarities between Hispanic and Euro-American samples.

Further research is necessary to replicate and explore the discrepancy between persistence at puzzles and persistence at shape-sorter and cause–effect tasks. It may be that these primarily low-income Hispanic children have not been exposed to puzzles at home and that this lack of exposure limits persistence. Such speculation would be at odds with the novelty hypothesis, however. An alternative explanation might have to do with the strangeness of the situation for the child. The visit to the laboratory was a new experience for most of the children, as was the behaviour of the tester (i.e. the limited affect). This novelty may have unduly influenced the child's initial behaviour. After adjusting to the experimenter's 'strange' behaviour, the children may have been able to focus more on the tasks presented to them (i.e. the shape-sorter and cause–effect tasks).

The comparisons for persistence and pleasure scores from the mastery tasks demonstrate the problems inherent in using subcultural or cross-cultural studies to establish the generalizability of measures. Two outcomes are possible. One is that there would be no differences between the samples, as seems to be the case with the persistence scores. While researchers may be tempted to conclude that such a finding establishes the generalizability of the measures, such a conclusion would not be valid from only one study. Our research methods allow the disconfirmation, but not the acceptance of the null hypothesis, so the conclusion of no

Table 7.2 Comparison of persistence scores to normative range

Score is:	Puzzle tasks (n)	%	Shape sorter tasks (n)	%	Cause–effect tasks (n)	%	Overall tasks (n)	%	Expectation %[a]
Below −1 SD	(5)	29	(2)	12	(1)	6	(8)	16	16
Above −1 SD, below mean	(5)	29	(5)	29	(4)	24	(14)	27	34
Above mean, below +1 SD	(6)	35	(6)	35	(8)	47	(20)	39	34
Above +1 SD	(1)	6	(4)	25	(4)	24	(9)	18	16

Notes: N = 17. Means and standard deviations for normative range are taken from Morgan et al. (1992). [a] Expectations are based on the assumption that persistence is a normally distributed characteristic.

differences is inappropriate until the findings are replicated. The second outcome is that the groups would show differences, as might be the case with the pleasure scores and the discrepancy between puzzles and the other two tasks here. Because random assignment to subcultural or cultural group is not possible, there are many variables, other than culture, which might be creating these differences. For example, if we were to control the novelty of the testing situation or materials, would Hispanics and Euro-Americans be different in pleasure or on puzzles? Thus, no firm conclusions about the generalizability of the standardized mastery motivation tasks can be drawn from this one study. However, the results are encouraging and suggest that, as adapted, the individualized method is appropriate for continued use with Hispanic populations.

THE DIMENSIONS OF MASTERY QUESTIONNAIRE

The Dimensions of Mastery Questionnaire (DMQ; Morgan *et al.*, this volume, Chapter 6) utilizes a second approach to measuring mastery motivation, namely adult ratings of children's behaviour via questionnaire.

Adaptation of the questionnaire

The adaptation of a questionnaire to an ethnic group with a different dominant language represents more of a challenge than the adaptation of standardized behavioural observations, because of the translation issues. When established questionnaires are utilized, the preferred method of adaptation uses a process of back translation (Brislin *et al.* 1973; Marín and Marín 1991). This method involves two bilinguals who work independently. The first takes the original version and translates it to the language of interest, the second then translates this version back to the original language, and the two same-language versions are compared. Discrepancies between the two must be resolved by modification of the translation. However, if the original version of the questionnaire can be modified, then a process of decentring (Werner and Campbell 1970) is better suited to produce an instrument culturally appropriate for both language groups (Marín and Marín 1991).

For the DMQ, the translation of the items was done at a time of revision, so the decentring process was used. The questionnaire was first translated into Spanish. There was a potential for misinterpretation of idioms in the English version. Because of this problem and the inadequacy of literal translations, slight changes were made to some items in translation. For instance, the wording for items 1 and 36 was changed from *practices* in the English version to *repeats*, because there was a concern that the word 'practice' could be interpreted as meaning that these skills had been fully mastered by the child and not as referring to the process of learning a new skill. The change in these two items was subsequently adopted in a revision of the English version, a change which is consistent with the decentring process, but would not be allowed in a back translation.

An item for which there was no adequate translation into Spanish was item 6. In this case, the original English version reads, 'Is a little slow catching on to things'. There is no equivalent phrasing in Spanish for 'catching on to things', so a literal translation was inappropriate. The Spanish version ('Se tarda un poco al tratar de entender las relaciones entre las cosas') can be translated back into English as 'Takes a while longer when trying to understand associations among things'.

In addition to issues of clarification, changes were made in wording to make items correct for both genders by adding the proper ending to adjectives and using he or she where appropriate. The revised items were translated back into English once again by someone unfamiliar with the original English version. As a final step in the decentring process, any discrepancies in meaning which were observed between the original and the back translation were discussed by bilingual judges and resolved. The result is two versions of the questionnaire which are culturally appropriate and linguistically equivalent.

Assessment of mastery motivation

While the decentring adaptation of the DMQ occurred several years ago, no data were available concerning the psychometric properties of the DMQ when used with Hispanics. Thus, two samples of Hispanic mothers were asked to provide ratings of their child's behaviour using the DMQ. The first were the seventeen mothers or care-givers of the children described in the previous section. These women completed the DMQ while their child was being tested with the standardized mastery tasks; ten completed a second DMQ at the time of retesting.

The second sample consisted of 68 Puerto Rican and Dominican mothers from studies of maternal teaching behaviours (Planos 1993; Vargas 1991). The education of these mothers ranged from fourth grade to college, with the median level being high-school graduation. The age of the children ranged from 27 to 66 months, with a mean of 48.5 months.

The mothers in both samples completed the DMQ in the language of their choice, with 38 being completed in English and 47 in Spanish. There were no mean differences between the mothers' ratings in English and those in Spanish, nor was there a relationship between maternal ratings and level of education or child's age.

The DMQ yields three persistence ratings, for object, social/symbolic and gross motor tasks, along with the affective component of mastery

Table 7.3 Dimensions of Mastery Questionnaire (DMQ) reliability data

	Coefficient alpha			
DMQ scale	All DMQs (n = 85)	Spanish DMQs (n = 47)	English DMQs (n = 38)	Test retest (n = 10)
Object-oriented persistence	0.81	0.83	0.75	0.69
Social/symbolic persistence	0.78	0.81	0.75	0.61
Gross motor persistence	0.74	0.75	0.76	−0.13
Pleasure	0.36	0.37	0.38	0.58
Competence	0.57	0.68	0.39	0.86

pleasure and a competence rating. The stability and internal consistency estimates of these scores are presented in Table 7.3. Except for the negative stability of gross motor persistence, the stability of the scores is reasonable, as are the internal consistency estimates of the persistence scales. As the alpha coefficients are approximately equal or higher for the Spanish version, the decentring procedure seems to have been successful.

As a preliminary evaluation of validity, the persistence and pleasure scores from the DMQ were compared to the scores on the structured tasks for the seventeen children in the first sample. The care-givers' ratings of their children's mastery pleasure were related to the child's mastery pleasure on the standardized tasks, $r = 0.37$. Surprisingly, the maternal ratings of persistence and competence were negatively related to persistence and competence scores on the tasks, $r = -0.46$ for object-oriented persistence, $r = -0.24$ for social-symbolic persistence, $r = -0.18$ for gross motor, and $r = -0.24$ for competence. The relationship between maternal ratings of pleasure and child affective behaviour on the tasks is about equal to those found by Morgan *et al.* (this volume, Chapter 6) in their studies comparing the DMQ to the mastery tasks. However, the negative correlation of the maternal ratings and the child behaviour undermines the potential validity of the measures for Hispanic populations, although it is not clear whether the problem lies with the DMQ, the standardized tasks, or both measures, or is the result of the small sample size.

A preliminary answer to this question comes from a comparison of the maternal DMQ ratings with maternal ratings of the child's temperament and maternal behaviour in a structured teaching task. Scores from the Dimensions of Temperament Survey-Revised (DOTS-R; Windle and Lerner 1986) were available for twenty-seven of the Puerto Rican and Dominican mothers participating in the studies of maternal teaching behaviour (Planos 1993; Vargas 1991). The DOTS-R is a maternal report temperament scale with fifty-four items and nine scales. Two scales on

Table 7.4 Correlations between maternal DMQ ratings and maternal teaching behaviours and temperament ratings

| | DMQ scale | | | |
| | Persistence | | | |
Variable	Object oriented	Social/ symbolic	Gross motor	Pleasure
Temperament dimension:				
Mood	n.a.	n.a.	n.a.	0.30
Orientation	0.19	0.02	0.13	n.a.
Teaching behaviour:				
Praise	0.45*	–	–	0.20
Inquiries	0.44*	0.27	0.24	0.50**
Negative verbalizations	–	–	–	0.27
Modelling	−0.44*	−0.43*	−0.52**	−0.40*
Directives	0.25	–	–	0.22

Notes: N = 31 for temperament and N = 29 for teaching behaviours. Correlations less than 0.20 are not included for teaching behaviours. *p < 0.05. **p < 0.01. – = < 0.02.

the DOTS-R are related to mastery motivation, orientation (which is indexed by distractibility and persistence items) and mood (which contains items relating to affect). The correlations between the DMQ and the DOTS-R are shown in Table 7.4. None of the relationships was significant, but all were in the expected positive direction or very negligible.

Scores from the Maternal Teaching Observation Technique (MTOT; Laosa 1980) were also available for twenty-nine mothers in this sample. The MTOT is a structured observation of maternal behaviours (e.g. praise, modelling, visual cues) during the teaching of a cognitive-perceptual task (copying Tinkertoy models) to young children. Frequencies of the maternal behaviours were coded by two raters to yield a frequency-per-minute score for each of the behaviours. The overall inter-rater reliability for the behavioural codes was 0.90.

Morgan, Maslin-Cole *et al.* (1990) found that negative and mixed affect exchanges of mothers and their 18-month-old toddlers were negatively related to persistence and pleasure, while positive exchanges were positively related to persistence and pleasure. Thus, we expected that negative verbal behaviours on the MTOT would be negatively related to persistence and pleasure, while praise was expected to be positively related. The correlations obtained are presented in Table 7.4. As expected, praise was positively related to object-oriented persistence, $r(27) = 0.45$, p < 0.05. Likewise, inquiries showed a positive relationship with object-oriented persistence, $r(27) = 0.44$, p < 0.05 and with pleasure, $r(27) = 0.50$, p < 0.01. Interestingly, modelling was negatively related to object-oriented, social symbolic and gross motor persistence, r (27) = − 0.44, p < 0.05, r (27) = − 0.43, p < 0.05, r (27) = − 0.52, p < 0.01, as well as being negatively related to pleasure, r (27) = − 0.40, p < 0.05. While not the subject of a priori expectations, these relationships are consistent with the definition of mastery motivation as being an intrinsic force, while modelling represents extrinsic control from the adult.

The pattern of relationships between the DMQ and the DOTS-R shows only a limited correspondence, but the relationship between the DMQ and MTOT is generally as expected, and thus provides support for the DMQ. Thus, it seems that the negative relationships between the DMQ and the tasks are more likely to be an artefact of the small sample size than a problem with the DMQ or the structured tasks. When considered separately, there is evidence supporting both the reliability and the validity of the two measures of mastery motivation.

THE ROLE OF CROSS-CULTURAL RESEARCH IN MASTERY MOTIVATION STUDIES

Our research with Hispanic samples involved investigation of mastery motivation from a cross-cultural perspective. Our procedures and findings from both the standardized mastery motivation tasks and the DMQ illustrate both the benefits and problems inherent in taking a construct derived from one cultural group and attempting to apply it to a new group. As such, our study reminds us of the proper role and interpretation of cross-cultural or subcultural research in psychological studies.

The ultimate goal of psychology is the understanding of behaviour; this goal will best be met through research that focuses on both the explanation and the interpretation of behaviour (Washington and McLoyd 1982). In psychology, the search for causes of behaviour has most successfully utilized the classic experimental design. This involves the manipulation of and random assignment to levels of the independent variable to see effects on the dependent variable – the behaviour of interest. In cross-cultural psychology, cultures are the independent variables, but culture is a status variable which cannot be manipulated easily or randomly assigned. Thus, cross-cultural research is not ideal for investigations which search for explanations of behaviour.

Cross-cultural research holds more promise for enhancing the interpretation of behaviour (Busch-Rossnagel 1992). When cross-cultural or subcultural work on different ethnic groups is conducted to examine the population generalizability of the tests or results, the findings are likely to yield factors which are confounded with the variables of interest. Our research has suggested two such factors: the confusion between difficulty level and novelty, and that between the tester's behaviour and the cultural expectation for non-verbal expression. The confusion may be seen as an impediment to clear interpretation, or as the avenue for identifying areas for further exploration – the approach suggested here.

In addition, cross-cultural research can be useful to basic research when the environments explored are maximally different along the psychological dimensions of interest (Busch-Rossnagel 1992). For example, middle-class Euro-American mothers show little variability in the materials they provide for children's play. If we are interested in the effect of difficulty or novelty on children's mastery motivation, then we need to find environments which show variability in the provision of play materials. Such environments are likely to be from different ethnic or cultural groups.

However, a search for variability via inclusion of different ethnic groups alone may lead to the further confusion of variables. In this example, family income and play materials are likely to be confused. However, if the psychological concept underlying the relationship between culture and behaviour is specified (for example, novelty or difficulty level of play materials), then the assumption of variability can be tested and potential confounding variables can be controlled (Busch-Rossnagel 1992).

We might, however, expect that the complexity of toys provided to children is influenced not only by family incomes, but also by the socialization goals of the parents and the techniques which they believe will be successful in achieving those goals. Such parental beliefs form part of the subjective culture (Triandis 1972) or subjective ecosystem (Diaz-Guerrero and Diaz-Loving 1990), and are related to parental education (and therefore to family income) and to cultural values. Thus, the cultural values which identify Hispanics as a group – namely time orientation, collectivism and so on – are likely to be related to mastery motivation. For example, the notion of mastery motivation examined here presupposes individual effort. In a culture where collectivism is valued as it is by Hispanics, then persistence and other indications of mastery motivation may have different meanings. Future research has the challenge of focusing on the meaning of such constructs in the Hispanic culture and relating them to mastery motivation as currently defined.

Thus, cross- or sub-cultural research on mastery motivation can help us to consider what psychological processes underlie the task pleasure and task persistence we observe. We have seen that three proximal processes (namely task difficulty, task novelty, and non-verbal expression in care-giving behaviour), together with several distal influences (socialization goals, parenting techniques and cultural values) influence mastery motivation. Future research, not only with Hispanics and other ethnic minority groups, but also with majority samples, should examine these processes to enhance our understanding of mastery motivation in all cultures.

NOTES

The research reported here was supported by Biomedical Research Support Grants from Fordham University to the first author and was begun during a Summer Faculty Fellowship, also to the first author and supported by Fordham University.

1 The testing materials are described in Morgan *et al.* 1992.
2 The most recent revision of the individualized method uses a two-minute criterion period, rather than one minute, to ensure moderate difficulty level. However, in the research described here and in other chapters in this volume using the individualized method (Maslin-Cole *et al.*, Chapter 11, Hauser-Cram, Chapter 12), the one-minute criterion was used.
3 The new puzzles are described in the most recent revision of Morgan *et al.* 1992.
4 The Spanish version of the instructions may be obtained from the authors.

REFERENCES

Barrett, K. C. and Morgan, G. A. (in press) 'Continuities and discontinuities in mastery motivation during infancy and toddlerhood: a conceptualization and review', in R. H. MacTurk, G. A. Morgan and E. J. Hrncir (eds) *Mastery Motivation: Conceptual Origins and Applications*, Norwood, NJ, Ablex.

Brislin, R. W. (1976) 'Comparative research methodology: Cross-cultural studies', *International Journal of Psychology* 11, 215–29.

Brislin, R. W., Lonner, W. J. and Thorndike, R. M. (1973) *Cross-cultural Research Methods*, New York, Wiley.

Busch-Rossnagel, N. A. (1992) 'Commonalities between test validity and external validity in basic research on Hispanics', in K. F. Geisinger (ed.) *Psychological Testing of Hispanics*, Washington, DC, American Psychological Association.

Diaz-Guerrero, R. and Diaz-Loving, R. (1990) 'Interpretation in cross-cultural personality assessment', in C. R. Reynolds and R. W. Kamphaus (eds) *Handbook of Psychological and Educational Assessment of Children: Personality, Behavior, and Context*, New York, Guilford Press.

Fitzpatrick, J. P. (1987) *Puerto Rican Americans: The Meaning of Migration to the Mainland*, 2nd edition, Englewood Cliffs, NJ, Prentice-Hall.

Hall, E. T. (1983) *The Dance of Life*, Garden City, NY, Anchor Books.

Hofstede, G. (1980) *Culture's Consequences*, Beverly Hills, CA, Sage Publications.

Laosa, L. M. (1980) 'Maternal teaching strategies in Chicano and Anglo-American families: the influence of culture and education on maternal behavior', *Child Development* 51, 759–65

Marín, G. and Marín, B. V. (1991) *Research with Hispanic Populations*, Newbury Park, CA, Sage Publications.

Morgan, G. A., Harmon, R. J. and Maslin-Cole, C. A. (1990) 'Mastery motivation: its definition and measurement', *Education and Development* 1, 318–39.

Morgan, G. A., Maslin, C. A. and Harmon, R. J. (1987) 'Mastery motivation tasks: a manual for 15- to 36-month old children', unpublished manuscript, Colorado State University.

Morgan, G. A., Busch-Rossnagel, N. A., Harmon, R. J. and Maslin-Cole, C. A. (1992) 'Individualized assessment of mastery motivation: manual for 15 to 36 month old children', unpublished document, Bronx, NY, Fordham University, Department of Psychology.

Morgan, G. A., Maslin-Cole, C. A., Biringen, Z. and Harmon, R. J. (1991) 'Play assessment and mastery motivation in infants and young children', in C. Schaefer, K. Gitlin and A. Sandgrund (eds) *Play Diagnosis and Assessment*, New York, Wiley.

Morgan, G. A., Maslin-Cole, C. A., Downing, K. and Harmon, R. J. (1990) 'Antecedents of mastery and prediction of behavior problems (summary)', *Program and Proceedings of the Developmental Psychobiology Research Group Fifth Biennial Retreat* 5, 15–16.

Morgan, G. A., Maslin-Cole, C. A., Harmon, R. J., Busch-Rossnagel, N. A., Jennings, K. D., Hauser-Cram, P. and Brockman, L. M. (1992) 'Assessing perceptions of mastery motivation: The Dimensions of Mastery Questionnaire, its development, psychometrics and use', unpublished document, Colorado State University, Human Development and Family Studies Department.

Planos, R. (1993) 'Correlates of teaching strategies in low-income Dominican and Puerto Rican mothers', unpublished document, Fordham University.

Redding, R. E., Morgan, G. A. and Harmon, R. J. (1988) 'Mastery motivation in infants and toddlers: is it greatest when tasks are moderately challenging?', *Infant Behaviour and Development* 11, 419–30

Triandis, H. C. (1972) *The Analysis of Subjective Culture*, New York, Wiley.

Vargas, M. (1991) 'Predictors of maternal teaching strategies in Puerto Rican mothers', unpublished dissertation, Fordham University.

Washington, E. and McLoyd, V. C. (1982) 'The external validity of research involving American minorities', *Human Development* 25, 324–39

Werner, O. and Campbell, D. T. (1970) 'Translating, working through interpreters and the problem of decentering', in R. N. Cohen and R. Cohen (eds) *A Handbook of Method in Cultural Anthropology*, New York, American Museum of Natural History.

White, R. W. (1959) 'Motivation reconsidered: the concept of competence', *Psychological Review* 66, 297–333.

Windle, M. and Lerner, R. M. (1986) 'Reassessing the dimensions of tempermental individuality across the life-span: the Revised Dimensions of Temperament Survey (DOTS-R)', *Journal of Adolescent Research* 1, 213–330.

Yarrow, L. J. and Messer, D. J. (1983) 'Motivation and cognition in infancy', in M. Lewis (ed.) *Origins of Intelligence*, 2nd edition, Hillsdale, NJ, Erlbaum.

Chapter 8

Social and motivational development in deaf and hearing infants

Robert H. MacTurk

In several influential papers, Robert White (1959, 1963) offered a critique of traditional drive theories of motivation and conceptualized the existence of an intrinsic drive to engage and control the environment. This drive toward competence, which he termed *effectance motivation*, sparked efforts to operationalize the concept and to develop an appropriate methodology, beginning in the early 1970s. Some preliminary studies of effectance motivation in school-aged children were conducted in the early 1970s by Susan Harter and colleagues (Harter 1975; Harter and Zigler 1974), but it was not until the late 1970s that a concerted effort was made to operationalize the concept and develop a methodology appropriate for the study of the motivational characteristics of young infants. The results of these efforts, with normally developing hearing infants and with developmentally delayed hearing infants, served to validate a methodology by showing moderate relationships to standardized measures of competence (Messer *et al.* 1986; Yarrow *et al.* 1983), and by linking parental behaviours to their infant's motivation to master the environment (Jennings *et al.* 1979; McCarthy and McQuiston 1983; Yarrow *et al.* 1982, 1984).

Two aspects of this series of investigations are relevant here. First, their primary focus was on the infants' motivation to explore the inanimate environment, with relatively little attention paid to social motivation or socially mediated expressions of motivated behaviour. Second, the focus of the validation studies employed samples of infants with known or suspected cognitive and/or physical impairments.

The infant's early experience with the social environment is considered to be the foundation upon which subsequent developmental competence is built. Over the years, a rich literature has been developed which charts the infant's acquisition of social skills, their correlates, and consequences of variations in the social environment on later development. Despite this background, the social facets of mastery motivation have been addressed only infrequently. Although the situation in which mastery motivation was assessed minimized social interaction with the tester and mother, several researchers have explored the social aspects of motivated behaviour (MacTurk *et al.* 1985; Maslin and Morgan 1985; Morgan *et al.* 1991; Vondra and Jennings 1990; Wachs 1987). These investigations established the importance of the social domain and prompted our curiosity about the combining of socially oriented behaviours into infants' object-related activities.

The rationale for previous investigations with atypical populations rested on the assumption that their motivation to interact with the environment and their ability to benefit from their attempts to gain mastery are depressed. Strong support for this assumption is contained in the series of reports by MacTurk and colleagues (1985, 1987) on the motivational characteristics of infants born with Down syndrome. Additional studies of premature infants, physically handicapped children and mentally retarded children also provide convergent evidence that handicapped infants and children suffer deficits in their motivated behaviour (Harmon *et al.* 1984; Jennings *et al.* 1985).

Although these investigations have furthered our confidence in the validity of the methodology employed to assess mastery motivation, they provided little knowledge about the range of motivated behaviour or the origins of observed deficits. We know, for example, that the presence of an atypical infant may profoundly affect the nature of the early interpersonal environment, as Koester and Meadow-Orlans (1990) have discussed in some detail. The effects of maternal behaviour on infant mastery and achievement motivation have been documented in several studies (Butterfield and Miller 1984; Harmon and Culp 1981; Redding *et al.* 1990). However, it remains difficult to draw firm conclusions concerning the origins of the observed deficits. This is because of the interaction between the functional limitations a particular condition may place on a child and the parent's reactions to that child.

The interactions between parents and handicapped infant, in general, and deaf infants, in particular, are typically characterized as being less rich and more directive or intrusive (Field 1987; Lederberg 1984; Schlesinger 1985; Wedell-Monnig and Lumley 1980). Not only is the range of interactive variation restricted but the opportunities to control, direct and otherwise affect the environment are restricted by the external controls imposed by an overly intrusive parent. Both of these characteristics may serve to undermine the infants' motivation to learn from their interactions with the environment.

However, this emphasis on a deficit model of development may cause us to ignore the possibility that atypical children may have particular, domain-specific strengths that ameliorate the effects of physical, mental or sensory impairments. This point was demonstrated powerfully by Fraiberg's (1974) work with normally developing blind infants. She found that blind infants use their hands to communicate a wide range of affective expressions normally carried on the face in sighted infants.

Other research with sensory-impaired infants examined the possible adaptive strategies exhibited by deaf infants to control the environment. It may be that deaf infants, like blind infants, develop compensatory behaviours in an effort to obtain the same information from two sensory channels that hearing infants obtain from three.

The lack of auditory contact may be especially problematic for these infants because an important precursor of intellectual competence (exploratory behaviour) is a responsive environment. This is an area that has received a great deal of attention and has repeatedly been shown to be important for social/emotional and cognitive development. Virtually all previous studies examined responsiveness in hearing infants and employed measures requiring auditory contact – for example, parental vocal responsiveness (McCarthy and McQuinston 1983) or measures that confound physical responsiveness and vocal responsiveness (Bell and Ainsworth 1972; Riksen-Walraven 1978). Researchers have never addressed the possible effects of deafness in an effort to understand the range of adaptive skills that infants may develop. Vision is the most obvious channel for deaf infants' adaptations.

The results of a pilot study of mother–infant interaction suggested that important differences exist between deaf and hearing infants in their use of the visual channel. Meadow-Orlans et al. (1987) found a decided shift from 3 to 6 months in deaf infants' attention to objects when compared with hearing infants. At 3 months of age, both the deaf and hearing infants spent most of their time looking at their mothers' faces in face-to-face interaction. At 6 months of age, the deaf infants spent twice as much time looking at objects rather than their mothers' faces, whereas the hearing infants spent only 3 per cent more time in object attention.

Additional studies of the motivational characteristics of deaf infants amplified the results from the preliminary investigations. MacTurk and Trimm's (1989) study of a small sample of deaf and hearing 12-month-olds found that, while the groups spent equal amounts of time visually attending to objects, the deaf infants spent more time looking at the objects prior to their first physical contact with them. More importantly, the deaf infants engaged with the social environment and displayed a positive emotional response to the situation sooner than the hearing infants. In addition, positive affect was more likely to be followed by a social behaviour for the deaf infants, a transition which never occurred with the hearing infants.

The results of these previous investigations uniformly point to the importance of addressing the social aspects of infants' interactions with objects as a means of furthering our understanding of the early development of atypical infants. The aim of this report is to describe the development of mastery motivation in a sample of normally developing deaf infants from hearing families, and to examine the responses to a lack of auditory contact with the environment.

DATA COLLECTION

The data contained in this report were obtained as part of a longitudinal investigation of the early development of deaf infants born to hearing families. The general aims of this larger study were to describe the early social, motivational and language development of deaf infants, and involved a series of observations in a laboratory setting when they were 9, 12 and 18 months old. The data contained in this report were obtained from assessments of mastery motivation which were conducted at 9 and 12 months.

Recruitment and sample characteristics

Early severe hearing loss is an extremely low-incidence condition in otherwise normally developing infants, and one which is usually not diagnosed until delays in language acquisition become apparent (Stein *et al.* 1983). To recruit the target sample size of twenty deaf infants with hearing parents within a reasonable length of time required a multi-site, collaborative recruitment strategy. In addition to recruitment efforts at the Gallaudet University, four experienced research groups (University of Texas-Dallas, University of Pittsburgh, Georgia State University-Atlanta, and University of Massachusetts-Amherst) agreed to collaborate in the recruitment and videotaping of the deaf infants.

Once a family with an infant who met the criteria for inclusion was identified, a letter of invitation was sent with a postcard for the parents to return if they were interested in participating. After each visit to an off-site laboratory, the respective research assistants mailed a videotape, informed consent, medical and audiological release forms, and background information data forms to the Gallaudet research staff. All video-tape coding was performed by the research staff at Gallaudet.

The sample includes twenty deaf infants with hearing parents (DIHP) and a control group of twenty hearing infants with hearing parents (HIHP) matched on sex and mother's education. All of the infants were developing normally, as assessed by the Alpern–Boll Developmental Profile (Alpern *et al.* 1980). Most came from middle-class families with both parents present in the home. Table 8.1 contains the background information for each group.

Fifteen of the deaf infants had a hearing loss in the severe to profound

Table 8.1 Demographic characteristics: means and standard deviations by group

	HIHP (N = 20)	DIHP (N = 20)
Birthweight (in grams)	3481.5 (505.7)	3047.0 (1041.1)
Birth order (% firstborn)	50%	55%
Sex (% males)	60%	60%
Mother's age	32.2 (4.4)	31.2 (3.5)
Mother's education (years)	16.6 (2.3)	15.9 (2.1)
Father's age	33.7 (4.9)	33.8 (4.9)
Father's education (years)	17.9 (1.9)	15.4 (2.6)

Note: Standard deviations are shown in brackets.

range (greater than a 71 dB loss); five had a more moderate loss (26 to 70 dB loss). Hearing loss was confirmed by age 7 months in all cases (mean age at time of diagnosis was 2.8 months). All were enrolled in early intervention programmes by the time they were 10 months old.

Procedures

At each age, the infants were presented with a series of four toys in a fixed order for three minutes each (Table 8.2). During the administration of the tasks, infants sat on their mother's lap at a feeding table, and the examiner sat across from the mother and infant. At the start of each session, the infant was given a warm-up toy for approximately one minute. Following this, the examiner demonstrated a toy to the infant. If no interest was shown within the first minute, it was demonstrated again. After the initial demonstration, the examiner sat quietly while the child played with the toy. The mother was instructed not to interact with or otherwise encourage her child.

Each mastery motivation assessment session was videotaped from behind a one-way mirror. These videotapes were subsequently coded using a remote-controlled Panasonic AG–6300 videocassette recorder connected to an IBM-compatible personal computer running a data-acquisition and recording program. The onset of each behaviour change was keyed into the PC's keyboard while the time (in 1/30 second intervals) was obtained from the videotape control pulse. The resulting data set

Table 8.2 Tasks for assessing mastery motivation

Toy	Task
Toy behind barrier[a]	An attractive lion squeeze toy is placed behind a clear plastic rectangular screen (approximately 6 inches wide and 18 inches high) within reach of the child. The infant may obtain the toy by reaching around the barrier.
Busy poppin' pals[b]	A yellow rectangular box with five pop-up doors that may be opened by operating the manipulanda (push buttons, dials, levers).
Peg board[a]	A yellow plastic rectangular board with six holes on top and six yellow pegs which fit into the holes. The toy is presented with the pegs in the holes and the infant is to remove the pegs. This object is an item from the Bayley Scales of Infant Development. The major diference is that when the Bayley is administered, the goal is to insert the pegs in the holes.
Farm door[b]	A plastic barn with double doors on the front that are latched. A small plastic animal is hidden inside and can be obtained by unlocking the latch and opening the doors.
Discovery cottage[c]	A brightly coloured house with a small front door and a hinged roof. Two dolls are hidden in slots located behind the door and under the roof, and may be obtained by opening the door or raising the roof.
Shapes and slides[c]	A brightly coloured box with three holes on the top where dolls of different shapes are placed. Levers are provided which, when pressed, release the doll down a slide.

Notes: To equalize the stimulus value of the objects for both groups of infants, all noise-making components have been silenced. [a]Presented at 9 months. [b]Presented at 9 and 12 months. [c]Presented at 12 months.

represents a time-based, sequential record of the infant's actions during the mastery motivation assessment session.

The mastery motivation coding system (Table 8.3) was designed to capture the full range of an infant's behaviour during an observation session and was divided into three general categories:

1 object codes – behaviours which are directed toward the toy;
2 social codes – behaviours which are directed towards the mother or examiner;
3 affect codes: – the infant's facial expressions of emotional state (smiling, fussing, interest, etc.).

The coding system was designed to permit simultaneous recording of

Table 8.3 Mastery motivation laboratory behaviour categories

Measure	Behaviour
Look	Only look at object.
Explore	Touch, mouth or hold object.
Manipulate	Active manipulation or examination of object (includes banging, shaking, or hitting object).
Task-directed	Task-related activity (including grasping, holding, or reaching for object). To qualify as a task-directed activity, the action must be related to the specific properties of the object.
Goal-directed	Goal-directed activity; this category is more specific than the task-directed behaviours. Here, the behaviour must (1) be related to specific properties of the object, and (2) if continued, lead to success.
Success	Obtains object or solves problem presented by toy.
Social	Looks and/or vocalizes to experimenter or mother. Also includes leaning back on mother and rejecting or offering object.
Off-task	Engaged with non-task object.

Facial expressions:
  Negative (cry, fuss)
  Obscured
  Neutral
  Interest/excitement
  Positive (smile, laugh)	

any combination of behaviours in the three categories. As a rule, no two behaviours within a category can happen at the same time, but they may co-occur between categories (for example, in the social codes, a baby cannot look at mother and look at examiner at the same time but may explore the object and smile at the same time). The actual coding was performed at the individual behaviour level and combined during the initial data-processing phase to yield the summary measures for each toy. The onsets[1] of each coded event were summed across the full three minutes of toy presentation, then the average across the four toys was computed to yield the measures reported here.

The object codes were derived in part from studies of exploratory behaviour (Switzky *et al.* 1974) and served as the basis for the ob' associated activities ('explore' and 'manipulate'). The next tw' (task- and goal-directed) were derived from general theories o' (Atkinson 1957; Hunt 1965; Piaget 1952) and observ' behaviour during the administration of standard' assessments (Yarrow *et al.* 1975). The levels were con' with the categories 'explore', 'manipulate', 'task-related' and 'goal-directed' ordered in relation to the degree of skill required of the infant. For example, exploring and manipulating the discovery cottage would include such behaviours as mouthing one of the dolls, banging or pushing the cottage, or holding the object while looking at the examiner. The task-related and goal-directed behaviours, on the other hand, consisted of activities which were related to the design of the toy and directed towards a possible solution. Examples of these with the discovery cottage would be attempting to open the door or roof (behind which are small dolls, visible through the windows), opening and closing the door or roof, or attempting to replace the doll in its original position.

The behaviours directed towards the examiner or mother were considered to be a form of social referencing in which infants used adults' emotional responses as guides to continued interaction with the objects (Clyman et al. 1986; Feinman 1982).

Affect was included in the social measure for both theoretical and empirical reasons. Facial expressions are considered to be a window to the infant's emotional appraisal of events (Izard 1971) and thus provide important information concerning infant state. In addition, our preliminary work with this population and the importance of positive affect in general (McCall 1972) led us to focus on positive affective displays in the context of social interaction.

Measures

On the basis of previous investigations of mastery motivation (Jennings et al. 1979; Yarrow et al. 1983), we focused on four measures: (1) explore; (2) persist; (3) success; and (4) social smile (social behaviours which co-occurred with positive affect).

1 Exploratory behaviours are common measures of infants' behaviour with objects and have often been employed as a measure of the infant's interest in learning about the characteristics of objects and the environment (McCall et al. 1977; Ruff 1984).
2 Persistence in goal-directed behaviour is the primary measure of mastery motivation. Task persistence has long been considered an index of motivation (Tolman 1932). More recently, Atkinson (1957), Feather (1962) and Weiner et al. (1980) have pointed to persistence as the defining characteristic of motivated behaviour. Thus, we assumed that the frequency of attempts to master a task was a valid index of mastery motivation.
3 Success with an object indexed the child's competence.
4 Social smiling was selected as the social measure for both theoretical and empirical reasons. White (1959) was quite explicit in stating that,

while the effectance motivation system was intrinsic to the organism, it was maintained by the positive feelings of efficacy derived from solving problems. This contention was supported by MacTurk *et al.* (1985), who found that task persistence resulted in positive affect but success did not. Morgan's (Morgan *et al.* 1990) assessments of mastery pleasure also produced similar findings.

Reliability

Inter-rater reliability was assessed by having two trained observers independently code 16 per cent ($N = 13$) of the eighty mastery assessment videotapes. These estimates were computed on the frequency of the individual measures and the Pearson product–moment correlations ranged from 0.60 for 'explore' to 0.96 for 'success', with a mean correlation of 0.82.

DATA ANALYSIS

The data were analysed in several phases.[2] Preliminary analyses were conducted to test for the presence of systematic differences according to research site, level of hearing loss, and sex differences. The descriptive phase consisted of a 2 (group) × 2 (age) repeated measures analysis of variance (MANOVA). In addition, correlational analyses were conducted to examine the interrelations among the measures for each group at each age. The final analysis examined the predictive relations among the measures for each group.

Preliminary analyses

Alpern–Boll Developmental Profile (Alpern *et al.* 1980) physical development and self-help sub-scales were converted into mean developmental quotients for the two ages. The physical development mean quotients were 114 and 108 for the deaf and hearing infants, respectively ($t = 1.52$, ns). The self-help mean quotients were 106 and 112 for the deaf and hearing infants, respectively ($t = -1.02$, ns).

The majority of the infants were seen in the laboratory on the Gallaudet University campus ($N = 10$). Therefore, the subjects were divided into two groups and analysed using Student's *t*-test. This analysis revealed no significant differences (above what would be expected by chance alone) on the measures of mastery motivation. Similar analyses were conducted on hearing level and infant sex. Again, no significant differences were detected.

Table 8.4 Mastery motivation measures for deaf and hearing infants at 9 and 12 months: means, standard deviations and repeated measures MANOVA significance levels

| | Deaf infants | | Hearing infants | | ANOVA effects | | |
	9	12	9	12	Group	Age	Group × age
Explore	13.61 (3.57)	14.89 (4.42)	13.79 (2.71)	12.78 (4.02)	n.s.	n.s.	n.s.
Persist	14.20 (3.66)	17.55 (6.14)	13.99 (3.16)	15.90 (5.98)	n.s.	<0.01	n.s.
Success	3.00 (1.77)	4.08 (2.20)	3.50 (1.76)	4.65 (2.60)	n.s.	<0.01	n.s.
Social smile	1.41 (1.52)	2.46 (1.94)	1.72 (1.52)	1.69 (1.96)	n.s.	n.s.	n.s.

Note: Deaf infants: *N* = 19; hearing infants: *N* = 20. Standard deviations are shown in brackets.

Group differences

The repeated measures MANOVA revealed no significant group differences or group-by-age interactions for any of the measures (Table 8.4). A main effect for age was detected for the frequency of 'persist' and 'success'. Both measures displayed a significant increase from 9 to 12 months – 14.10 to 16.73 (F (1, 37) = 7.81) and 3.25 to 4.37 (F(1, 37) = 8.00) for 'persist' and 'success', respectively. These results supported our expectation that hearing status among healthy, normally developing infants does not affect their motivation to explore objects nor their engagement with the social environment.

Contemporaneous correlations

9-month intercorrelations

The correlations among the measures for the deaf infants revealed one significant relationship, 'explore' with 'persist' (Table 8.5). The remainder were statistically independent, except for a moderate relationship between the frequency of 'social smile' and 'persist'. This is in sharp contrast with the pattern of relationships found among the hearing infants.

For the hearing infants, all of the object engagement measures were highly correlated with each other. This suggests that the hearing infants' actions with the objects were relatively undifferentiated and that the mastery assessment was tapping a general exploratory behaviour system as opposed to a more sophisticated motivational system. In addition, the correlations between 'social smile' and object engagement were all in the negative direction; those infants who looked and smiled at the examiner or mother frequently were those who were less persistent.

In some respects, given the logic of the coding system and the operational definition of persistence (which required visual attention to the object), this was to be expected. Since, by definition, social behaviours could not co-occur with persistent, task-directed behaviours, it is almost

Table 8.5 Intercorrelations for the 9-month measures of mastery motivation and social smiles for the deaf and hearing infants

	Explore	Persist	Success	Social smile
Explore	–	**0.72***	**0.60**	**−0.08**
Persist	0.81***	–	**0.70***	**−0.31**
Success	0.35	0.22	–	**−0.11**
Social smile	0.26	0.40+	−0.04	–

Notes: +p < 0.10. **p < 0.01. ***p < 0.001. Correlations for the deaf infants (n = 20) are below the diagonal; correlations for the hearing infants (n = 20) are in **bold** and above the diagonal. − = 1.00.

a given that more of one class of behaviour must reduce the available time to engage in other classes. However, the deaf infants displayed a positive relationship between their persistent, goal-directed activities and social smiling. It appears that the deaf infants were skilled at combining the rival demands of these two domains; it also appears that an increased reliance on social sources of feedback led to a diffusion of the mastery-related activities, as evidenced by the low correlations between the object measures.

12-month intercorrelations

In some respects the pattern of intercorrelations obtained from the 12-month assessment mirrored the earlier results (Table 8.6). The deaf infants displayed a pattern of correlations that was similar to the hearing infants' at 9 months. This pattern of correlations is also in keeping with the hierarchical conceptualization of the levels of object engagement; 'explore' was correlated with 'persist', and 'persist' with 'success'. The hearing infants, on the other hand, maintained the pattern of task involvement observed at the earlier age.

The major change from 9 to 12 months centres on the relationships between social smiling and the object-related behaviours. This is especially evident for the hearing infants. Where, before, social smiling was unrelated to the child's attempts to master the toys, now it appears to be an integral part of their repertoire. For the deaf infants, a similar pattern of relations held, both at the earlier age and in comparison with the hearing infants.

The results of the data obtained from the 12-month-old hearing infants imply that the relative importance of socially directed behaviours in the context of attempts to master the environment undergoes a significant transformation during the interval from 9 to 12 months – a similar finding to that of an earlier report about 6- and 12-month-old infants (MacTurk et al. 1987). This is in contrast to our finding here of a transformation towards increased domain-specific independence for the deaf infants over

Table 8.6 Intercorrelations for the 12-month measures of mastery motivation and social smiles for the deaf and hearing infants

	Explore	Persist	Success	Social smile
Explore	–	0.90***	0.78***	0.53*
Persist	0.81***	–	0.88***	0.44*
Success	0.19	0.62**	–	0.38+
Social smile	0.29	0.26	0.26	–

Notes: +p < 0.10. *p < 0.05. **p < 0.01. ***p < 0.001. Correlations for the deaf infants (N = 19) are below the diagonal; correlations for the hearing infants (N = 20) are in **bold** and above the diagonal.

the same time span. We see that, at 9 months, social smiling accounts for 16 per cent of the observed variance in the index of mastery motivation for the deaf infants and 9 per cent for the hearing infants. At 12 months, the situation is reversed. Now only 7 per cent of the variation in mastery motivation may be explained by the frequency of social smiling for the deaf infants, and 19 per cent is explained for the hearing infants.

We are unsure of why this might be. It may be that the deaf infants are showing a delay in their ability to process two competing sources of information about their environment. Though this developmental-delay argument may have some merit, we feel that these results support a conclusion that the deaf infants have developed a unique set of compensatory behaviours. Hearing infants have access to environmental information through three main channels (visual, tactile and auditory), all of which may be processed simultaneously. The deaf infants must develop skills which enable them to acquire information in a sequential manner.

As Wood (1982) has suggested, deafness prevents the child from simultaneously exploring the world visually *and* receiving the vocal narrative that often accompanies such activity. Thus, for the deaf infant, visual attention to an object or person, and communication about that object or person, must typically occur in a sequential rather than a parallel fashion. This places an increased strain on the infants' developing attention, memory and integrative capacities, possibly diminishing their early interactions with both the animate and inanimate environment. However, as may be seen from the results presented here, those deaf infants who are better able to integrate the social–object sequences appear to have a relative advantage over their deaf peers, who were not as adept with this sequencing skill.

Cross-age correlations

Turning to the predictive relations among the measures, an interesting pattern of differences emerges. For the hearing infants (Table 8.7), all of the significant cross-age correlations were between measures of task involvement. Not only did 'explore', 'persist' and 'success' show a high

Table 8.7 Cross-age correlations for the hearing infants

	12 months			
9 months	Explore	Persist	Success	Social smile
Explore	0.60**	0.33	0.35	0.18
Persist	0.56**	0.46*	0.48*	0.30
Success	0.72***	0.63**	0.61**	0.39+
Social smile	0.08	0.06	−0.02	−0.06

Notes: +$p < 0.10$. *$p < 0.05$. **$p < 0.01$. ***$p < 0.001$. $N = 20$.

Table 8.8 Cross-age correlations for the deaf infants

9 months	12 months			
	Explore	Persist	Success	Social smile
Explore	−0.01	0.18	0.11	0.00
Persist	0.19	0.22	−0.03	0.17
Success	0.14	0.19	0.01	0.09
Social smile	0.56**	0.55**	0.34	0.44+

Notes: +$p < 0.10$. **$p < 0.01$. $N = 20$.

degree of cross-age stability, but persistence at 9 months predicted success at 12 months as earlier success predicted later persistence. This is consistent with White's (1959) and Yarrow's (Yarrow *et al.* 1983) contention that mastery motivation serves to support competence and the rewards of mastery (or competence) serve to maintain the motivation to master the environment.

The deaf infants (Table 8.8), in comparison, displayed virtually no cross-age stability in any of the measures of task engagement. However, social smiling at 9 months was predictive of later 'explore' and 'persist', and showed a moderate degree of stability. These findings represent a curious situation, in which social smiling was unrelated to the deaf infants' organization of object-directed activities contemporaneously, yet led to higher levels of task engagement at the later age. As stated earlier, we feel that these cross-age correlations support our contention that, for the deaf infants, the integration of social behaviours into the ongoing stream of object-related activities represents an adaptation to their lack of auditory contact with the environment. There were no mean differences between the groups in their deployment of object or social interaction at either age, but there were differences in how these behaviours were related. This raises the question of whether or not the same behaviour has the same psychological meaning for the two groups of infants.

CONCLUSIONS

Two explanations could account for these results, and they lead to very different conclusions. One explanation involves a reformulation of the measures, and the other involves a reinterpretation of the mastery-motivation assessment situation.

We had originally conceptualized the social measure as representing a form of social referencing, in which the adult's social signals are used to assist the infant's appraisal of their performance. This adequately explains the observed relationships for the hearing infants but may not be entirely correct for the deaf infants; social smiling for the deaf infant may represent social motivation and not social referencing. Cross-situational support for this is contained in a report by MacTurk (1992), who found that social bids during an episode of maternal still-face in a mother–infant interaction at 9 months of age was highly correlated with later persistence in deaf infants but not in hearing infants. In general, those deaf infants who persisted in their attempts to control their social environment, regardless of the situation, were also more motivated to control the inanimate environment.

This supports the conclusion that the deaf infants have developed a set of compensatory strategies to overcome their reduced contact with the environment. As indicated earlier, hearing infants experience a social and object environment that provides sources of feedback which may be processed simultaneously. Deaf infants, on the other hand, experience a social and object environment which requires adaptations to enable the infant to process environmental signals sequentially. Though this adaptation does not register in terms of mean differences, it may register in terms of its consequences, both across ages and across situations.

The alternative explanation involves a rethinking of the meaning of the assessment situation itself. The original research paradigm (i.e., serial presentation of toys and minimal social interaction) was designed to examine the infants' self-directed attempts to master the objects. This benign interpretation may mask some subtle and unforeseen dynamics which may differentially affect the two groups.

In many respects, the lack of responsiveness by the adults combined with the close proximity is similar to the still-face episode during the typical mother–infant, face-to-face interaction situation. Tronick (Tronick and Gianino 1986) describes maternal still-face as a moderate stressor which permits the infant's adaptive resources to be observed. It has been suggested that the mastery assessment parallels the still-face episode. Just as the mother's presence combined with her non-responsiveness produces uncertainty in the infant, the presence of the mother and examiner combined with non-interaction in a situation where mutual toy play would be the normative condition might also produce uncertainty.

This uncertainty did not affect overall distribution of mastery-related behaviours between the groups, but did affect the relation between behaviours. The picture that emerges from the pattern of correlations for the hearing infants is one of a focus on their interactions with the objects. Although they did not explore the toys more than the deaf infants, their behaviour was more predictable from knowing the other behaviours.

The deaf infants, on the other hand, showed a more unpredictable pattern of interaction. The correlations suggest that their object-related and socially directed activities were statistically independent of one another. This independence of social and exploratory/mastery behaviours suggests that social smiling may serve a different psychological function for deaf infants. Social smiling for the hearing infants may represent a signal to participate in child's exploration of the object, especially since social smiling was not correlated with success. If the mastery-assessment situation is, in fact, similar to episodes of maternal still-face, the deaf infants may be seeking visual feedback concerning their performance in an effort to reduce greater situational ambiguity. In this sense, the formal definition of social referencing may be a more appropriate explanation for the observed predictive relationships between social and object behaviour. If the hypothesis that social referencing represents a coping strategy is true, then the deaf infants who were able to integrate social/coping behaviours into their ongoing stream of object-related activities at 9 months were able to devote more of their efforts to exploration and goal-directed activities at 12 months. This explanation rests on the assumption that the deaf infants were more stressed during the mastery assessment than their hearing peers.

Koester and Trimm (1991), for example, found that during the still-face episode, 9-month-old deaf infants spent more time in self-regulatory or self-comforting behaviours than their hearing counterparts. Gianino and Meadow-Orlans (1987) report a similar finding in 6-month-old deaf infants with deaf mothers. The conclusions derived from these findings was that, under conditions of interactional uncertainty, the deaf infants were more stressed than hearing infants. This was most probably due to a greater reduction in sensory input. Our current research efforts involves a closer examination of stress-markers in deaf infants from deaf or hearing families in a variety of situations (including the mastery-motivation assessment) to address the origins of these group differences.

In summary, the results of this investigation provide additional evidence in support of the existence of a specific motivational system. This system is sensitive to individual differences, shows a moderate degree of cross-age stability, and provides important information about how various groups of infants negotiate one of the most important tasks of development; the achievement of competence.

NOTES

This research was supported by the Division of Maternal and Child Health, Bureau of Health Care Delivery and Assistance (Grant No. MCJ–110563) and the Gallaudet Research Institute.

1 Previous reports measured these behaviours in terms of the time spent (expressed as a percentage-duration) engaged in each of the variables. This approach introduces dependencies in the data, since the total duration must add up to 100 per cent. This is especially problematic with the contemporaneous correlations, because a high correlation between two measures means a low correlation between two others, thus making the interpretation difficult. The use of frequencies reduces this problem.

2 A videotape of one deaf infant at 12 months was uncodable for technical reasons. The data for this subject was included for the 9-month analyses but not in the cross-age analyses.

REFERENCES

Alpern, G. D., Boll, T. J. and Shearer, M. S. (1980) *Manual, Developmental Profile II*, revised edition, Aspen, CO, Psychological Development Publications.

Atkinson, J. W. (1957) 'Motivational determinants of risk-taking behavior', *Psychological Review* 64, 359–72.

Bell, S. M. and Ainsworth, M. (1972) 'Infant crying and maternal responsiveness', *Child Development* 43, 1171–90.

Butterfield, P. M. and Miller, L. (1984) 'Read your baby: a follow-up intervention program for parents with NICU infants', *Infant Mental Health Journal* 5, 107–116.

Clyman, R. B., Emde, R. N., Kempe, J. E. and Harmon, R. J. (1986) 'Social referencing and social looking among twelve-month-old infants', in T. B. Brazelton and M. W. Yogman (eds) *Affective Development in Infancy*, Norwood, NJ, Ablex.

Feather, N. T. (1962) 'The study of persistence', *Psychological Bulletin* 59, 94–115.

Feinman, S. (1982) 'Social referencing in infancy', *Merrill-Palmer Quarterly* 28, 445–70.

Field, T. (1987) 'Interaction and attachment in normal and atypical infants', *Journal of Consulting and Clinical Psychology* 55, 853–9.

Fraiberg, S. (1974) 'Blind infants and their mothers: an examination of the sign system', in M. E. Lewis and L. A. Rosenblum (eds) *The Effect of the Infant on its Caregiver*, New York, Wiley.

Gianino, A. and Meadow-Orlans, K. P. (1987) 'Stress and self-regulation in six-month-old deaf and hearing infants with deaf mothers', poster presented at the Biennial Meeting of the Society for Research in Child Development, Baltimore, MD.

Harmon, R. J. and Culp, A. M. (1981) 'The effects of premature birth on family functioning and infant development', in I. Berlin (ed.) *Children and Our Future*, Albuquerque, University of New Mexico Press.

Harmon, R. J., Pipp, S. L. and Morgan, G. A. (1984) 'Mastery motivation in perinatal risk infants', invited presentation at a NICHHD conference on mastery motivation in infancy and early childhood, Bethesda, MD.

Harter, S. (1975) 'Developmental differences in the manifestation of mastery motivation on problem solving tasks', *Child Development* 46, 370–8.

Harter, S. and Zigler, E. (1974) 'The assessment of effectance motivation in normal and retarded children', *Developmental Psychology* 10, 169–80.

Hunt, J. McV. (1965) 'Intrinsic motivation and its role in psychological development', in D. Levine (ed.) *Nebraska Symposium on Motivation. Vol. 13*, Lincoln, NE, University of Nebraska Press.

Izard, C. E. (1971) *The Face of Emotion*, New York, Appleton-Century-Crofts.

Jennings, K. D., Connors, R. E., Stegman, C. E., Sankaranarayan, P. and Mendelsohn, S. (1985) 'Mastery motivation in young preschoolers: effect of a physical handicap and implications for educational programming', *Journal of the Division for Early Childhood* 9, 162–9.

Jennings, K., Harmon, R., Morgan, G., Gaiter, J. and Yarrow, L. (1979) 'Exploratory play as an index of mastery motivation: relationships to persistence, cognitive functioning and environmental measures', *Developmental Psychology* 15, 386–94.

Koester, L. S. and Meadow-Orlans, K. P. (1990) 'Parenting a deaf child: stress, strength and support', in D. Moores and K. P. Meadow-Orlans (eds)

Educational and Developmental Aspects of Deafness, Washington, DC, Gallaudet University Press.

Koester, L. S. and Trimm, V. M. (1991) 'Face-to-face interactions with deaf and hearing infants: do maternal or infant behaviors differ?', paper presented at the Biennial Meeting of the Society for Research in Child Development, Seattle, WA.

Lederberg, A. R. (1984) 'Interaction between deaf preschoolers and unfamiliar hearing adults', *Child Development* 55, 598–606.

MacTurk, R. H. (1992) 'Relations between mother–infant interaction and the organization of mastery motivation in 9- and 12-month deaf and hearing infants', poster presented at the 8th International Conference on Infant Studies, Miami Beach, FL.

MacTurk, R. H. and Trimm, V. M. (1989) 'Mastery motivation in deaf and hearing infants', *Early Education and Development* 1, 19–34.

MacTurk, R. H., McCarthy, M. E., Vietze, P. M. and Yarrow, L. J. (1987) 'Sequential analysis of mastery behavior in 6- and 12-month-old infants', *Developmental Psychology* 23, 199–203.

MacTurk, R. H., Hunter, F. T., McCarthy, M. E., Vietze, P. M. and McQuiston, S. (1985) 'Social mastery motivation in Down syndrome and nondelayed infants', *Topics in Early Childhood Special Education* 4, 93–109.

Maslin, C. A. and Morgan, G. A. (1985) 'Measures of social competence: toddlers' social and object orientation during mastery tasks', presented at the Biennial Meeting of the Society for Research in Child Development, Toronto.

McCall, R. B. (1972) 'Smiling and vocalization in infants as indices of perceptual-cognitive processes', *Merrill-Palmer Quarterly* 18, 341–7.

McCall, R. B., Eichorn, D. H. and Hogarty, P. S. (1977) 'Transitions in early mental development', *Monographs of the Society for Research in Child Development* 42 (3), Serial No. 171).

McCarthy, M. E. and McQuiston, S. (1983) 'The relationship of contingent parental behaviours to infant motivation and competence', paper presented at the Biennial Meeting of the Society for Research in Child Development, Detroit, MI.

Meadow-Orlans, K. P., MacTurk, R. H., Prezioso, C. T., Erting, C. J. and Day, P. S. (1987) 'Interactions of deaf and hearing mothers with three- and six-month-old infants', paper presented at the Biennial Meeting of the Society for Research in Child Development, Baltimore, MD.

Messer, D. J., McCarthy, M. E., McQuiston, S., MacTurk, R. H., Yarrow, L. J. and Vietze, P. M. (1986) 'Relation between mastery behavior in infancy and competence in early childhood', *Developmental Psychology* 22, 336–72.

Morgan, G. A., Harmon, R. J. and Maslin-Cole, C. A. (1990) 'Mastery motivation: definition and measurement', *Early Education and Development* 1, 318–39.

Morgan, G. A., Maslin-Cole, C. A., Biringen, Z. and Harmon, R. J. (1991) 'Play assessment of mastery motivation in infants and young children', in C. E. Schaefer, K. Gitlin and A. Sandgrund (eds) *Play Diagnosis and Assessment*, New York, Wiley.

Piaget, J. (1952) *The Origins of Intelligence in Children*, New York, International Universities Press.

Redding, R. E., Harmon, R. J. and Morgan, G. A. (1990) 'Maternal depression and infants' mastery behaviors', *Infant Behavior and Development* 13, 391–6.

Riksen-Walraven, J. M. (1978) 'Effects of caregiver behavior on habituation rate and self-efficacy in infants', *International Journal of Behavioral Development* 1, 105–30.

Ruff, H. A. (1984) 'Infants' manipulative exploration of objects: effects of age and object characteristics', *Developmental Psychology* 20, 9–20.

Schlesinger, H. S. (1985) 'Deafness, mental health, and language', in F. Powell, T. Finitzo-Hieber, S. Friel-Patti and D. Henderson (eds) *Education of the Hearing Impaired Child*, San Diego, College-Hill.

Stein, L., Clark, S. and Kraus, N. (1983) 'The hearing-impaired infant: patterns of identification and habilitation', *Ear and Hearing* 4, 232–6.

Switzky, H. N., Haywood, H. C. and Isett, R. (1974) 'Exploration, curiosity, and play in young children: effects of stimulus complexity', *Developmental Psychology* 10, 321–9.

Tolman, E. C. (1932) *Purposive Behavior in Animals and Man*, New York, Appleton-Century.

Tronick, E. Z. and Gianino, A. F. (1986) 'The transmission of maternal disturbance to the infant', in E. Z. Tronick and T. Field (eds) *Maternal Depression and Infant Disturbance*, New York, Wiley.

Tronick, E. Z., Als, H. and Brazelton, T. B. (1980) 'Monadic phases: a structural descriptive analysis of infant–mother face-to-face interaction', *Merrill-Palmer Quarterly* 26, 3–24.

Vondra, J. I. and Jennings, K. D. (1990) 'Infant mastery motivation: the issue of discriminant validity', *Early Education and Development* 2, 340–53.

Wachs, T. D. (1987) 'Specificity of environmental action as manifest in environmental correlates on infant's mastery motivation', *Developmental Psychology* 23, 782–90.

Wedell-Monnig, J. and Lumley, J. M. (1980), 'Child deafness and mother–child interaction', *Child Development* 51, 766–74.

Weiner, B., Kun, A. and Benesh-Weiner, M. (1980) 'The development of mastery, emotions and morality from an attributional perspective', in W. A. Collins (ed.) *Minnesota Symposium on Child Psychology. Vol. 14*, Hillsdale, NJ, Erlbaum.

White, R. W. (1959) 'Motivation reconsidered: the concept of competence', *Psychological Review* 66, 297–333.

White, R. W. (1963) 'Ego and reality in psychoanalytic theory', *Psychological Issues* 3, 1–40.

Wood, D. J. (1982) 'The linguistic experiences of the pre-lingually hearing-impaired child', *Journal of the British Association of Teachers of the Deaf* 6, 86–93.

Yarrow, L. J., Rubenstein, J. L. and Pedersen, F. A. (1975) *Infant and Environment: Early Cognitive and Motivational Development*, Washington, DC, Hemisphere, Halsted, Wiley.

Yarrow, L. J., Morgan, G. A., Jennings, K. D., Harmon, R. J. and Gaiter, J. L. (1982) 'Infant's persistence at tasks: relationships to cognitive functioning and early experience', *Infant Behavior and Development* 5, 131–42.

Yarrow, L. J., McQuiston, S., MacTurk, R. H., McCarthy, M. E., Klein, R. P. and Vietze, P. M. (1983) 'Assessment of mastery motivation in the first year of life: contemporaneous and cross-age relationships', *Developmental Psychology* 19, 159–71.

Yarrow, L. J., MacTurk, R. H., Vietze, P. M., McCarthy, M. E., Klein, R. P. and McQuiston, S. (1984) 'Developmental course of parental stimulation and its relationship to mastery motivation during infancy', *Developmental Psychology* 20, 492–503.

Chapter 9

The construct validity of measures of social mastery motivation

Terri T. Combs and Theodore D. Wachs

While mastery motivation during child and adulthood may be viewed as differentiated into various motives, this differentiation is not thought to occur until post-infancy (Dweck and Elliot 1983; White 1959). Hence, infant mastery motivation has traditionally been considered to be a global individual characteristic. Given the predominance of this global viewpoint it is not surprising that research on infant mastery motivation has focused primarily on object-mastery behaviours (e.g. Jennings *et al.* 1979; Yarrow *et al.* 1975, 1982, 1983, 1984).

In terms of alternative types of mastery motive, Harter (1981) has proposed that mastery motivation should be examined separately in the cognitive, social and physical domains. While Harter was speaking primarily about school-aged children, Wachs and Combs (in press) have argued that separate social and object dimensions of mastery motivation are also identifiable during infancy. Their argument is based on evidence suggesting that early object and social mastery motivation have independent *developmental courses*, independent *developmental correlates* and independent *environmental predictors*. While existing evidence suggests that mastery motivation is differentiated into social and object mastery during infancy, the strength of this evidence is limited by ambiguity in the measurement and conceptualization of the social mastery construct. These ambiguities are considered in the following sections.

THE MEASUREMENT OF SOCIAL MASTERY MOTIVATION

MacTurk *et al.* (1985) defined social mastery motivation as 'the motivation to generate, maintain, and influence the course of social interactions', while Wachs (1987) defined it as the persistence of children's attempts to obtain adult attention. Common to both definitions are measures of the amount of social interaction that a toddler displays in a standard situation. The greater the amount of social interaction, the higher the judged level of social mastery motivation. The relation of *context* to this type of behaviour is not yet clear.

The context in which social mastery motivation has been measured has involved two dimensions: (1) social v. object nature of the *tasks*, and (2) structured v. free play *format*. In terms of *task* factors, MacTurk *et al.* (1985) measured the amount of socially directed behaviour during object and social tasks (e.g. peek-a-boo), and found differences between normal infants and infants with Down's syndrome in the amount of social behaviour displayed during object tasks but not during social tasks. Given these results, MacTurk *et al.* considered only social behaviour during social tasks to be indicative of social mastery motivation.

In terms of play *format*. recent evidence from our laboratory indicates that proportionately more socially directed behaviour and less object-directed behaviour occurred during a free-play situation than during a structured-play situation. Even more critically, our findings indicate that the nature of mastery play may vary in free-play and structured-play situations. Based on a principle components analysis on the play behaviour of sixty-four 12-month-old toddlers (see Table 9.1), separate object and social mastery factors emerged when toddlers were tested in a structured-play situation (Factors I and IV). In free play not only did separate object and social mastery factors not appear, but it was also unclear whether socially oriented infants were showing mastery or 'pseudo-mastery' behaviours. That is, infants high on Factor I, while showing high levels of social mastery behaviours, also displayed high levels of social orientation and distress along with low levels of exploratory object play and object mastery. Interpretation of this component suggests that these infants seemed to show a high degree of socially directed behaviour because of distress, rather than because of a desire to interact competently with the social environment. Supporting this interpretation, Combs (1987) found that fussy-difficult temperament was positively related to social mastery motivation measures in free play but not in structured settings.

Besides emphasizing the importance of context, the above results also suggest that we may need to pay attention to the quality (affective tone) as well as the quantity of social mastery motivation. Conceptually, positive affect shown during mastery behaviour is thought to be an indication of the pleasure derived from the behaviour. Affect is considered to be an important component of mastery motivation (Morgan and Harmon 1984) and is viewed as separable from the persistence aspect of mastery motivation (Barrett *et al.*, this volume, Chapter 5). Both positive and negative affect may play a role in mastery motivation (Barrett *et al.*, this volume). Mastery pleasure during object play has been included in object mastery measures (Morgan *et al.* 1987) and has been found to be related to task-directed behaviour (Morgan *et al.* 1988). For the most part, in studies that assess social mastery, the quantity of social interactions has been assessed without assessing affective tone during the procedure.

Table 9.1 Factor analysis of duration measures in structured and free-play
situations

Behaviours* Structured play:	Factors and factor loadings			
	I	II	III	IV
Object mastery	0.86	–	–	–
Active object exploration	– 0.85	−0.41	–	–
Passive object watching	−0.59	0.63	–	–
Object pre-mastery	0.43	−0.42	−0.55	–
Passive social orientation	–	0.80	–	–
Social mastery	–	0.43	–	0.48
Off-task	–	–	−0.91	–
Distress	–	–	–	−0.69
Social-object mastery	–	–	–	0.66
Eigenvalue	2.29	1.63	1.19	1.06
% variance	25.5%	18.2%	13.3%	11.9%
Factor name	Object mastery	Passivity- inhibition	Off-task behaviour	Social mastery
Free play:				
	I	II	III	
Passive social orientation	0.90	–	–	
Active object exploration	−0.80	–	–	
Distress	0.74	–	–	
Social mastery	0.64	–	0.42	
Object pre-mastery	−0.50	–	0.50	
Off-task	–	0.79	–	
Passive object watching	–	0.74	–	
Object mastery	–	−0.53	–	
Social-object mastery	–	–	0.85	
Factor name	Person orientation under stress	Passivity/ off-task	General mastery	
Eigenvalue	3.12	1.65	1.21	
% variance	34.7%	18.3%	13.5%	

Notes: Loadings < 0.40 are not shown (–). *A definition for each mastery code is found
in Table 9.2.

Further, as seen in the next section, there is also a potential confounding
between social mastery and development in other affect-related domains.

SOCIAL MASTERY MOTIVATION AND RELATED CONSTRUCTS

Mastery motivation and security of attachment

Ainsworth (1975) has defined attachment as an enduring affectional tie
that one person forms to another person. Attachment behaviours are
distinct from attachment but are theorized to lead to attachment; they

will promote contact with the care-giver, and contact in turn will lead to the development of an attachment bond between the infant and care-giver. Many attachment behaviours, such as signalling (e.g. vocalizing), would be coded as social mastery behaviours in laboratory assessment procedures. Although social mastery motivation and attachment share many behavioural indicators, their goals differ. While the goal of attachment is to feel secure (Bretherton 1985), the goal of social mastery motivation is to interact effectively with and have an effect on the social environment.

Some investigators have already looked at the relation between attachment and *object mastery motivation*. However, the results of these studies are highly inconsistent (see Riksen-Walraven *et al.*, this volume, Chapter 10, for review). The relation between security of attachment and object mastery motivation has been found to differ depending on whether insecurely attached subjects are classified as anxious/resistant or anxious/avoidant (Frodi *et al.* 1985; Riksen-Walraven *et. al.*, this volume), the dimension of object mastery motivation that is assessed (Maslin *et al.* 1986), the classification of the mother as depressed or non-depressed (Popper *et al.* 1992) and the sex of the child (Riksen-Walraven *et al.*, this volume). The relation between attachment behaviours and *social mastery behaviours* is also not yet well understood. Popper *et al.* (1992) have reported that more secure attachments are associated with higher social-object mastery motivation (the child trying to get the adult involved in joint toy play), but this relation holds only for girls.

Social mastery motivation and temperament

Temperament has been defined by Buss and Plomin (1984) as inherited personality traits that appear early in life. Specific temperament character-istics may influence the infant's choice of activities and goals, which may in turn be related to the infant's motivational orientation. Conceptually, sociability is one aspect of temperament that appears likely to be related to social mastery motivation. Sociability is defined by Buss and Plomin (1984) as the tendency to prefer the presence of others to being alone. Highly sociable children are expected to direct more of their attention to the people in their environment than are less sociable children. Due to sociable infants' preference for being with people and sharing activities with people (Buss and Plomin 1984), they should receive higher social mastery motivation scores than less sociable children.

Mastery motivation, attachment and temperament: an empirical test

To investigate these issues we have assessed the convergent and discrimin-ant validity of different measures of social mastery motivation in relation to object mastery, attachment and temperament. To assess convergent validity, three different measures of social mastery motivation were compared. One involved using a standard observation procedure, adapted from previous studies on social mastery motivation; the other two relied on maternal report, using both a questionnaire and a Q-sort assessment. Significant positive relations between different measures of social mastery motivation would be evidence for convergent validity. Additionally, by looking at relations between specific social behaviours coded on these measures, we hoped to gain a more precise view of the nature of social mastery motivation. To test discriminant validity, we looked at the relation of social mastery motivation to measures of object mastery, attachment, sociability and difficult temperament. Significant positive correlations between the three measures of social mastery motivation with those of attachment, temperament and object mastery would be evidence against the discriminant validity of existing measures of social mastery motivation.

Subjects were 85 18-month-old toddlers (42 males) and their parents. All toddlers came from middle-class socio-economic backgrounds, were full-term, and had no known developmental delays.

The assessment of mastery

Infant mastery motivation initially was assessed by observing each toddler twice, in sessions which took place approximately two weeks apart, in a structured laboratory procedure. The procedure followed an identical format during both administrations, utilizing a series of four object tasks and four social tasks, but using slightly different toys during the second session to avoid confounding toy familiarity with session. For the object tasks, the experimenter demonstrated each toy and then asked the child to try it. The four object tasks consisted of two toys that required practising emerging skills and two toys that required the use of problem-solving skills. For one session, a ring-stacking toy, a milk bottle containing four plastic balls, nesting eggs, and a form-fitter toy were used. Toys for the other session included a stacking toy shaped like Snoopy, a board with four different kinds of latch, a shape sorter, and nesting cups of graduated sizes. Each toy was presented for three minutes. Parents were asked to avoid initiating interactions with the toddler and to avoid trying to get the toddler involved with the toys. They were allowed to respond when the infant initiated an interaction or tried to get them involved with a toy.

The social tasks consisted of games that made use of mutual involvement in social interactions. Games for the social tasks were selected on the basis of two criteria: (1) they gave the toddlers an opportunity to practise a behaviour involved in social mastery, and (2) they were found to be interesting and engaging to 18-month-old toddlers. Two of the four games selected involved turn taking: (1) rolling a ball back and forth with an adult, and (2) rolling a car or animal on wheels back and forth with an adult. The remaining two games involved imitation, a skill dependent on both cognitive-developmental level and motivation (Yando *et al.* 1978). To reduce the influence of cognitive level on performance, imitation tasks were selected that were well within the cognitive capabilities of an average 18-month-old toddler. The two tasks were: (1) imitating an adult pretending to drink from a tea cup, stir with a spoon, and pour from a pitcher, and (2) imitating an adult tapping wooden blocks or drumsticks.

For the social tasks, the experimenter briefly explained each game to the parents, who were then given 30 seconds to encourage their child to play the game with them. Following this 30-second period, there was a 60-second period during which the parent responded but did not initiate social interactions with the child. Then followed another 30-second period of active encouragement, and another 60-second period in which the parent only responded to the child. Total length of time for each task was three minutes.

The coding of mastery tasks

Two coding systems were used to assess the toddlers' behaviour, one using duration codes and the other using frequency codes (see Table 9.2). Duration codes were used to assess the toddlers' persistence and complexity of play with toys and the amount of their interactions with people. The duration coding system contained nine mutually exclusive codes, three of which were social. The coding system was primarily a measure of object play, with social codes (except for social-object) only being coded during times when toddlers were not actively playing with the toys. Two levels of purely social behaviour, passive and active, were coded. The third code, social-object, was used when adult–child interactions involving a toy were taking place. Frequency codes were used to take a more detailed look at toddler affect and the kinds of social interaction that took place between the toddler and the parent and between the toddler and the examiner. While there was overlap between behaviours coded by the frequency and duration coding systems, the latter was sampling a smaller subset of the social behaviours, while the former measured four kinds of social interaction that toddlers had with their parents and the examiner, as well as toddler affect. Interactions were coded according to whether they were directed towards the parent or the examiner, and by whether they were maintaining or initiating an interaction with the adult. A time sampling technique was used to record the presence or absence of positive and negative affect during thirty-second time blocks. Inter-observer reliabilities on the codes described in Table 9.2 ranged from 0.84 to 0.96.

Table 9.2 Mastery motivation codes

Code	Description

Mastery motivation duration codes:

0   *Non-involvement.* The infant may be looking elsewhere in the room, involved in non-task play, or showing gross motor behaviour.

1   *Passive object* interaction. The child may look at a toy without touching it, passively touch or hold a toy, or mouth a toy without obvious attempts at exploration.

2   *Active object* interaction. This category refers to situations where the child is actively involved with a toy but not in such a way as to produce an effect for which the toy is designed, solve a problem or practise skills. It includes such things as exploration, banging, hitting, or dropping a toy.

3   *Object pre-mastery* behaviours. These are basically task-related behaviours that are precursors of mastery. They include relating two parts of the toy, grasping or holding the relevant parts of the toy, or reaching for relevant parts of the toy.

4   *Object mastery behaviours.* These include goal-directed behaviours by which the child is able to produce an effect, solve a problem, or re-set a problem or task.

5   *Social-object mastery.* The major criterion distinguishing this category is the child's attempt to get an adult involved with him or her in dealing with the object. It includes such behaviours as the child showing or handing an object to the adult or involving him or her in some kind of reciprocal play with a toy.

6   *Active social mastery.* This characterizes a child who is predominantly interested in interactions with adults (caretaker or experimenter) rather than toys. It includes behaviours such as the child looking and vocalizing to an adult, touching an adult, and smiling or whining at an adult without active toy involvement.

7   *Passive social orientation.* This involves a child attempting to interact with the adult (caretaker or experimenter) but not with the same degree of activity as in code 6. This could involve the child leaning back against the adult or looking at him or her without affect or vocalization.

8   *Uncodable* behaviours. This code is to be used when the observer cannot use other codes because it is impossible to see what the child is doing, or if the mother is actively directing the child's activities.

9   *Active distress.* This involves sustained loud crying with no active interaction with objects or adults.

Mastery motivation observation frequency codes:

TIM   *Toddler initiation of interaction directed towards parent.* Both verbal (vocalizes and looks at parents) and non-verbal (touches parent, reaches for parent without vocalizing, offers object without vocalizing) interactions are scored. Initiations are scored only when the parent is not actively interacting with the

	toddler in the three seconds immediately preceding the toddler's interaction attempt. Separate initiation attempts are scored when there are three or more seconds without social interaction between initiation attempts.
TIE	*Toddler initiation of interaction directed towards examiner.* The same as TIM, but directed towards the examiner.
TMM	*Toddler maintenance interaction directed towards parent.* This is used when the parent has been interacting with the child within the three seconds prior to the toddler's interaction behaviour. Both verbal (vocalizes while looking at parent, vocalizes in imitation of mother) and non-verbal (look, touch, imitate parent) interactions are scored.
TME	*Toddler maintenance interaction directed towards examiner.* The same as TMM, but directed towards the examiner.
POSAFF	*Positive affect.* This is scored if the toddler smiles or laughs. Coded once per 30-second time period.
NEGAFF	*Negative affect.* This is scored if the toddler whines, cries, frowns, looks sad or fusses. Coded once per 30-second time period.

Non-task measures of social mastery and related characteristics

Besides observation, two parental report measures of social mastery were obtained. The Dimensions of Mastery Questionnaire (DMQ) (Morgan *et al.*, this volume, Chapter 6) includes sub-scales to assess both general mastery motivation and specific aspects of mastery motivation. One of these sub-scales, *social persistence*, was used as a measure of social mastery. Object mastery was measured by combining two others – combinatorial persistence and means–end persistence.

Social mastery motivation was also assessed, using a social mastery motivation criterion sort for the Attachment Behavior Q-sort, Revision 2.0 (Waters and Deane 1985). The original Q-sort was developed primarily as a measure of security of attachment. However, the Q-sort includes items which assess not only attachment but also affectivity, social interaction, object manipulation, independence, dependency, social perceptiveness and endurance/resiliency. From this pool of items we can obtain a description of the child's behaviour in many different domains. Measures of a domain can be obtained by comparing an individual child's behaviour with an ideal sort for that domain (Waters 1987).

For the present study, a criterion sort of social mastery motivation was developed by asking seven researchers actively involved in the study of motivation to sort the Waters and Deane Q-sort for a hypothetical toddler having the highest possible level of social mastery motivation.[1] The resulting criterion sort for social mastery motivation had high internal consistency (alpha = 0.91). Percentage agreement across raters was calculated by determining whether the percentage of items placed by one rater in a category was the same as or adjacent to the category in which it was placed by a second rater. Percentage agreement between individual raters ranged from 46.6 per cent to 70.0 per cent, with an average inter-rater agreement of 60.5 per cent. There were some items for which raters' differences in scoring seemed to reflect genuine disagreement concerning the nature of social mastery motivation. For example, one item is 'Child cries as a way of getting mother to do what he wants'. Four raters scored the item as involving high social mastery, two raters scored the item as low, and one gave an intermediate score. Disagreements such as these further point out the need for more precise descriptions of the nature of social mastery motivation.

The ninety-item Q-sort was completed at home by one of the toddler's parents. The parent was instructed to sort the set of ninety cards into nine piles of ten cards each. Pile 1 was to contain the cards that were most unlike their child, pile 9 was to have cards that were most like their child, and piles 2–8 were to have cards that were in between. The correlation between individual toddlers' Q-sorts and the social mastery motivation criterion Q-sort was used as a measure of each individual toddler's level of social mastery motivation.

Security of attachment was also assessed using the Attachment Behavior Q-sort, Revision 2.0 (Waters and Deane 1985). The same parent descriptions of the child's behaviour that were obtained for the social mastery measure were used for the attachment measure. However, to assess attachment security, they were compared to the criterion sort for security of attachment rather than to the criterion sort for social mastery motivation.

Sociability was assessed using the Colorado Childhood Temperament Inventory (CCTI) (Rowe and Plomin 1977). The CCTI is a thirty-item parental rating scale which assesses temperament across six domains. The internal consistency of the sociability scale appears satisfactory (alpha = 0.88). Rowe and Plomin (1977) have reported a one-week test-retest reliability of 0.58 for the sociability scale.

The Infant Characteristics Questionnaire (ICQ) (Bates et al. 1979) was used to measure infant difficultness. The ICQ contains thirty-two items rated on seven-point scales, which collapse into four temperament dimensions. The fussy-difficult scale has an internal consistency alpha coefficient of 0.79 and a thirty-day test-ratest reliability of 0.70 (Bates et al. 1979).

After the first mastery session in our laboratory, the experimenter explained to the mother how to sort and record the Attachment Behavior Q-sort. The mother was asked to observe her child at home, carry out the Q-sort based on her observations, and return the sorted items to the laboratory when they made their second visit. The mother also was given the DMQ, the ICQ and the CCTI to take home to complete and return at the second session.

Table 9.3 Means and standard deviations for observation duration and
frequency codes

Code name	Mean number of seconds	SD
Duration codes:		
Non-involvement	69.9	64.5
Passive object	488.6	151.8
Active object	1018.2	164.9
Object pre-mastery	250.7	67.9
Object mastery	738.9	156.4
Social-object mastery	104.8	57.3
Active social mastery	59.4	43.3
Passive social	85.2	53.3
Active distress	14.9	47.9
Frequency codes:		
Toddler initiations towards parent	29.7	13.9
Toddler initiations towards examiner	35.7	16.8
Toddler maintenance towards parent	74.1	31.9
Toddler maintenance towards examiner	13.1	17.1
Positive affect	19.0	10.7
Negative affect	5.6	7.0

Convergent validity

Means and standard deviations for observations measures can be seen in
Table 9.3. The distinction between 'social' and 'object' tasks appeared to
be artificial for the set of tasks used in the observation. While the average
number of social interactions was higher in social than in object tasks
(118 v. 33), no differentiation between object and social tasks appeared
in the factor structures when factor analysis of the codes was performed
with object and social scores kept separate. Correlations between social
and object scores were also significant and positive, giving further evidence that scores should be combined. Therefore, analyses were made
with data collapsed across social and object tasks.

In terms of *convergent validity* (relations between social mastery
measured during observations, on the DMQ, and with the Q-sort), a
complex set of finding emerged (see Table 9.4). The two questionnaire
measures of social mastery were unrelated to each other. Neither the
DMQ social mastery sub-scale nor the Q-sort social mastery score was
related to toddlers' initiations of interactions or to affect. There were
some relations with the other observational codes. The correlation

Table 9.4 Correlations between social codes

Codes	Q-sort	DMQ
DMQ social persistence	–	–
Social-object mastery (Dur)	–	0.20[t]
Active social mastery (Dur)	0.21[t]	–
Passive social (Dur)	–	0.22*
Toddler initiations to parent (TIM)	–	–
Toddler initiations to examiner (TIE)	–	–
Toddler maintenance to parent (TMM)	0.27*	–
Toddler maintenance to examiner (TME)	−0.22*	–
Positive affect	–	–
Negative affect	–	–

Notes: Dur = Duration. [t] $p < 0.10$. * $p < 0.05$. – = Non-significant.

between DMQ social persistence and passive social behaviour was significant and positive, and the correlation of DMQ social persistence with social-object mastery was close to reaching significance. Q-sort social mastery was significantly positively related to toddler maintenance interactions with the parent and negatively related to toddler maintenance interactions with the examiner. The correlation between Q-sort social mastery and active social mastery bordered on significance.

Further analysis suggested that the lack of relation between the DMQ social persistence scores and the frequency of social interactions during play observation may be partly due to sex differences. For males, DMQ social persistence was significantly and positively related to the overall number of interactions ($r = 0.36$, p <0.05); the corresponding correlation for females was negative and non-significant ($r = - 0.22$), (ns) and the difference between the male and female correlation was statistically significant ($z = 2.67$, p < 0.01). Similarly, for males, DMQ social persistence was positively related to the number of interactions with the parent ($r = 0.34$, p < 0.05). For females, DMQ social persistence was significantly and *negatively* related to the total number of interactions with the parent ($r = - 0.35$, p < 0.05), and the difference between male and female correlations was again significant ($z = 3.14$, p < 0.01).

Principal components analysis using a varimax rotation was performed on the observation and questionnaire social codes, in order to get a clearer picture of the overlap between measures and the nature of the dimensions of social behaviour that were assessed (factor loadings > 0.40 were used for interpretation). These results are shown in Table 9.5. The first factor was labelled *object involvement with parents*. Behaviours loading positively on this factor included initiation and maintenance interactions with the parent and social-object interaction. Negative affect had a high negative loading. The second factor most closely describes behaviour consistent with the definition of social mastery motivation, and was called

Table 9.5 Factor analysis of social mastery motivation codes

Social mastery codes	Factors and factor loadings			
	I	*II*	*III*	*IV*
Social-object mastery (Dur)	0.84	–	–	–
TMM (Freq)	0.74	–	−0.48	–
TIM (Freq)	0.70	–	–	–
Negative affect (Freq)	−0.62	–	–	–
Positive affect (Freq)	–	0.79	–	–
TIE (Freq)	–	0.74	–	–
Active social mastery (Dur)	–	0.71	–	–
TME (Freq)	–	–	0.84	–
Q-sort social mastery	–	–	−0.59	–
DMQ social persistence	–	–	–	0.74
Passive social (Dur)	–	–	–	0.69
Eigenvalue	2.89	1.60	1.45	1.22
% variance	26.3%	14.5%	13.1%	11.1%
Factor name	Object involvement with parent	Active positive social orientation	Examiner preference	Passive social orientation

Notes: Dur = Duration. Freq = Frequency. Loadings < 0.40 are not shown (–).

active positive social orientation. This factor was characterized by positive loadings on active social interactions, social initiation towards the examiner, and high positive affect. The third factor was less clear, but the loading pattern suggested a label of *examiner preference*. Negative loadings were shown for Q-sort social mastery and toddler maintenance to mother, while toddler examiner maintenance had a high positive loading. The fourth factor, *passive social orientation*, was characterized by positive loadings on DMQ social mastery and passive social orientation during play. Implications of this complex pattern of convergent validity findings for the measurement of social mastery motivation are discussed in the final section.

Divergent Validity

In terms of divergent validity a more consistent picture appeared, with few relations found between social mastery and related constructs. Object mastery was measured in the observation session and by the DMQ questionnaire. Contrary to expectations, the two measures were unrelated to each other. However, as predicted, their relations with the social codes were generally non-significant or negative. Observed object mastery was significantly and negatively correlated with passive social behaviour ($r = -0.32$, $p < 0.01$). Correlations bordering on significance were found between observed object mastery and negative affect ($r = -0.21$, p <

0.10) and observed object mastery and toddler maintenance interactions towards the parent ($r = 0.18$, p < 0.10). The DMQ object mastery sub-scale was not significantly related to any of the social codes. Trends were seen between DMQ object mastery and toddler maintenance interactions towards the parent ($r = -0.22$, p < 0.06) and between DMQ object mastery and social-object mastery ($r = -0.19$, p < 0.08).

Attachment security was highly related to Q-sort social mastery, very probably due to the high correlation between the ideal criterion sorts for attachment security and social mastery motivation ($r = 0.61$, p < 0.001). The relations between security of attachment and the remaining social codes were non-significant, although a few trends did appear. Positive affect was positively correlated ($r = 0.20$, p < 0.08) and negative affect was negatively correlated with attachment security ($r = -0.20$, p < 0.08). For males only two other trends appeared, namely a positive relation between attachment security and initiation interactions with the examiner ($r = 0.26$, p < 0.10) and a negative relation between attachment security and maintenance interactions with the examiner ($r = -0.28$, p < 0.08). No such trends appeared for females.

Difficult temperament, as measured on the ICQ, was related to affect but not to any of the interaction codes. The temperament-affect directionality was as expected, with difficultness being positively related to negative affect ($r = 0.29$, p < 0.05) and negatively related to positive affect ($r = -0.24$, p < 0.05).

CCTI sociability was significantly positively related to Q-sort social mastery ($r = 0.28$, p < 0.05). The relations of sociability to the other codes were not significant but showed some interesting trends. Positive correlations were found between sociability and toddler initiation to examiner ($r = 0.20$, p < 0.08), positive affect ($r = 0.19$, p < 0.09), and active social mastery ($r = 0.18$, p < 0.10).

A second principal components analysis was performed, this time including the object mastery and related constructs along with the social codes. This analysis allowed us to assess the independence of social mastery behaviours from the possibly related but theoretically independent constructs of object mastery, attachment security and temperament. Six factors were retained according to the mineigen criterion (see Table 9.6). Again factor loadings > 0.40 were used for interpretation. The first factor was named *parental social perception* and was characterized by positive loadings on three parental report measures: Q-sort social mastery, Q-sort attachment and CCTI sociability. The second factor was called *parent preference*, and was characterized by positive loadings on interaction with the mother and negative loadings on interaction with the examiner. The third factor was named *social orientation*, and was characterized by a positive loading on social object play and DMQ social mastery, and negative loadings in observed negative affect and DMQ

Table 9.6 Factor analysis of social mastery, object mastery and related constructs

Codes	Factors and factor loading					
	I	II	III	IV	V	VI
Q-sort social mastery	0.83	–	–	–	–	–
Q-sort attachment	0.79	–	–	–	−0.42	–
CCTI sociability	0.60	–	–	–	–	–
TME (Freq)	–	−0.78	–	–	–	–
TMM (Freq)	–	0.77	–	–	–	–
TIM (Freq)	–	0.71	–	–	–	–
Social-object mastery (Dur)	–	–	0.80	–	–	–
Negative affect (Freq)	–	–	−0.59	–	0.56	–
DMQ object mastery	–	–	−0.56	–	–	–
DMQ social mastery	–	–	0.41	–	–	–
TIE (Freq)	–	–	–	0.75	–	–
Positive affect (Freq)	–	–	–	0.72	–	–
Active social mastery (Dur)	–	–	–	0.68	–	–
ICQ difficultness	–	–	–	–	0.86	–
Passive social (Dur)	–	–	–	–	–	0.80
Object mastery (Dur)	–	–	–	–	–	−0.79
Eigenvalue	3.05	2.13	1.61	1.46	1.36	1.18
% variance	19.0%	13.3%	10.1%	9.2%	8.5%	7.4%
Factor name	Parental social perception	Parent preference	Social orientation	social mastery	Difficult/ low attachment	Passivity

Notes: Dur = Duration. Freq = Frequency. Loadings < 0.40 are not shown (–).

object mastery. The fourth factor suggested a *social mastery* dimension, being characterized by positive loadings on initiation to examiner, positive affect and social interactions directed toward the parent. The fifth factor was labelled as *difficult/low attachment*, and was characterized by positive loadings on ICQ difficultness and negative affect during observation and a negative loading on attachment. The final factor was labelled *passivity* and was characterized by a positive loading on passive social orientation and a negative loading on object mastery during observation.

DISCUSSION

Previous theory and research suggests that a conceptual distinction between social and object mastery should be made. The proposed differentiation between social and object mastery was supported in the present research by the distinction found between object and social mastery behaviours. Indeed, the only relations found between object and social mastery were negative. Therefore, rather than functioning as a single dimension for toddlers, social and object mastery motivation were expressed independently of one another.

Our divergent validity results further suggest the existence of an independent domain of infant social mastery motivation. For the most part, what we are calling social mastery does not appear to be the same thing as attachment, sociability or difficult temperament. Trends, but no significant correlations, were found between social mastery in a structured-play situation and these constructs. Factor analysis further suggested that social mastery behaviours were separable from object mastery, attachment, sociability and difficult temperament.

While the present results support the conceptual validity of the construct of social mastery motivation, they also highlight problems in regard to the measurement of this construct. From the convergent validity factor analysis that was done on our social mastery measures, we can make at least four conclusions about the measurement of social mastery motivation. First, social mastery depends in part on who is the social partner. The quantity of interactions a toddler had with his or her parent was not necessarily related to the quantity of interactions he or she had with the examiner. This distinction is shown by the fact that both a parental preference factor and an examiner preference factor appeared. Second, the nature of mastery motivation may change as a function of the measurement context – free v. structured play. The factor structure defining dimensions of mastery motivation observed during structured play clearly differs from the factor structure observed during free play. Third, while social mastery factors do appear, the same factors do not characterize parent perception and observation measures. This may be due to our final problem, namely ambiguities in what is measured by parental report measures. For example, our Q-sort social mastery measure seems to tie into a more general parental preference factor, encompassing attachment and sociability as well as mastery. DMQ social persistence seems to measure a passive, social orientation rather than active social mastery motivation. Further work needs to be done to develop or refine parental report measures so that there is greater agreement between observed and reported behaviour. This may entail further refinement of the DMQ or perhaps the development of a Q-sort where the items are more specifically tailored to the construct of mastery motivation.

Going beyond strictly measurement issues, the present results also suggest the validity of including affect in measures of social mastery. Specifically, our results indicate that positive affect was significantly and positively related to at least one measure of active social mastery. Negative affect tended to load on the opposite pole of social-object mastery behaviours. These findings suggest that the expression of positive affect is a component of social mastery that should be included in assessment procedures.

We might ask how these findings help to guide future attempts to define social mastery behaviours. One issue that was raised during construction of the Q-sort social mastery criterion sort was whether a child who cried as a way of getting his or her mother to do what he or she wanted was displaying social mastery behaviour. In the factor analyses that were performed, crying or negative affect loaded with insecure attachment and difficulty rather than social mastery. Taking an active role in social interactions and attempting to involve adults in object play was associated with frequent smiling and laughing. Therefore, even though a form of social manipulation is taking place when a child cries to get her or his way, it does not appear to be a behaviour characteristically related to social mastery.

These findings also suggest that a structured play setting can alleviate some of the 'pseudo-mastery' linked with distress that may appear in a free-play setting. Future research could profitably elaborate on these hypotheses by examining contingencies between parent–child social interactions, child affect and child mastery.

Another dimension of social behaviour that appeared in the factor analysis was the active/passive distinction. Active social interaction was separable from a more passive social orientation. When interpreting these findings, we need to remember that our observation social tasks were primarily based on 'playing together'. The degree of activity on the part of the toddler was essentially the degree of intensity or involvement in play with another person, rather than the degree of control that the toddler had in the interaction. The assumption of an active role in interactions could also be thought of as how much an individual tries to control an interaction. We did not attempt to measure this type of behaviour. The role of control of either the course of social interactions or of another person's behaviour in social mastery behaviours is an issue which still needs to be explored.

Although t-tests indicated that the average scores for males and females were generally not significantly different on the observational measures or on the parental report measures, males and females did show interesting differences in the patterns of relations between different measures. In particular, when comparing the DMQ social persistence score to observed social behaviour, males showed an expected positive relation but females showed an unexpected negative relation. That is, parental reports of motivational orientation more closely fit observed mastery behaviour for boys than for girls. This raises the possibility that parents may have different expectations for and support different motivational styles for males and females. Although the genesis of mastery motivation has not been looked at in this way, both cross-cultural (Whiting and Edwards 1988) and developmental research (Hoffman 1988) do suggest that male and female children may well encounter different types of socialization experience, which may be rooted in different parental goals and values concerning the two sexes. Future research needs to look at how parents conceptualize mastery in male and female toddlers, and what types of different mastery-related rearing style they may be displaying to their

NOTES

1 Social mastery criterion Q-sorts provided by Lois Brockman, Terri Combs, Kay Jennings, Susan McQuiston, George Morgan, Peter Vietze and Theodore Wachs.

REFERENCES

Ainsworth, M. (1975) 'The development of infant–mother attachment', in B. Caldwell and H. Riciutti (eds) *Review of Child Development Research. Vol. 3*, Chicago, University of Chicago Press.

Bates, J., Freeland, C. and Lounsbury, M. (1979) 'Measurement of infant difficultness', *Child Development* 50, 794–803.

Bretherton, I. (1985) 'Attachment theory: retrospect and prospect', *Monographs of the Society for Research in Child Development* 50 (1–2, Serial No. 209).

Buss, A. and Plomin, R. (1984) *Temperament: Early Developing Personality Traits*, Hillsdale, NJ, Erlbaum.

Combs, T. (1987) 'Fussy-difficult temperament and toddler mastery motivation', paper presented at the Midwestern Psychological Association, Chicago.

Dweck, C. and Elliot, E. (1983) 'Achievement motivation', in P. Mussen (ed.) *Handbook of Child Psychology. Vol. 4: Socialization, Personality and Social Development*, New York, Wiley.

Frodi, A., Bridges, L. and Grolnick, K. (1985) 'Correlates of mastery related behavior: a short-term longitudinal study of infants in their second year', *Child Development* 56, 1291–8.

Harter, S. (1981) 'A model of mastery motivation in children: individual differences and developmental change', *Minnesota Symposia on Child Psychology* 14, 215–55.

Hoffman, L. (1988) 'Changes in family role, socialization and sex differences', in G. Handel (ed.) *Childhood Socialization*, New York, Aldine de Gruyter.

Jennings, K., Harmon, R., Morgan, G., Gaiter, J. and Yarrow, L. (1979) 'Exploratory play as an index of mastery motivation: relation to persistence, cognitive functioning, and environmental measures', *Developmental Psychology* 15, 386–94.

Lewis, M. and Feiring, C. (1989) 'Infant mother and mother infant interaction behavior and subsequent attachment', *Child Development* 60, 831–7.

MacTurk, R., Hunter, F., McCarthy, M., Vietze, P. and McQuiston, S. (1985) 'Social mastery motivation in Down Syndrome and nondelayed infants', *Topics in Early Childhood Special Education* 4, 93–109.

Maslin, C., Bretherton, I., and Morgan, G. (1986) 'The influence of attachment security and maternal scaffolding on toddler mastery motivation', paper presented at the International Conference on Infant Studies, Beverly Hills, CA.

Morgan, G. and Harmon, R. (1984) 'Developmental transformations in mastery motivation: measurement and validation', in R. Emde and R. Harmon (eds) *Continuities and Discontinuities in Development*, New York, Plenum.

Morgan, G., Harmon, R. and Maslin, C. (1987) 'Measuring mastery motivation in infants and young children', poster presented at the International Society of Behavioral Development, Tokyo.

Morgan, G., Maslin, C., Ridgeway, D. and Kang-Park, J. (1988) 'Toddler mastery motivation and aspects of mother–child affect communication', poster presented at the 5th Biennial Retreat of the Development Psychobiology Research Group, Estes Park, CO.

Popper, S., Cohn, J. and Campbell, S. (1992) 'Do securely attached infants show higher mastery motivation?', paper presented to the International Conference on Infant Studies, Miami Beach, Fl.

Rowe, D. and Plomin, R. (1977) 'Temperament in early childhood', *Journal of Personality Assessment* 41, 150–6.

Wachs, R. D. (1987) 'Specificity of environmental action as manifest in environmental correlates of infant's mastery motivation', *Development Psychology* 23, 782–90.

Wachs, T. D. and Combs, T. (in press) 'The domains of mastery motivation', in R. MacTurk (ed) *Mastery Motivation: Conceptual Origins and Applications*, Norwood, NJ, Ablex.

Waters, E. (1987) 'Open workshop on Q-sort methods for assessing attachment behavior', paper presented at the Biennial Meeting of the Society for Research in Child Development, Baltimore, MD.

Waters, E. and Deane, K. (1985) 'Defining and assessing individual differences in attachment relationships: Q-methodology and the organization of behavior in infancy and early childhood', in I. Bretherton and E. Waters (eds) 'Growing points of attachment theory and research', *Monographs of the Society for Research in Child Development*, 50 (1–2), Serial No. 209).

Wenar, C. (1978) 'Social initiative in toddlers', *Journal of Genetic Psychology* 132, 231–46.

White, R. (1959) 'Motivation reconsidered: the concept of competence', *Psychological Review* 66, 297–333.

Whiting, B. and Edwards, C. (1988) 'A cross-cultural analysis of sex differences in the behavior of children age 3 through 11', in G. Handel (ed.) *Childhood Socialization*, New York, Aldine de Gruyter.

Yando, R., Seitz, V. and Zigler, E. (1978) *Imitation: A Developmental Perspective*, Hillsdale, NJ, Erlbaum.

Yarrow, L., Morgan, G., Jennings, K. and Harmon, R. (1982) 'Infants' persistence at tasks: relationships to cognitive functioning and early experience', *Infant Behavior and Development* 5, 131–41.

Yarrow, L., Rubenstein, J. and Pedersen, F. (1975) *Infant and Environment: Early Cognitive and Motiviational Development*, New York, Halsted Press.

Yarrow, L., McQuiston, S., MacTurk, R., McCarthy, M., Kelin, R. and Vietze, P. (1983) 'Assessment of mastery motivation during the first year of life: contemporaneous and cross-age relationships', *Developmental Psychology* 19, 159–71.

Yarrow, L., MacTurk, R., Vietze, P., McCarthy, M., Klein, R. and McQuiston, S. (1984) 'Developmental course of parental stimulation and its relation to mastery motivation during infancy', *Developmental Psychology* 19, 159–71.

Part III

Attachment and social processes

Chapter 10

Mastery motivation in toddlers as related to quality of attachment

J. Marianne Riksen-Walraven, Hans Th. Meij, Juchke van Roozendaal and Jeannette Koks

TWO THEORETICAL VIEWS ON THE EFFECTS OF EARLY EXPERIENCE UPON MASTERY MOTIVATION

This chapter addresses the question of to what extent a secure attachment relationship during infancy is related to mastery motivation in toddlerhood. Mastery motivation is conceived here in a rather broad sense, as the motivation to know, act upon and master the environment. What we mean by mastery motivation is closely related to White's (1959) conception of effectance or competence motivation, which was elaborated further by Harter (1978). White emphasized that the motivation to interact competently with the environment must be seen as a universal and innate drive. Although White mentioned the role of life experiences upon the development of effectance motivation, he did not explicitly pay attention to the existence and development of inter-individual differences in the strength of the motive. In recent years, however, much effort has been invested in the assessment of mastery motivation and in the development and stability of inter-individual differences in this area (Morgan *et al.* 1990). In addition, a considerable number of studies have focused upon the effects of children's experiences on the development of their motivation to explore and master the environment. With regard to the effects of experience within infancy, research has been conducted from two different theoretical perspectives, suggesting different mechanisms to explain and specify the effects of experience upon the development of mastery motivation.

Personal agency beliefs as influences on mastery motivation

Within the first theoretical viewpoint, personal agency beliefs, such as perceptions of control, perceptions of competence, and self-efficacy expectations, are proposed to mediate the effects of experience upon the child's motivational development (Bandura 1977; Ford and Thompson 1985; Lewis and Goldberg 1969; Riksen-Walraven 1978; Skinner 1986;

Watson 1966). According to this point of view, infants experience their acts as effective because the acts elicit responses in the environment. This will promote the development of a generalized sense of the self as an effective agent, which in turn provides the motivational basis for exploration and mastery of the environment. Consequently, responsiveness of the environment is considered as the most influential determinant of the development of competence motivation in infancy. It was shown that enhancement of responsiveness in parents indeed fostered competence motivation in their children in the first year of life (Riksen-Walraven 1978). Heckhausen (this volume, Chapter 4) further specifies which experiences may contribute to the development of perceived competence beyond infancy.

The influence of attachment quality on mastery motivation

The conceptual framework of attachment theory offers a different explanation for the effects of early experience upon a child's motivation to explore and master the environment. In attachment theory, mastery motivation is viewed as being under the control of the exploratory behavioural system. The exploratory system controls behaviour 'which promotes learning to know and to deal with features of the environment, including persons other than attachment figures' (Ainsworth *et al.* 1978: 22). The working of the exploratory system is presumed to be inversely related to activation of the attachment behavioural system, which has a set goal of maintaining a sense of security. When an infant feels secure, his or her attachment system is at a low level of activation, and this accounts for the phenomenon described by Ainsworth as 'using the mother as a secure base for exploration' (1978: 22). The level of activation of the attachment behavioural system has to be low for the exploratory system to be engaged at full capacity.

At the end of the first year of life, infants exhibit important interindividual differences in 'felt security', presumably reflecting the caregiver's sensitive responsiveness to the infant's attachment behaviours. It is argued that *securely attached* infants have learned to expect their caregiver to be accessible and to provide reassurance and comfort. Therefore they should feel relatively secure when they are observed in an exploration or mastery situation while the attachment figure remains present. This allows the exploration system to function at high levels, so exploration and mastery behaviour can be expected, if challenging stimuli are available. *Anxious-resistant* infants are supposed to have experienced a history of inconsistent accessibility of their attachment figure, leading to a feeling of insecurity and to chronic activation of their attachment system, which, of course, is at the cost of exploration. Hence, these infants can be expected to show low levels of motivation in exploration and mastery situations, even when the care-giver is present. *Anxious-avoidant* infants are assumed to have experienced a care-giving history of rejection or neglect, leading to the expectation of unavailability of the care-giver and to the tendency to avoid this attachment figure, especially in times of stress and discomfort. In fact, the avoidant children may have learnt to suppress their attachment behaviour whenever they feel insecure. Because this insecurity is not reduced by comfort in contact with the attachment figure, the exploration system of the anxious-avoidant child may not be activated at high levels in stressful or unfamiliar situations. Ainsworth *et al.* (1978: 320) state that the tendency to avoid the care-giver leads the child 'to turn to the neutral world of things, even though displacement exploratory behavior is devoid of the true interest that is inherent in nonanxious exploration'. It might be predicted that, when anxious-avoidant children are in an exploration or mastery situation with their care-giver, they will explore or play with the available objects, maybe even for longer periods of time than a securely attached child. But, compared with a secure child, the avoidant child should show less signs of real interest or motivation, such as eagerness, affective engrossment and sustained and focused attention.

EMPIRICAL EVIDENCE FOR THE RELATION BETWEEN MASTERY MOTIVATION AND QUALITY OF ATTACHMENT

Empirical data on the relationship between attachment quality and mastery motivation do not yield a very consistent picture. The strength and direction of the relationship vary across different behavioural manifestations of mastery motivation. Only for the *anxious-resistant* children does a clear picture emerge. Resistant children score consistently lower than their secure and avoidant counterparts on a variety of measures reflecting mastery motivation, such as exploratory competence (Tracy *et al.* 1980), task-directedness (Maslin-Cole and Spieker 1990), and persistence and enthusiasm during problem solving (Erickson and Farber 1983).

Securely attached children score higher than insecure children (both anxious-resistant and anxious-avoidant) on a number of measures, especially on those reflecting qualitative aspects of play and exploration. Security of attachment was found to be associated with breadth, variety and level of symbolic play (Tracy *et al.* 1980), mean duration of bouts of symbolic play (Matas *et al.* 1978), high quality of play (Harmon *et al.* 1979), concentrated play (Suess *et al.* 1992), 'executive capacity' in free play (Belsky *et al.* 1984), and amount of 'sophisticated exploration' (van den Boom 1988). These measures, reflecting quality of exploration and play, certainly have a motivational component, but differences between secure and insecure children may as well be caused or inflated by differences in cognitive development.

Scores for ego-resiliency, based on judgements by pre-school teachers, have been used as measures of competence in studies examining the predictive power of attachment security in infancy with respect to adaptation in the pre-school. Ego-resiliency has been defined as 'analysis of the "goodness of fit" between situational demands and behavioural possibility, and flexible invocation of the available repertoire of problem-solving strategies' (Block and Block 1980: 48). This may be considered as a competence construct with a strong motivational component. Arend et al. (1979), and Sroufe (1983) have reported higher ego-resiliency scores in pre-schoolers with secure attachment histories. Similarly, Waters et al. (1979) found security of attachment to be associated with higher scores for ego-strength/effectance, a construct related to the concept of ego-resiliency and used as an index of effectance motivation. However, Easterbrooks and Goldberg (1990) found no relationship between ego-resiliency and attachment security.

Thus, securely attached children tend to score higher than children with insecure attachment relationships on measures reflecting competence during free play and exploration, and on measures of ego-resilience and ego-strength/effectance, based upon overall judgements of their behaviour in the natural setting of the pre-school. To our knowledge, there is only one study in which secure children were found to score higher than anxiously attached children upon measures of mastery motivation during structured mastery tasks. Maslin-Cole and Spieker (1990) reported a significant correlation between attachment security and ratings of the child's goal-directedness and attention span in tasks especially designed for the purpose of assessing mastery motivation.

When the group of securely attached children is contrasted with the anxious-avoidant group, an interesting pattern emerges. Avoidant children are found to score higher than secure children on measures reflecting amount of time spent in interaction with the objects available in exploration, play and mastery situations. They appear to be more active in free play than secure children (Harmon et al. 1979) and show significantly more object interaction during structured tasks (Maslin-Cole and Spieker 1990). This finding is not surprising in the light of the hypothesized tendency of avoidant children to 'turn to the neutral world of things'. But, contrary to the expectations, there is no evidence that avoidant children are less motivated than secure children in their interactions with objects. In some studies, the reverse even seems to be true. On measures of persistence, which are generally accepted as valid indicators of mastery motivation (Morgan et al. 1990, 1991), avoidant children are found to score as high as or even higher than secure children (Erickson and Farber 1983; Maslin-Cole and Spieker 1990). Finally, children in the anxious-avoidant group appeared to show higher levels of engrossment or engagement during play with symbolic toys than secure children, which also points into the direction that anxious-avoidant children may be even more mastery-motivated than children with a secure attachment relationship.

The results discussed above underscore the importance of paying due attention to the operationalization of mastery motivation when examining its relationship with attachment quality (for a review on this issue see Morgan *et al.* 1990). In our own study, to be presented in the next section, we explored the relationship between different aspects of mastery behaviour displayed within the same setting. Therefore, we used scores on rating scales devised to tap motivational aspects of mastery as well as scores reflecting completeness and level of exploration of the objects presented during the tasks.

Furthermore, we assessed mastery motivation in two settings, differing in level of caretaker participation. In some of the aforementioned studies of the relationship between attachment quality and mastery motivation, the child's mastery motivation was assessed on a task allowing or even requiring the active participation of the care-giver. In these studies, the relationship between attachment quality and mastery motivation may be inflated because of the differential effects of the quality of care-giver–child interaction between secure and insecure dyads during the assessment procedure. Matas *et al.* (1978), for example, found that securely attached toddlers were more compliant and engaged in less negativism and aggression towards their mothers during problem-solving tasks. In order to examine the effect of the level of care-giver participation in the task upon the child's mastery motivation, we observed the child in two different settings. First, the child's mastery motivation was rated during an exploration task where the care-giver was present, but was not allowed to participate. A second rating of the child's mastery motivation was obtained during a task where a problem had to be solved in cooperation with the care-giver. Because, in earlier longitudinal studies of the development of mastery motivation, sex-differences in patterns correlations have been found (cf. Jennings *et al.* 1984), in the present study all analyses were conducted separately for boys and girls.

A LONGITUDINAL STUDY OF MASTERY MOTIVATION AT 30 MONTHS IN RELATION TO ATTACHMENT QUALITY AT AGE 1

The sample consisted of 77 firstborn, lower-class children (41 boys, 36 girls) and their primary care-givers (76 mothers, 1 father). The subjects participated in a longitudinal study when they were 6, 9, 12, 18 and 30 months old. The present report only uses data from 12 months and 30 months.

At the age of 12 months, the infants were observed with their primary care-giver in the Ainsworth Strange Situation (Ainsworth *et al.* 1978), a procedure designed to assess the organization of attachment behaviour under increasingly stressful circumstances. According to the criteria described by Ainsworth *et al.*, infants were classified as secure, insecure-avoidant, or insecure-resistant. Sixty-one subjects (80 per cent) were classified as secure, 15 were classified as insecure-avoidant (20 per cent), while there were no insecure-resistant classifications. One infant (a boy) turned out to be unclassifiable, so that all analyses involving attachment classifications were performed on 76 subjects. Inter-rater agreement between two previously trained observers equalled 94, 96 and 100 per cent for avoidant, secure and resistant classifications, respectively. There were no sex-differences in attachment classification.

Assessment of mastery motivation during exploration

At the age of 30 months, the child's exploratory behaviour was observed during a laboratory visit. Before the exploration episode started, care-giver and child had been observed during a series of instruction tasks in the same experimental room. At the onset of the exploration session, the experimenter placed a modified version of Banta's (1970) 'curiosity box' on the floor in front of the child, at a distance of about one metre from the chair the care-giver was sitting on, and encouraged the child to play with it. The wooden curiosity box (40 × 30 × 25 cm) was painted in different bright colours and contained a number of manipulative devices with interesting cause–effect contingencies, some of them difficult to discover. There were, for example, push-buttons operating a counter with a reset, a turning-wheel controlling the illumination level of different compartments within the box, marbles which could be pushed through a tube, and a joystick. One compartment within the box contained a squeaky toy that could only be felt through a small hole. One of the sides contained a door with a complicated magnetic lock, which could be opened and closed. A second door, seemingly giving access to an other compartment of the box, could not be opened, because a key did not fit into the lock.

During the exploration session, parents were allowed to respond to their children's social exchanges, but were asked not to touch the box, nor to give directions to the children or comments on their behaviours. The whole episode, lasting eight minutes and starting at the moment the child touched the box for the first time, was recorded on videotape.

The videotapes were scored using a five-point rating scale we developed to assess the child's *mastery motivation* during exploration of a novel object. All tapes were rated by two independent observers (first and fourth author), and inter-rater agreement exceeded 80 per cent. Table 10.1 shows that the scale focuses upon motivational aspects of the child's exploration and disregards other aspects of exploratory behaviour, such as variety and completeness of the child's exploration and the level or

Table 10.1 Rating scale for mastery motivation during exploration

Scale point	Definition
1	The child spends very little time exploring the object. If there are any moments of exploration, the child is passive and listless and seems to have an extreme lack of confidence in his or her behaviour. There is no evidence of pleasure or excitement. Sometimes the object even seems to elicit negative emotions in the child.
2	The child devotes more than just a few moments to exploration. Exploration is superficial, sometimes seemingly 'mechanical', and never with eagerness. The child may show some moments of active interest, for instance when repeating an effective manipulation, but never shows enthusiasm or excitement. The child shows a lack of confidence and gives up easily.
3	This rating is given if there is inconsistence in the behavioural manifestation of mastery motivation. Two different patterns of inconsistence are distinguished. The *first* pattern is characterized by the alternation of brief periods of eager exploration and periods of disinterest. The child spends relatively little time on exploration, but shows moments of active engagement and enthusiasm during exploration. In the *second* pattern, there seems to be a lack of harmony between the child's affect and behaviour. The child spends relatively long periods of time in exploration, but without overt signs of pleasure or excitement. In both patterns the child may show a lack of confidence in his or her behaviour.
4	The child devotes much of the time to exploration and shows co-ordination between affect and behaviour during most of the session. The child is generally eager and confident, and enjoys his or her discoveries.
5	Throughout the session, the child explores with great enthusiasm and eagerness. The child changes his or her posture and position frequently and energetically in the service of exploration. He or she seems very confident and self-reliant and shows pleasure and excitement if effects are discovered.

Notes: The scale reflects the degree to which a toddler shows mastery motivation during exploration of a novel object. It is assumed that mastery motivation in toddlers during exploration is reflected in (1) amount of time spent on exploration, (2) eagerness, involvement, investment of effort in exploration, (3) displays of confidence and self-reliance, and (4) enthusiasm and excitement during exploration. The level of competence or sophistication of the child's exploratory behaviours should not be taken into account for this rating.

sophistication of the exploratory behaviours. We do not regard these latter measures as appropriate measures of mastery motivation, because they may confound children's mastery motivation with their cognitive or fine motor competence or with their activity level.

Because we wanted to explore the relationship between mastery motivation displayed during exploration and other aspects of the child's exploration, the same episodes were scored with the aid of a more detailed coding system. In the observational system, twenty-nine different parts of the box were distinguished. Four levels of exploration were defined: (1) global inspection or touching one single part of the box, (2) detailed inspection or focused manipulation of one single part of the box, (3) simple relational exploration, defined by manipulation of one part of the box, combined with manipulation or inspection of another part, and (4) detailed relational exploration, described as relating two different parts of the box through different kinds of manipulation, or examining the interrelationship between more than two parts of the box. Each successive exploratory behaviour of the child was scored on one of the levels described above, and it was registered at which part of the box the exploration was directed. Inter-rater agreement (first and second author) equalled 67, 91, 81 and 82 per cent, for the four different levels of exploration. On the basis of these codings, for each child two scores were computed, one reflecting *completeness* of exploration (total number of different parts of the box explored by the child during the whole episode) and one indicating the *mean level* of exploration shown during the session (mean of all codings, ranging from 1 to 4).

Assessment of mastery motivation during a task requiring cooperation

During the same laboratory visit the care-giver and child were observed during a problem-solving task which required them to work together. The task involved catching as many fish as possible from a 'pool' (a carpet with a diameter of 1.5 metres) within a period of five minutes, without 'getting wet feet'. The fish could be caught with a magnet, attached at the midpoint of a rope which had to be held at opposite ends by the care-giver and child.

Care-giver and child behaviours were rated from videotape by two independent observers (first and third author) on a number of seven-point rating scales, designed by Erickson *et al.* (1985). For all scales, inter-rater reliability exceeded 0.80. For this chapter, three child ratings were used for constructing a composite score reflecting mastery motivation during the cooperation task: (1) *persistence* at the task, reflected in sustained attention, involvement and effort invested in task-directed behaviour, (2) *enthusiasm*, expressed in vigour, eagerness to reach the goal and enjoyment of success, and (3) *self-reliance*, reflected in a display of personal initiative and self-confidence while approaching the task. On conceptual grounds, supported by the size of the correlations between the scales (0.86 between persistence and enthusiasm, 0.53 between persistence and self-reliance, and 0.63 between enthusiasm and self-reliance), we decided to sum the scores on the three rating scales in order to obtain one composite score for *mastery motivation* during the cooperation task.

Conceptually, this score seems highly comparable to our rating of the child's mastery motivation during exploration.

Results

Consistency of mastery motivation across measures and tasks

There were no sex-differences in the means of the four scores of mastery motivation and exploration in the two different settings. The pattern of interrelations among these variables, however, differed considerably for boys and girls; therefore, the results are reported separately for each sex. Table 10.2 shows that the intercorrelations among the four measures are quite different in boys and girls. In fact, the only point of similarity between the sexes displayed in Table 10.2 is the positive correlation, during the session with the curiosity box, between the rating of mastery motivation and the score for completeness of exploration. This means that both boys and girls rated high on mastery motivation during exploration of the curiosity box, paid attention to many different parts of the box while exploring it. The mean level of sophistication of the exploratory behaviours displayed, however, shows a quite different pattern of associations with the other three measures in boys and girls. In fact, level of exploration appears to be unrelated to all three other measures in girls,

Table 10.2 Means and intercorrelations of mastery scores at 30 months for the whole sample, and separately for boys and girls

Mastery score	2	3	4	M	SD
Total sample (n = 77):					
1 Exploration: completeness	0.04	0.54**	−0.15	18.14	4.27
2 Exploration: level		0.34**	0.28**	2.38	0.23
3 Exploration: mastery motivation			0.19*	3.30	1.16
4 Cooperation: mastery motivation				12.91	5.29
Boys (n = 41):					
1 Exploration: completeness	0.26*	0.53**	0.08	17.78	4.27
2 Exploration: level		0.61**	0.42**	2.41	0.22
3 Exploration: mastery motivation			0.30*	3.24	1.22
4 Cooperation: mastery motivation				13.22	5.57
Girls (n = 36):					
1 Exploration: completeness	−0.16	0.56**	−0.42**	18.56	4.29
2 Exploration: level		0.05	0.10	2.33	0.24
3 Exploration: mastery motivation			0.05	3.36	1.10
4 Cooperation: mastery motivation				12.56	5.00

Notes: * p < 0.05, one-tailed. ** p < 0.01, one-tailed.

while it shows a significant positive correlation with all three other measures in boys.

Another remarkable difference between boys and girls concerns the relationship between the ratings of the child's mastery motivation in the two different settings. As shown in Table 10.2, mastery motivation was relatively stable across settings in boys. In girls, however, mastery motivation during the exploration task proved to be unrelated to mastery motivation shown during the task requiring cooperation with the caregiver.

Mastery motivation and quality of attachment

In order to investigate the effect of attachment quality upon the different mastery scores, we used four separate 2 (attachment quality, A v. B) × 2 (sex) ANOVAs (Analyses of Variance). There were no differences between secure and insecure-avoidant children with regard to completeness and level of exploration, nor were there significant interaction effects, nor a main effect of attachment quality on the ratings of mastery motivation. However, a significant interaction effect of attachment quality by sex upon mastery motivation during exploration was found, $F(1, 75)$ = 8.816, p = 0.004. Mean mastery motivation scores for secure and anxious-avoidant girls equaled 3.57 and 2.33, respectively, $t(34)$ = 2.73, p = 0.01. There was no significant difference between mastery motivation scores in secure and avoidant boys (mean ratings of 3.06 and 3.78, respectively). Thus, attachment security is associated with higher scores for mastery motivation during exploration in girls, but not in boys.

With regard to the relation between attachment quality and the child's mastery motivation during the task requiring cooperation with the caregiver, a comparable trend was found (mean scores for secure boys and anxious-avoidant boys 13.10 and 13.11, respectively; mean scores for secure girls and anxious-avoidant girls 12.80 and 11.33, respectively). In this case, however, the interaction effect of attachment quality by sex did not reach significance: $F(1,75)$ = 0.221.

DISCUSSION

The empirical investigation presented in this chapter provides little support for our hypothesis, derived from attachment theory, that attachment security promotes mastery motivation in toddlers. Although our findings are not consistent with attachment theory, they agree with findings from previous empirical studies, reviewed in the first part of this chapter. There, we had to conclude that there is little evidence that avoidant children are less motivated than secure children in their interactions with objects. Furthermore, our results agree with the findings presented by

Maslin-Cole *et al.* (this volume, Chapter 11), who also had to conclude that attachment security did not consistently predict mastery motivation in toddlers. Of course, our data do not permit conclusions regarding mastery motivation in anxious-resistant children, because in our sample only secure and avoidant children were found.

From our study, we can infer that quality of attachment appears to play *some* role in determining toddlers' level of mastery motivation, but only in girls. Of course, we have to confine this conclusion to mastery motivation in the domain of *objects*, because we did not assess the child's motivation to influence the *social* environment. During the exploration task the care-giver was uninvolved, and in the fishing game, which required cooperation with the parent, we assessed children's motivation to catch the fish, not their motivation to cooperate. Perhaps the predictive power of attachment quality is stronger in regard to mastery motivation in the social domain. In general, attachment security has been found to predict social competence better than competence in other domains (Lamb 1987).

A most conspicuous finding of our study is the gender difference, in relation to both the impact of attachment quality on the development of mastery motivation, and the comparison of mastery motivation exhibited by the children in different settings. In boys, mastery motivation showed some consistency across settings, but appeared to be independent of quality of attachment. For girls, on the other hand, the predicted relationship between attachment security and higher degrees of mastery motivation was observed: securely attached female toddlers were significantly more mastery-motivated than anxious-avoidant girls in an exploration task where the attachment figure was present, although uninvolved. Similarly, the securely attached girls seemed to be more highly motivated during problem solving in cooperation with the care-giver, although in this case the difference with the anxious-avoidant girls was not significant. However, there was no relation between the girls' mastery motivation rated in the two different settings.

Searching for similar gender differences in other studies, we were impressed by the fact that very few investigations have reported consequences of attachment quality separately by sex. Suess *et al.* (1992) found such differences in a recent study of the relationship between attachment quality at age 1 and quality adaptation at age 5. Certainly, with regard to *overall* scores of competent functioning in the pre-school, the predictive power of attachment quality was similar for boys and girls, but for most of the *specific* variables, such as amount of concentrated play, the influence of attachment quality proved to be stronger in girls. LaFreniere and Sroufe (1985) also report that high competence in pre-school was more strongly related to security of attachment for girls than for boys. However, it should be kept in mind that LaFreniere and Sroufe focused primarily upon the domain of *social competence*, which should be carefully distinguished from that of *object mastery* (see Combs and Wachs, this volume, Chapter 9).

In our study, mastery motivation in girls, but not in boys, was related to quality of attachment to the care-giver as well as to the level of care-giver participation in the task used to assess the child's mastery motivation. These findings suggest that mastery motivation in young girls is sensitive to social experience. Earlier findings with regard to differential stability in mastery motivation for boys and girls may be cited in support of this viewpoint. Jennings *et al.* (1984: 458) observe that 'behaviors related to mastery motivation . . . have generally been found to be more stable for boys in the early years than for girls'. Remarkable gender differences in stability of competence were also found in our own, previous, longitudinal research. In a sample of one hundred 9-month-old infants, measures of competence motivation were obtained during exploration and during an operant learning task (Riksen-Walraven 1978). When the children were 7, 10 and 12 years old, their ego-resiliency was judged by teachers using the California Child Q-set designed by Block and Block (1980). Competence motivation at 9 months predicted subsequent ego-resiliency in boys, but not in girls. The correlation of the exploration score in infancy with ego-resiliency in boys was 0.45 at age 7 ($n = 47$), 0.43 at age 10 ($n = 43$), and 0.32 at age 12 ($n = 42$) (Riksen-Walraven 1991; van Aken and Riksen-Walraven 1992). Results from the same longitudinal study, pertaining to the long-term effects of early intervention in the domain of parent–child interaction, also support the assumption that competence motivation is less susceptible to the influence of social experience in boys than in girls. An intervention programme enhancing responsiveness of parents towards their infant was shown to have a positive effect upon the infant's competence motivation. In both boys and girls, competence motivation was enhanced by the intervention, in comparison with controls (Riksen-Walraven 1978). For boys, however, this enhancement was subsequently found to be temporary, while in girls remarkable long-term effects of the early intervention were observed. Girls from the experimental group, whose social experience was modified by the intervention in the first year of life, were significantly more ego-resilient than controls at the ages of 7, 10 and 12 years (Riksen-Walraven 1991).

If it is true that mastery motivation for boys is not as sensitive to social experience in early development as for girls, their development may be largely promoted by their transactions with the *inanimate* environment. A corollary of this assumption is that innate differences are more clearly reflected in the development of mastery motivation in boys, because initial differences in aptitude are reinforced by mastery experience in the world of objects, a self-perpetuating process.

We have not yet mentioned the possibility that gender differences in susceptibility of mastery motivation to social experience might be due to differential *rearing* of boys and girls. Perhaps girls are *made* more sensitive to social experience, because parents are more responsive to their social overtures than to independent mastery attempts. It may be that boys *learn* to focus upon experiences in the physical domain, because their parents provide them with challenging toys and respond more to their successes and failures during exploration and mastery attempts. The greater stability observed in boys' mastery motivation in the early years might be caused by a greater consistency in independence training by parents of boys, as Jennings *et al.* (1984) suggested. However, the assumption of sex-related differences in parental treatment has not been supported by much convincing empirical evidence. In a recent, extensive meta-analysis of studies concerning sex-differentiated socialization, Lytton and Romney (1991) found very few differences in parental treatment of boys and girls.

A possible explanation for the lack of integrated mastery motivation in girls might be found in the nature of the play materials used in the tasks. This argument pertains especially to the curiosity box, which may be considered a relatively 'masculine' toy. Is it possible that boys are more attracted to or acquainted with this kind of toy, as Block (1983) suggested in her review of sex-differentiated socialization? We think that our data contradict the assumption that the boys were more attracted to the curiosity box than the girls, because no gender differences in mean scores for mastery motivation during exploration of the box were found. This is in agreement with Maccoby and Jacklin's (1974) conclusion that there is no consistent evidence for sex-differences in toy preference before the age of 30 months. Another possible explanation is that girls are less acquainted with toys like the curiosity box, because parents provide sex-typed toys for their children. This might explain the lack of correlation in girls between mastery motivation and competence (level and completeness) during exploration of the box: although girls may be interested in 'masculine' toys and motivated to explore them, many of them do not have the opportunity to develop competence in dealing with them. However, in our study, girls appeared to be as competent as boys during exploration of the curiosity box. Furthermore, there is no consistent evidence that parents buy sex-typed toys for their children before age 3 (Maccoby and Jacklin 1974).

The results of our investigation have several implications for future research. First, our findings underscore the need to make a distinction between social and object mastery motivation. A second suggestion is that, in studies examining the effects of experience upon children's motivational development, more attention should be paid to the interaction of children with their non-social environment. Most studies investigating the effects of children's daily experiences upon their motivational development have focused on their interactions with their social environment. The role of mastery experiences in interaction with objects has rarely been acknowledged as an important determinant of motivational development (Karniol 1989). Yet, observation of children's interactions with the physical world might contribute substantially to our understanding of the development and stability of inter-individual differences in object mastery motivation. Finally, our results indicate the need to pay more attention to sex differences in the development and behavioural manifestation of mastery motivation in the early years.

NOTES

Portions of this chapter were presented at the eleventh biennial meeting of the International Society for the Study of Behavioral Development, Minneapolis, Minnesota, 3–7 July, 1991.

We would like to thank C. F. M. Van Lieshout and J. J. Fahrenfort for their helpful comments on an earlier version of this chapter.

Requests for reprints should be addressed to J. Marianne Riksen-Walraven, Department of Psychology, University of Nijmegen, P. O. Box 9104, 6500 HE Nijmegan, The Netherlands.

REFERENCES

Ainsworth, M. D., Blehar, M. C., Waters, E. and Wall, S. (1978) *Patterns of Attachment: A Psychological Study of the Strange Situation*, Hillsdale, NJ, Erlbaum.

Arend, R., Gove, F. L. and Sroufe, L. A. (1979) 'Continuity of individual adaptation from infancy to kindergarten: a predictive study of ego-resiliency and curiosity in preschoolers', *Child Development* 50, 950–9.

Bandura, A. (1977) 'Self-efficacy: toward a unified theory of behavioral change', *Psychological Review* 84, 191–215.

Banta, J. T. (1970) 'Tests for the evaluation of early childhood education: the Cincinnati autonomy test battery', in J. Hellmuth (ed.) *Cognitive Studies, Vol. 1*, New York, Brunner/Mazel.

Belsky, J., Garduque, L. and Hrncir, E. (1984) 'Assessing performance, competence, and executive capacity in infant play: relations to home environment and security of attachment', *Developmental Psychology* 20, 406–17.

Block, J. H. (1983) 'Differential premises arising from differential socialization of the sexes: some conjectures', *Child Development* 54, 1335–54.

Block, J. H. and Block, J. (1980) 'The role of ego-control and ego-resiliency in the organization of behavior', in W. Collins (ed.) *Development of Cognition, Affect, and Social Relations: Minnesota Symposia on Child Psychology. Vol. 13*, 39–101, Hillsdale, NJ, Erlbaum.

Easterbrooks, M. E. and Goldberg, W. A. (1990) 'Security of todler–parent attachment: relation to children's sociopersonality functioning during kindergarten', in M. Greenberg, D. Cicchetti, and E. Cummings (eds) *Attachment in the Preschool Years: Theory, Intervention, Research*, Chicago and London, University of Chicago Press.

Erickson, M. F. and Farber, E. A. (1983) 'Infancy to preschool: continuity of adaptation in high-risk children', paper presented at the meeting of the Society for Research in Child Development, Detroit, MI.

Erickson, M. F., Sroufe, L. A. and Egeland, B. (1985) 'The relationship between quality of attachment and behavior problems in preschool in a high-risk sample', in I. Bretherton and E. Waters (eds) 'Growing points of attachment theory and research', *Monographs of the Society for Research in Child Development* 50, 147–67.

Ford, M. E. and Thompson, R. A. (1985) 'Perceptions of personal agency and infant attachment: toward a life-span perspective on competence development', *International Journal of Behavioral Development* 8, 377–406.

Harmon, R. J., Suwalski, J. D. and Klein, R. P. (1979) 'Infants' preferential response for mother versus an unfamiliar adult', *Journal of the American Academy of Child Psychiatry* 18, 437–49.

Harter, S. (1978) 'Effectance motivation reconsidered: toward a developmental model', *Human Development* 21, 34–64.

Jennings, K. D., Yarrow, L. J. and Martin, P. P. (1984) 'Mastery motivation and cognitive development: a longitudinal study from infancy to 3½ years of age', *International Journal of Behavioral Development* 7, 441–61.

Karniol, R. (1989) 'The role of manual manipulative stages in the infant's acquisition of perceived control over objects', *Developmental Review* 9, 205–33.

LaFreniere, P. J. and Sroufe, L. A. (1985) 'Profiles of peer competence in the preschool: interrelations between measures, influences of social ecology, and relation to attachment history', *Developmental Psychology* 21, 56–69.

Lamb, M. E. (1987) 'Predictive implications of individual differences in attachment', *Journal of Consulting and Clinical Psychology* 55, 817–25.

Lewis, M. and Goldberg, S. (1969) 'Perceptual-cognitive development in infancy: a generalized expectancy model as a function of mother–infant interactions', *Merrill-Palmer Quarterly* 15, 81–100.

Lytton, H. and Romney, D. M. (1991) 'Parents' differential socialization of boys and girls: a meta-analysis', *Psychological Bulletin* 109, 267–96.

Maccoby, E. E. and Jacklin, C. N. (1974) *The Psychology of Sex Differences*, Stanford, CA, Stanford University Press.

Maslin-Cole, C. A. and Spieker, S. J. (1990) 'Attachment as a basis for independent motivation', in M. Greenberg, D. Cicchetti and E. Cummings (eds) *Attachment in the Preschool Years: Theory, Intervention, Research*, Chicago and London, University of Chicago Press.

Matas, L., Arend, R. A. and Sroufe, L. A. (1978) 'Continuity of adaptation in the second year: the relationship between quality of attachment and later competence', *Child Development* 49, 547–56.

Morgan, G. A., Harmon, R. J. and Maslin-Cole, C. A. (1990) 'Mastery motivation: definition and measurement', *Early Education and Development* 1, 318–40.

Morgan, G. A., Maslin-Cole, C. A., Biringen, Z. and Harmon, R. J. (1991) 'Play assessment of mastery motivation in infants and young children', in C. E. Schaefer, K. Gitlin and A. Sandgrund (eds) *Play Diagnosis and Assessment* New York, Wiley.

Riksen-Walraven, J. M. (1978) 'Effects of caregiver behavior on habituation rate and self-efficacy in infants', *International Journal of Behavioral Development* 1, 105–30.

Riksen-Walraven, J. M. (1991) 'Die Entwicklung kindlicher Kompetenz im Zusammenhang mit sozialer Unterstützung' [Development of competence in children in relation to social support] in F. J. Monks and G. Lehwald (eds) *Neugier, Erkundung und Begabung bei Kleinkindern*, München and Basel, Ernst Reinhardt Verlag.

Skinner, E. A. (1986) 'The origins of young children's perceived control: mother contingent and sensitive behavior', *International Journal of Behavioral Development* 9, 359–82.

Sroufe, L. A. (1983) 'Infant–caregiver attachment and patterns of adaptation in the preschool: the roots of maladaptation and competence' in M. Perlmutter (ed.) *Minnesota Symposia on Child Psychology. Vol. 16*, Hillsdale, NJ, Erlbaum.

Suess, G. J., Grossmann, K. E. and Sroufe, L. A. (1992) 'Effects of infant attachment to mother and father on quality of adaptation in preschool: from dyadic to individual organisation of self', *International Journal of Behavioral Development* 15, 43–65.

Tracy, R. L., Farish, G. D. and Bretherton, I. (1980) 'Exploration as related to infant–mother attachment in one-year-olds', paper presented at the International Conference on Infant Studies, New Haven.

van Aken, M. A. and Riksen-Walraven, J. M. (1992) 'Parental support and the development of competence in children', *International Journal of Behavioral Development* 15, 101–23.

van den Boom, D. C. (1988) 'Neonatal irritability and the development of attachment: observation and intervention', doctoral dissertation, University of Leiden.

Waters, E., Wippman, J. and Sroufe, L. A. (1979) 'Attachment, positive affect, and competence in the peer group: two studies in construct validation', *Child Development* 50, 821–9.

Watson, J. S. (1966) 'The development and generalization of contingency awareness in early infancy: some hypotheses', *Merrill-Palmer Quarterly* 12, 123–35.

White, R. W. (1959) 'Motivation reconsidered: the concept of competence', *Psychological Review* 66, 297–323.

Chapter 11

Toddler mastery motivation and competence

Links with attachment security, maternal scaffolding and family climate

Christine Maslin-Cole, Inge Bretherton and George A. Morgan

This chapter reports results from a short-term longitudinal study examining the influence on toddler mastery motivation and competence of three aspects of the early social environment: mother–child attachment security, maternal scaffolding behaviour, and family climate. This study extends previous research, first, by including multiple measures of mastery motivation derived from free play, structured tasks and maternal perceptions; second, by repeating measures at two points during toddlerhood to allow for prediction over time and assessment of stability of key measures; and third, by employing multiple regression to determine predictability of outcome measures using several measures of the child's early social environment.

DISTINGUISHING MASTERY MOTIVATION AND COMPETENCE

We have previously defined mastery motivation as a psychological force that stimulates an individual to attempt independently, in a focused and persistent manner, to solve a problem or master a skill that is at least moderately challenging for him or her (Morgan *et al.* 1990). A recent extension of our definition (Barrett and Morgan in press; Barrett *et al.*, this volume, Chapter 5) identifies two aspects of mastery motivation: (1) an instrumental aspect, which involves behaviours aimed at controlling and/or mastering the environment and reflects qualities such as persistence, engrossment and sustained attention while attempting to reach a goal or striving to gain control, and (2) an expressive aspect, which includes emotional responses displayed while striving towards a goal, after attaining or failing to attain a goal, or in response to attempts to gain control over ongoing events. Typical measures of each aspect in object-related contexts include persistence at challenging tasks (instrumental aspect) and smiling during or after reaching a goal (expressive aspect).

Measures of persistence and mastery pleasure have generally not been found to be highly correlated (e.g. Barrett *et al.*, this volume, Chapter 5; Morgan *et al.*, this volume Chapter 6; Redding *et al.* 1988). However, we consider mastery pleasure and other indicators of the expressive aspect of mastery motivation to be conceptually related to the instrumental component because they reflect a child's emotional responses during attempts to master a task or solve something challenging (Morgan *et al.* 1990). Perhaps the failure to find consistent correlations between these two aspects of mastery motivation is due to variations in the origin of each or in the factors that influence each aspect's expression. We hoped this study would shed light on this issue by identifying differential predictors of each aspect of mastery motivation.

Substantial research and theory suggests a motivational component in the development of cognitive competence, especially during infancy (e.g. Barrett and Morgan in press; Scarr 1981; Ulvund 1980; Yarrow and Messer 1983). We have attempted to distinguish these two concepts in order to understand variations in their developmental course and antecedents better (Morgan *et al.* 1990). We have also attempted to disentangle mastery motivation and competence empirically by individualizing the difficulty of tasks presented to each child and assessing persistence using only those levels of difficulty that are moderately challenging for a particular child (Morgan *et al.* 1992). We included measures of competence in order to test intercorrelations of competence and mastery motivation variables and to determine the extent to which the predictor variables for mastery motivation and competence differ.

SOCIAL INFLUENCES ON MASTERY MOTIVATION

Robert White's (1959) classic view of early effectance motivation emphasized an intrinsic motive, presumably universal to the human species, as giving rise to a child's desire to master his or her environment. However, the extent to which environmental factors influence individaul variation and the possible pathways these factors may follow remain open questions. In particular, arguments for considering the effects of socializing agents on individual expressions of mastery motivation have begun to recently appear (see Heckhausen, this volume, Chapter 4), and a number of social environmental influences can be considered candidates for explaining individual differences.

Attachment theory (e.g. Bowlby 1982; Bretherton 1985) asserts that the infant's sense of perceived security regulates separation from the attachment figure, allowing exploration of the environment. Securely attached infants maintain a balance between exploration and attachment behaviours, while the balance is disrupted for anxiously attached infants (Ainsworth *et al.* 1978). Avoidant infants tend to choose object interaction over interaction with the attachment figure (Ainsworth *et al.* 1978; Maslin-

Cole and Spieker 1990) even in times of stress (Sroufe and Waters 1977). Resistant infants tend to explore and manipulate objects in limited ways (Hazen and Durrett 1982; Main 1983), returning to the attachment figure to seek and resist contact ambivalently when distressed (Ainsworth *et al.* 1978).

Infants who easily separate to explore, relative to those infants who separate with difficulty, might be at an advantage for developing the kind of focused and persistent interactions with objects that characterize mastery motivation. However, a preparedness for exploration is not synonymous with high mastery motivation, especially during late infancy and toddlerhood. The ability to explore independently from an attachment figure may be a prerequisite to developing persistent and focused interactions with objects, but is not sufficient by itself. Infants and toddlers who easily separate from their attachment figure may prefer social interactions over object interactions, or may interact with objects without the focused engrossment characteristic of high mastery motivation. In this study, we predicted that security of attachment would be related to toddler instrumental mastery motivation and toddler competence, in part on the basis of previous research (e.g. Matas *et al.* 1978). We were unsure whether the positive parent–child emotional interactions that typically accompany a secure attachment would influence expressive aspects of child mastery motivation.

Active parental attempts to encourage motivation, such as scaffolding (Maslin 1987; Wood *et al.* 1976), might be expected to influence a child's willingness to persist independently towards a challenging goal. In particular, it might be expected that a parent's direct encouragement and attempts to enhance child motivation during joint play would favourably influence a child's motivation when working alone on a challenging task or activity. Likewise, good technical assistance about how to do a task or good emotional support in the face of frustration might contribute to a child's developing sense of effectance with objects. We made several specific predictions:

1 that active maternal encouragement (motivational support) would influence the instrumental aspect of mastery motivation;
2 that maternal emotional support during challenging tasks would influence the expressive aspect of mastery motivation;
3 that active maternal teaching and assistance (technical support) would influence child competence.

Family climate, which we define as the qualities characterizing organization, structure and tone of family interactions, might also be expected to influence a child's independent attempts towards a goal. A child may internalize parental or family beliefs about success in challenging situations, and parental modelling in goal-related situations may influence a child's subsequent motivation in the face of challenge. In addition, both parental availability for providing active support during challenging tasks and the affective tone of interactions with significant family members may influence a young child's emerging sense of self-esteem. We hypothesized that a stressful marital relationship, evidenced by low marital satisfaction, consensus or cohesion, would adversely influence toddler instrumental and expressive mastery motivation. However, we made no specific predictions about the influence of family adaptability or cohesion on motivation or competence measures.

Finally, we included child temperament measures as possible predictors of both mastery motivation and competence. Several conceptualizations of temperament include a construct similar to the instrumental component of mastery motivation (e.g. attention span/persistence, Thomas and Chess 1977) and some researchers argue for an appreciable genetic role underlying at least some temperamental differences (e.g. Buss and Plomin 1984; Plomin 1986). However, Thomas and Chess (1977) found little evidence of stability in persistence during infancy and the pre-school years, suggesting susceptibility of this aspect of motivational behaviour to environmental influences. In this study, we examined possible social influences on ratings of child attention span and persistence along with other indicators of the instrumental aspect of mastery motivation. Other aspects of temperament were included as possible predictors of both mastery motivation and competence, but no specific predictions were made.

RESEARCH QUESTIONS

In this research, we asked how well attachment security, maternal scaffolding effectiveness, qualities of the marital relationship, family adaptability and cohesion, and child temperament predict scores on measures of mastery motivation and competence. Four questions guided our work:

1 How are aspects of mastery motivation (both instrumental and expressive) and competence interrelated during toddlerhood? Are they stable from 18 to 25 months of age?
2 Which aspects of a child's early social environment best predict instrumental aspects of toddler mastery motivation?
3 Which aspects of a child's early social environment best predict expressive aspects of toddler mastery motivation?
4 Which aspects of a child's early social environment best predict toddler cognitive competence?

OVERVIEW OF THE STUDY

Subjects in this study were forty-one toddlers and their mothers, seen at 18 and 25 months of age. Subjects were primarily white and represented a range of socio-economic groups. All families were intact when recruited and all children were screened for prematurity and major health problems. Three subjects did not participate in the study at the second assessment age.

At 18 months, the procedure involved a home visit to interview the mother, administer the Bayley Mental Scale, and leave questionnaires for parents to complete. In addition, two laboratory visits were conducted to assess child free play and mother–child joint play and attachment security, and to administer structured mastery tasks. At 25 months, the procedure included a home visit similar to that at 18 months, and there was one laboratory visit to assess child free play and mother–child joint play, to administer structured mastery tasks, and to obtain a maternal attachment Q-sort about her child.

MEASURES OF MASTERY MOTIVATION

The instrumental and expressive aspects of mastery motivation were assessed in several ways. Structured mastery tasks (Morgan *et al.* 1992) were administered. At 18 months, toddlers were tested twice on separate days with three different types of task (puzzles or form boards, lock boards or cause-and-effect toys, and shape sorters) and scores were averaged across both testing sessions. At 25 months, three sets of structured tasks (puzzles, cause-and-effect toys, and shapes) were administered during a single testing session. Each set of tasks varied in difficulty from easy to quite hard; however, the testing method allowed a moderately challenging level of each task type to be selected for each child. (See Busch-Rossnagel *et al.*, this volume, Chapter 7, for a more complete description of the tasks and the testing method).

Two motivation measures were derived from the structured tasks for each child: *task persistence* (the number of fifteen-second intervals in which the child showed task-directed behaviour on the level or levels of each task judged to be moderately challenging for him or her) and *task mastery pleasure* (the number of fifteen-second intervals in which the child smiled and/or expressed excitement while working on a task or immediately following completion of part of a task). The task persistence score did not include looking at or simply exploring the task without attempting to use it in a goal-directed fashion.

Examiner ratings of toddler *goal-directedness* and *attention span* were made at each age, following structured mastery tasks and the Bayley Mental Scale, and using nine-point rating scales. The highest rating on the goal-directedness scale described a child who was very highly absorbed in tasks, who willingly repeated solutions to difficult tasks, and who stayed with tasks until completion. The highest rating on the attention-span scale described a child who watched task demonstrations by the tester closely, who listened carefully to all instructions, and who waited for instructions or demonstrations to be completed before beginning work on tasks. Maternal ratings of toddler *persistence* and *mastery pleasure* were obtained using scales from the Dimensions of Mastery Questionnaire (DMQ; Morgan *et al.*, this volume, Chapter 6).

Toddler free play was observed at each age with both combinatorial and symbolic toys for eight minutes with each toy type. Combinatorial toys included blocks, nesting cups and a shape sorter; symbolic toys included a toy tea-set, stuffed animals with a bed, and a toy phone. Toy types were presented separately, with the order of toy type counterbalanced for child sex and reversed at the second assessment age. The child's mother sat at the side of the room, remaining accessible to her child but instructed to encourage independent play if her attention was sought.

Each session was coded separately for engrossment and mastery pleasure from written transcripts. The *free-play engrossment* score indicated the number of seconds during each eight-minute free-play espisode when the child showed high or medium levels of engrossment, with the number of seconds rated as high engrossment receiving double weight. High engrossment reflected a toddler who gave an impression of full absorption in the play activity by looking intently at what he or she was doing and looking away only briefly to search for another piece to incorporate into play or to share a brief moment with mother. The *free-play mastery pleasure* score reflected the total number of positive vocalizations, gestures or facial expressions the child showed during play bouts with medium or high engrossment. A play bout consisted of a period of play with a specific toy or toy-set, or play organized around a particular activity. Detailed scoring instructions are provided in Bretherton (1988).

Inter-tester and inter-rater reliability was high for measures of mastery motivation. Testers achieved 80–100 per cent agreement for scoring task persistence and mastery pleasure during structured tasks. For free-play scoring, two independent raters achieved 92 per cent inter-rater agreement for engrossment scores. For ratings of attention span and persistence, examiners achieved greater that 85 per cent exact agreement and nearly 100 per cent agreement within one point on both scales (prior to ratings subjects in this study), and agreement was checked throughout data collection. For the Dimensions of Mastery Questionnaire, reliability and validity data are presented in Morgan *et al.* (this volume, Chapter 6).

MEASURES OF COMPETENCE

Toddler competence measures were also drawn from several sources. The *Bayley Mental Development Index* (MDI; Bayley 1969) was calculated at each age. A *task-competence score* was derived from the structured mastery tasks at each age (based on the number of correct solutions for each moderately challenging task, weighted for level of difficulty and summed across task types). At each age, *free-play competence* was scored separately for toddler free play with combinatorial and symbolic toys. Competence levels were obtained for each toy type by summing the scores for the two bouts of play assigned the highest play level. A seven-point combinatorial play competence scale (Bretherton and Wilcox 1988) was based on observations of the combinatorial play schemes shown by the toddlers in this study. At its low end, the combinatorial scale assessed exploratory actions such as hitting or banging; at its high end, the scale assessed high-level organizations such as putting rings on the ring stack in order by size or inserting several different complex shapes into the shape-sorter holes. An eight-point symbolic play competence scale (Bretherton et al. 1988) was based on Nicolich (1977) and a review of pretend play by the second author (Bretherton 1984). At its low end, the symbolic scale assessed use of objects in imitative schemes that are not yet clearly identifiable as pretence; at its high end, the scale assessed whether the toddler created sequences of pretence (such as putting a doll to bed), which also included pretend vocalizations or treating animals and dolls as children. Finally, *maternal ratings of child competence* were made at each age using the competence scale of the Dimensions of Mastery Questionnaire (Morgan et al., this volume, Chapter 6).

Inter-tester reliability for task competence scores was 82–100 per cent agreement on scoring solutions to tasks. For scoring of combinatorial play level, exact inter-rater agreement was 87 per cent, with 97 per cent agreement within one point. For scoring symbolic play level, exact inter-rater agreement was 82 per cent, with 94 per cent agreement within one point.

MASTERY MOTIVATION AND COMPETENCE FACTORS

Mastery motivation and competence measures were assigned to one of three conceptual categories: the instrumental aspect of mastery motivation, the expressive aspect of mastery motivation, or competence. Principal components factor analyses with varimax rotation were used to determine factors within each category at each age. These analyses yielded solutions with one to three factors per category (See Table 11.1). Factor scores were computed for all conceptually meaningful factors by normalizing each variable and then summing (unweighted) each subject's

Table 11.1 Means, standard deviations and factor loadings for instrumental measures of mastery motivation

Factor name and variables	$\bar{X}$	SD	Factor loading
18 months:			
Factor 1: Overall task-directedness (2.47, 31%)			
Goal-directedness rating (structured tasks)[a]	6.20	1.03	0.87
Task persistence score (structured tasks)[b]	6.70	1.91	0.85
Attention span rating (structured tasks)[a]	5.02	1.17	0.71
Goal-directedness rating (Bayley)[a]	6.44	1.20	0.52
Mother's ratings of persistence (DMQ)[c]	2.82	0.51	0.35
Factor 2: (unnamed) (1.46, 18%)			
Attention span rating (Bayley)[a]	5.68	1.40	0.83
Goal-directedness rating (Bayley)[a]	6.44	1.20	0.57
Mother's ratings of persistence (DMQ)[c]	2.82	0.51	−0.52
Free-play engrossment (combinatorial toys)[d]	457.50	245.63	−0.32
Factor 3: Free-play engrossment (1.12, 14%)			
Free-play engrossment (symbolic toys)[d]	427.84	183.38	0.80
Free-play engrossment (combinatorial toys)[d]	457.50	245.63	0.68
25 months:			
Factor 1: Overall task-directedness (2.30, 29%)			
Task persistence score (structured tasks)[e]	6.11	1.26	0.78
Goal-directedness rating (Bayley)[a]	6.59	1.19	0.77
Goal-directedness rating (structured tasks)[a]	6.65	1.16	0.73
Mother's ratings of persistence (DMQ)[c]	2.93	0.52	0.45
Attention span rating (structured tasks)[a]	5.32	0.97	0.41
Attention span rating (Bayley)[a]	6.08	1.44	0.36
Factor 2: (unnamed) (1.29, 16%)			
Attention span rating (Bayley)[a]	6.08	1.44	0.75
Attention span rating (structured tasks)[a]	5.32	0.97	−0.67
Free-play engrossment (combinatorial toys)[d]	750.22	180.27	−0.30
Factor 3: Free-play engrossment plus (1.12, 14%)			
Free-play engrossment (symbolic toys)[d]	676.05	219.20	0.76
Free-play engrossment (combinatorial toys)[d]	750.22	180.27	0.64
Mother's ratings of persistence (DMQ)[c]	2.93	0.52	0.35

Notes: Only variables with loadings of 0.30 and above are reported and were included in factor scores; all variables were equally weighted when summed. Eigenvalues and percentage variance accounted for follow the factor names. [a]Nine-point rating scale. [b]Average number of 15-second intervals for 4-minute tasks (max. = 16). [c]Average of five items (4-point rating scales). [d]Number of seconds during 8-minute episode; high engrossment weighted twice (max. = 960). [e]Average number of 15-second intervals for 3-minute tasks (max. = 12). n = 41 at 18 months. n = 38 at 25 months.

score on variables loading 0.30 or above on that factor. Composites were not computed for the second instrumental factor at each age (see Table 11.1), since these two factors were difficult to interpret and did not lend themselves to calculation of meaningful summary variables.

Instrumental factors

At both ages, the primary instrumental factor reflects covariation of measures typically used to tap the instrumental aspect of mastery motivation (i.e. persistence at structured tasks and ratings of both attention span and goal-directedness: see Table 11.1). Child engrossment during free play loaded on the third factor at both ages.

The emergence of a similar factor structure at both ages suggests some stability in the toddler period of different expressions of the instrumental aspect of mastery motivation. The consistent separate factoring of free-play engrossment suggests that while this factor clearly contains elements of task-directed action, it is a separate facet of focused effort towards goals. This factor appears to differ from the behaviours historically associated with mastery motivation. In addition, the factor structure reported here for the instrumental aspect offers preliminary support for an expanded view of mastery motivation (see Barrett and Morgan in press for a related discussion). Aspects of instrumental mastery motivation may be expressed in various ways (for example, a child manipulating a toy in a focused way during free play, or a child working persistently to complete a tester-defined task). Relevant behaviours may vary with development and across particular individuals and situations.

Expressive factors

At 18 months of age, all indices of the expressive aspect of mastery motivation covaried, suggesting a unitary construct at this age (see Table 11.2). It would appear that the 18-month-old who shows high levels of mastery pleasure in one mastery-related situation tends to show high levels in related situations.

At 25 months of age, type of situation seemed to influence covariation of expressive measures. Mastery pleasure expressed during free play (a relatively unstructured situation) was empirically distinct from that expressed in structured task situations. Mastery pleasure on the DMQ covaried with measures from structured situations, a consistent finding since DMQ mastery pleasure items largely reference task-related events.

Competence factors

At 18 months, covariation of competence variables appeared to be dependent upon the situational source (i.e. free play v. structured tasks) (see Table 11.3). The variables in the first factor primarily reflected child performance in structured testing situations and correspond to traditional measures of competence, while the variables in the second factor were drawn from unstructured free play.

Table 11.2 Means, standard deviations and factor loadings for expressive measures of mastery motivation

Factor name and variables	$\bar{X}$	SD	Factor loading
18 months:			
Factor 1: Overall mastery pleasure (1.73, 43%)			
Free-play mastery pleasure (combinatorial toys)[a]	3.00	3.11	0.68
Mother's ratings of mastery pleasure (DMQ)[b]	3.26	0.46	0.68
Free-play mastery pleasure (symbolic toys)[a]	1.82	2.26	0.64
Task mastery pleasure (structured tasks)[c]	0.65	1.07	0.62
25 months:			
Factor 1: Task pleasure (1.29, 32%)			
Task mastery pleasure (structured tasks)[d]	1.02	1.41	0.80
Mother's ratings of mastery pleasure (DMQ)[b]	3.24	0.45	0.79
Factor 2: Free-play pleasure (1.18, 30%)			
Free-play mastery pleasure (combinatorial toys)[a]	1.95	2.07	0.75
Free-play mastery pleasure (symbolic toys)[a]	1.43	1.86	0.74

Notes: Only variables with loadings of 0.30 and above are reported and were included in factor scores; all variables were equally weighted when summed. Eigenvalues and percentage variance accounted for follow the factor names. [a]Number of expressions during 8-minute episode. [b]Average of five items (4-point rating scales). [c]Average number of expressions during six 4-minute tasks. [d]Average number of expressions during three 3-minute tasks. $n = 41$ at 18 months. $n = 38$ at 25 months.

At 25 months, similarities in task demands and task type appeared to underlie the pattern of covariation. The first factor included three indices based, in large part, on combinatorial-related activity (Bayley MDI, structured mastery tasks, and free play with combinatorial toys). The second competence factor included performance on the Bayley mental scale, plus play level with symbolic toys and mother's rating of competence. Perhaps emerging language skills provide the thread of communality for the variables covarying on the second factor, since the MDI at this age more heavily reflects language ability than at 18 months, and advanced levels of symbolic play require more integration of language into play schemes than lower levels (see Bretherton *et al.* 1988). Furthermore, the competence questions on the DMQ primarily asked the rater to compare a child's general competence level to same-age peers, and we suspect that mothers may use language skill as the key comparison point as a toddler matures.

Table 11.3 Means, standard deviations and factor loadings for competence
measures

Factor name and variables	$\bar{X}$	SD	Factor loading
18 months:			
Factor 1: Task competence (1.92, 38%)			
Task competence score (structured tasks)[a]	143.52	28.50	0.85
Bayley MDI	112.51	15.27	0.84
Mother's ratings of competence (DMQ)[b]	3.19	0.42	0.59
Factor 2: Free-play competence (1.22, 24%)			
Free-play competence level (symbolic toys)[c]	8.34	2.03	0.80
Free-play competence level (combinatorial toys)[c]	7.55	2.15	0.69
25 months:			
Factor 1: Combinatorial competence (1.65, 33%)			
Task competence score (structured tasks)[a]	190.78	38.77	0.78
Free-play competence level (combinatorial toys)[c]	11.08	1.82	0.70
Bayley MDI	118.84	14.97	0.69
Factor 2: Symbolic competence (1.30, 26%)			
Mother's ratings of competence (DMQ)[b]	3.21	0.39	0.82
Bayley MDI	118.84	14.97	0.58
Free-play competence level (symbolic toys)[c]	10.46	2.38	0.57

Notes: Only variables with loadings of 0.30 and above are reported and were included in factor scores; all variables were equally weighted when summed. Eigenvalues and percentage variance accounted for follow the factor names. [a]Average weighted scores based on correct solutions and level of task (max. = 600). [b]Average of five items (4-point rating scales). [c]Sum of two highest scores; 7-point scale. $n = 41$ at 18 months. $n = 38$ at 25 months.

Cross-age stability and intercorrelations of factors

Figure 11.1 illustrates same-age correlations and cross-age stability for instrumental and expressive factors of mastery motivation and for competence factors. Factors tapping the expressive aspect of mastery motivation will be discussed first.

A strong cross-age correlation was found between overall mastery pleasure at 18 months and the task pleasure factor at 25 months. However, the 18-month overall mastery pleasure factor was not significantly related to the 25-month free-play pleasure factor. These results suggest continuity in one dimension of mastery pleasure, with the appearance of a new dimension at 25 months. Our results suggest that measures of the expressive aspect of mastery motivation are independent from both instrumental measures and competence, since no relevant same-age or cross-age correlations were significant. In other research, expressive measures (usually mastery pleasure) have generally been minimally related or

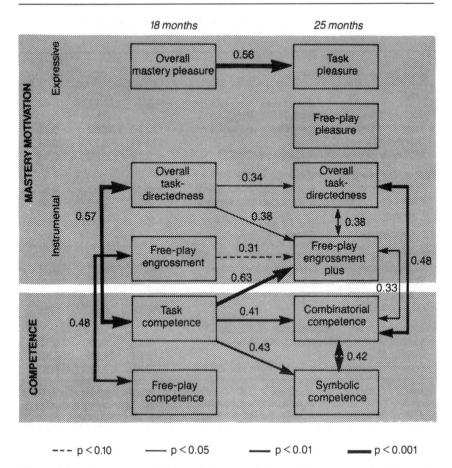

Figure 11.1 Cross-age stability and intercorrelations of mastery motivation and competence factors at 18 and 25 months

unrelated to instrumental measures (usually task persistence) and competence measures (Barrett *et al.*, this volume, Chapter 5; Morgan *et al.* 1992; Redding *et al.* 1988; Yarrow *et al.* 1982). However, Barrett (Barrett *et al.*, this volume, Chapter 5) reports a clear, positive relationship between young infants' rate of activating a simple jack-in-the-box and rate of smiling.

For the principle factor of the instrumental aspect of mastery motivation (overall task-directedness), modest stability was found. This finding is consistent with previous research in which stability of task-directedness (or related measures) in infancy and toddlerhood has generally been modest (e.g. Barrett *et al.*, this volume, Chapter 5; Thomas and Chess, 1977; Yarrow and Messer 1983).

The factors tapping engrossment during free play were only marginally stable across our seven-month observation interval. At 18 months, the overall task-directedness factor and the free-play engrossment factor were unrelated. In contrast, they were modestly related at 25 months, suggesting some overlap between these two representations of instrumental mastery motivation at the later age. However, it is important to note that these correlations may underestimate the true relationship between these two aspects of instrumental mastery motivation, since orthogonal factor analysis forces empirical independence. In addition, scores on the earlier (18-month) overall task-directedness factor predicted scores on the later (25-month) free-play engrossment plus factor. That is, those toddlers who, at the earlier age, persist well at challenging structured tasks with a small amount of adult support are able at the later age to persist independently during free play.

For competence factors, 18-month task competence was positively related to combinatorial competence at 25 months, a finding that is consistent with other research reporting fairly high cross-age stability in toddlerhood of competence measures tapping task-related, combinatorial-type skills (e.g. Barrett *et al.*, this volume, Chapter 5). Task competence at 18 months was also positively related to symbolic competence at 25 months. The second competence factor at 18 months, free-play competence, was not significantly related to either 25-month factor. The two competence factors at 25 months were positively related to each other, in part because both factors included the Bayley MDI.

Interestingly, no cross-age correlations between earlier motivation measures (either instrumental or expressive factors) and later competence factors were significant, indicating that in this study, at least, earlier motivation measures did not predict later competence. However, 18-month task competence was strongly related to free-play engrossment plus at 25 months, suggesting that toddlers who showed earlier competence with tasks showed high levels of motivation during free play seven months later.

Intercorrelations for same-age mastery motivation and competence factors showed strong positive relationships at 18 months (overall task-directedness and task competence; free-play engrossment and free-play competence) and at 25 months (overall task-directedness and combinatorial competence). These findings indicate positive relationships between instrumental aspects of mastery motivation and competence when the measures are drawn from similar settings (e.g. structured tasks or free play) or similar types of material (e.g. combinatorial type) at the same age.

MEASURES OF TODDLER SOCIAL ENVIRONMENT AND TEMPERAMENT

Attachment security was assessed at 18 months using the Ainsworth Strange Situation (see Ainsworth *et al.* 1978) and dyads were assigned to one of four classification groups: secure (group B), anxious-avoidant (group A), anxious-resistant (group C), disorganized-disoriented (group D). The proportions of securely attached and anxiously attached dyads were consistent with other non-risk samples (see Ainsworth *et al.* 1978). A five-point *security score* was computed: score 5 (most secure) = B3, score 4 = B1, B2, B4; score 3 = A2, C1; score 2 = A1, C2; score 1 (least secure) = D, A/C mix. At 25 months, attachment security was assessed using the Attachment Q-sort (Waters and Deane 1985). A security score was calculated for each child, based on agreement between the sort completed by the child's mother and the ideal sort.

Maternal scaffolding effectiveness was assessed at each age during two five-minute sessions of mother–toddler joint play (one session for combinatorial toys, one session for symbolic toys). Each mother was asked to choose a toy or activity that she thought would be a little beyond what her child could do independently, to show her child how to do it, and to encourage her child to keep working on it. Each mother was free to vary the difficulty of the chosen task as she saw fit.

Effectiveness ratings (based on an elaboration of Wood *et al.* 1976) were made for three aspects of scaffolding support: motivational, technical and emotional. The *motivational rating* reflected the mother's ability to recruit the child's attention, communicate the nature of the end goal and maintain direction towards the goal. The *technical rating* reflected the effectiveness of maternal demonstrations, simplification, marking critical features of the task, and organization. The *emotional rating* reflected maternal sensitivity to the child's emotional state, ability to reduce frustration, and contribution to the child's sense of accomplishment. A highly effective scaffolder was able to perceive accurately her child's needs for support and to vary the amount and type of assistance accordingly. A description of scaffolding rating scales is provided in Maslin 1987.

Three aspects of the marital relationship (*satisfaction, consensus* and *cohesion*) were assessed at each age using the Dyadic Adjustment Scale (Spanier 1976). At 25 months only, mothers completed the Family Adaptability and Cohesion Scales (Olson *et al.* 1979, 1982), which assess perceptions of *family adaptability* and *family cohesion*.

Five aspects of child temperament were assessed. Toddler *emotionality, activity level, shyness* and *sociability* were assessed using established scales from the Colorado Children's Temperament Inventory (Rowe and Plomin 1977). Toddler *difficultness* was assessed using relevant items from the Infant Characteristics Questionnaire (Bates *et al.* 1979) and the general rating from the Infant Temperament Questionnaire (Carey and McDevitt 1978).

Inter-rater reliability for attachment and scaffolding scoring was high. Attachment tapes were scored by the first two authors, who were each trained previously to score tapes of the Strange Situation reliably. A reliability check of randomly selected tapes indicated no substantial disagreements, and all questionable tapes were viewed by both scorers. For scaffolding scoring, all tapes were scored independently by two raters. High inter-rater agreement (86 per cent exact agreement and 92 per cent agreement within one point) was achieved before scoring began and was rechecked during scoring.

PREDICTION OF TODDLER MASTERY MOTIVATION AND COMPETENCE

Step-wise multiple regression was used to determine predictability of the mastery motivation and competence factors, using measures of the toddler's social environment and child temperament. Because of the exploratory nature of this study, the criterion chosen for entry of variables into the regression equation was less strict than usual (p for entry = 0.10), in order to get a more complete picture of the predictability of outcome variables.

Prediction of instrumental mastery motivation factors

Overall task-directedness at 18 months was predicted by same-age attachment security, scaffolding technical support with symbolic toys and child shyness (see Table 11.4). Other aspects of maternal scaffolding at this age were correlated with the overall task-directed factor, but did not meet the criteria for entry into the equation. Because the scaffolding variables are strongly intercorrelated, they did not make separate contributions to the regression equation. For the overall engrossment factor at 18 months, no predictor variables were entered into the equation. At 25-months, overall engrossment plus was predicted by same-age family cohesion and family adaptability (weighted negatively). No same-age variables met the criteria for entry into the regression equation for prediction of the 25-month factor overall task-directedness, nor did cross-age predictors for either overall task-directedness or overall engrossment plus.

The 18-month results predicting overall task-directedness suggest that a toddler's motivation to persist independently in the face of challenge is supported by his or her relationship with mother. This effect appears to be limited to the earlier assessment age; however, a less sensitive index of attachment security was used at the later age, which may account for the failure of attachment security to enter the regression equation. In

Table 11.4 Same-age and cross-age prediction of instrumental mastery motivation factors

Predictor variables	Same-age (18 months) Overall task-directedness (N = 41)	Same-age (25 months) Overall engrossment plus (N = 38)
	beta	beta
Attachment security	0.33	—
Scaffolding effectiveness:		
Combinatorial toys	—	—
Symbolic toys	0.32[a]	—
Marital:		
Satisfaction	—	—
Consensus	—	—
Cohesion	—	—
Family:		
Adaptability	N/A	−0.47
Cohesion	N/A	0.57
Child temperament:		
Emotionality	—	N/A
Activity level	—	N/A
Shyness	0.26	N/A
Sociability	—	N/A
Difficultness	—	N/A
Final statistics R	0.52	0.44
R^2	0.27	0.19
F	4.51**	4.58*

Notes: No predictor variables were entered into the equation for same-age prediction of overall engrossment (18 months) or overall task-directedness (25 months), or for cross-age prediction of overall task-directedness or overall engrossment plus. [a]Technical support. N/A = not applicable/not administered at this age. * $p \leqslant 0.05$. ** $p \leqslant 0.01$.
—— indicates betas less than 0.30.

our study, the best prediction resulted for cases in which a secure mother–child attachment relationship existed, good technical support during challenging tasks was provided, and the child tended to be shy. We speculate that active maternal scaffolding, when attuned to a child's particular needs and pace, provides a basis for a child's same-age independent efforts to master challenging tasks. Most probably, a secure attachment relationship enhances a scaffolder's ability to gauge the child's scaffolding needs and allows the child to be more receptive to maternal assistance. A shy child, especially when securely attached with a mother who scaffolds effectively, may be less active and more attuned to maternal support in a new situation, such as a laboratory playroom.

Maternal scaffolding support and the support derived from a secure attachment relationship may work in concert to facilitate child task-directedness. A child may internalize an overall sense of well-being from a secure attachment relationship, and incorporate specific beliefs about himself or herself as effective in the face of challenge from successful joint efforts at challenging tasks with mother (scaffolding). However, our results *do not* suggest that both a secure attachment and effective scaffolding by mother are necessary for a child to show high levels of task-directedness. Indeed, as reported elsewhere (Maslin-Cole and Spieker 1990), avoidantly attached infants (group A) showed the highest levels of engrossment during play with symbolic toys (at age 25 months only), although both the avoidant and secure groups were significantly higher than the resistant and disorganized groups. In addition, the avoidant group (at 18 months) showed significantly more object interaction (goal-directed behaviour plus exploration) during structured tasks than other attachment groups.

Moreover, our results do not suggest either that the ability to provide a secure base and good scaffolding skill covary, since security of attachment and scaffolding effectiveness were modestly correlated at best ($r = 0.17$ to 0.30 at 18 months; $r = 0.01$ to 0.19 at 25 months). Closer examination of our data showed that the best scaffolders at 18 months did have secure attachment relationships with their toddlers; however, all mothers showing secure attachment relationships with their toddlers at this age were not necessarily good scaffolders. Some mothers who had children judged to be securely attached were not particularly capable at the technical aspects of scaffolding (such as communicating critical features of a task or breaking the task down into manageable sub-steps). It appears that a secure attachment relationship (most probably the emotional attunement that typically accompanies security) may be a necessary but not sufficient prerequisite for the most effective levels of scaffolding.

It is not clear why aspects of the mother–toddler relationship failed to predict the 25-month factors of instrumental mastery motivation. Perhaps the child's movement towards increased physical and psychological autonomy results in less dependence on maternal support for independent motivation at 25 months than at 18 months. As children develop, persistence at tasks may be more strongly influenced by the child's internal representation of himself or herself as successful in the face of challenge than by the quality of concurrent adult support. If this were true, we would expect to see stronger cross-age stability for measures of persistence and engrossment, and perhaps greater cross-age correlations between earlier success at challenging tasks and later motivation to persist in the face of challenge, than found in this study.

Concerning prediction of the 25-month factor overall engrossment plus, we think it reasonable that high levels of family adaptability (perhaps approaching a chaotic lifestyle) combined with low family cohesion (tending towards disconnectedness) would adversely affect a child's ability to show sustained attention and could be expected to result in low engrossment during free play.

Prediction of expressive mastery motivation factors

For the single 18-month expressive mastery motivation factor, overall mastery pleasure, three variables were entered into the regression equation (see Table 11.5). Maternal emotional scaffolding support (with symbolic toys) and child activity level were both weighted positively, while maternal technical scaffolding support (with combinatorial toys) was weighted negatively. For same-age prediction of the 25-month factors, no variables entered the equation for predicting task pleasure or free-play pleasure.

The solution for predicting overall mastery pleasure at 18 months suggests that mothers who were emotionally expressive, attuned to their child, and facilitated give and take (all qualities of emotional scaffolding support) during play with symbolic toys, and who tended not to emphasize the technical aspects of play, had children who expressed more mastery pleasure in general at this age. Perhaps a physically active child would be more likely to be emotionally expressive as well, which would explain the contribution of activity level to this solution.

Interesting findings emerged for cross-age prediction of both 25-month expressive factors. The solution for predicting task pleasure from 18 to 25 months suggests that mothers who tended at the earlier age not to emphasize the technical aspects of play, but who were able to keep their children motivated towards an end goal (in some cases, taking on a role not unlike a cheerleader), had children who expressed more mastery pleasure during structured tasks at the later age. This solution also suggests that a tendency towards greater marital agreement, but less marital togetherness, facilitates children's expression of task pleasure. In comparison, the solution for free-play pleasure across ages suggests that two aspects of a child's earlier temperament which may promote emotional expressiveness – high activity level and absence of shyness – contributed to prediction of the amount of mastery pleasure a child expressed at the later age during free play. Like cross-age prediction of task pleasure, ability to keep a child motivated during joint play plus less marital togetherness contributed to prediction of later free-play pleasure.

Prediction of competence factors

The 18-month task competence factor was predicted by same-age maternal motivational scaffolding support (with symbolic toys) and child

Table 11.5 Same-age and cross-age prediction of expressive mastery motivation factors

Predictor variables	Same-age (18 months) Overall mastery pleasure (N = 41) beta	Cross-age Task pleasure (N = 38) beta	Cross-age Free-play pleasure (N = 38) beta
Attachment security	—	—	—
Scaffolding effectiveness:			
Combinatorial toys	-0.40[b]	0.76[a] -1.08[b]	—
Symbolic toys	0.60[c]	0.56[a]	0.24[a]
Marital:			
Satisfaction	—	—	—
Consensus	—	0.28	—
Cohesion	—	-0.42	-0.31
Family:			
Adaptability	N/A	N/A	N/A
Cohesion	N/A	N/A	N/A
Child temperament:			
Emotionality	—	—	—
Activity level	0.28	—	0.32
Shyness	—	—	-0.31
Sociability	—	—	—
Difficultness	—	—	—
Final statistics R	0.62	0.65	0.58
R²	0.38	0.42	0.34
F	7.60***	5.05***	4.54**

Notes: No predictor variables were entered into the equation for same-age prediction of task pleasure or free-play pleasure (both 25 months). [a]Motivational support. [b]Technical support. [c]Emotional support. N/A = not applicable/not administered at this age. ** $p \leq 0.01$. *** $p \leq 0.001$. — indicates betas less than 0.30.

sociability and difficultness, all of which were weighted positively (see Table 11.6). No variables were entered into the regression equation for the other 18-month competence factor, free-play competence. At 25 months, the symbolic competence factor was predicted only by same-age maternal motivational scaffolding support with symbolic toys. Cross-age prediction of the 25-month factor of combinatorial competence was provided by three 18-month variables: maternal emotional scaffolding support with symbolic toys and child emotionality (weighted positively) and marital satisfaction (weighted negatively). No cross-age predictors of 25-month symbolic competence met the criteria for entry into the regression equation.

For both task competence (18 months) and symbolic competence (25 months), the effectiveness of same-age maternal *motivational* support with symbolic toys emerged as the strongest contributor to prediction. However, an examination of the univariate correlations shows that all aspects of maternal scaffolding with both types of toy were positively correlated with these two factors ($r = 0.24 - 0.35$, $p = 0.08 - 0.01$ for task competence; $r = 0.24 - 0.41$, $p = 0.08 - 0.01$ for symbolic competence), suggesting a general contribution of effective scaffolding support to prediction of same-age child object competence. Attachment security did not emerge as a predictor variable for any of the competence factors. Apparently, security of attachment plays some role in how task-directed a child is (discussed above), but appears not to contribute to prediction of competence levels in this study.

Two aspects of child temperament were included in the regression equation predicting 18-month task competence. Sociability and effective maternal scaffolding together may moderate a fussy, dependent temperament (difficultness), thus allowing difficultness to make this unexpected contribution to the prediction of the task competence factor.

The results for cross-age prediction of combinatorial competence were, likewise, not expected. Rather than the quality of earlier *technical* support predicting later object competence, these results indicated that the quality of earlier *emotional* scaffolding support, with a different kind of toy type (symbolic), contributed to the prediction of scores on the combinatorial competence factor. This regression solution seems to suggest that poor marital satisfaction does not detract from the combined positive effects of maternal emotional support during difficult tasks and child emotionality on a child's developing competence.

CONCLUSIONS AND IMPLICATIONS

This study, like previous research, yielded evidence of moderate stability for measures of the instrumental aspect of mastery motivation and strong stability for the expressive aspect of mastery motivation. Measures of

Table 11.6 Same-age and cross-age prediction of competence factors

Predictor variables	Same-age (18 months) Task competence (N = 41) beta	Same-age (25 months) Symbolic competence (N = 38) beta	Cross-age Combinatorial competence (N = 38) beta
Attachment security	—	—	—
Scaffolding effectiveness:			
Combinatorial toys	0.51[a]	—	—
Symbolic toys	—	0.41[a]	0.47[b]
Marital:			
Satisfaction	—	—	-0.31
Consensus	—	—	—
Cohesion	—	—	—
Family:			
Adaptability	N/A	—	N/A
Cohesion	N/A	—	N/A
Child temperament:			
Emotionality	—	N/A	0.37
Activity level	—	N/A	—
Shyness		N/A	—
Sociability	0.28	N/A	—
Difficultness	0.28	N/A	—
Final statistics R	0.52	0.41	0.54
R^2	0.27	0.17	0.29
F	4.64**	8.01**	5.12**

Notes: No predictor variables were entered into the equation for same-age prediction of free-play competence (18 months), same-age combinatorial competence (25 months), or cross-age prediction of symbolic competence. [a]Motivational support. [b]Emotional support. N/A = not applicable/not administered at this age. ** $p \leq 0.01$. — indicates betas less than 0.30.

child competence showed less evidence of cross-age stability than reported in previous research, probably because the content of our competence factors changed somewhat with age. Measure-by-measure comparisons over time would give a more accurate picture of cross-age stability of competence for subjects in this study.

Measures of the instrumental aspect of mastery motivation and competence measures were fairly well correlated when assessed at the same age, which is consistent with previous research, although the correlations tended to be weaker for free play than for task-related measures. However, no evidence emerged for cross-age prediction of child competence from earlier levels of instrumental mastery motivation. The results of our study are not consistent with the notion that early mastery (or effectance) motivation enhances the development of later cognitive competence. It appears that early motivation in children, as measured in this study, does not propel a child towards greater levels of competence seven months later. If we were able to follow the development of competence in our subjects, perhaps a predictive effect of earlier motivation would appear one or two years later, as in other research (e.g. Yarrow et al. 1975).

No consistent predictors from the early social environment emerged for the instrumental aspect of mastery motivation. As a result, we are unable to draw specific conclusions about differential predictors of mastery motivation in task-related settings versus mastery motivation in free-play settings. Contrary to our expectations as well as to some previous research (e.g. Frodi et al. 1985; Matas et al. 1978), attachment security did not consistently predict mastery motivation or competence. While we found evidence that attachment security predicted same-age toddler task-directedness (at 18 months of age) in conjunction with effective maternal scaffolding and child shyness, earlier attachment security did not predict later mastery motivation or competence. Hence, for interactions with toys and challenging tasks at least, our results contradict a prevailing notion (cf. Matas et al. 1978; Sroufe 1979) that early attachment security serves to organize a child's later sense of efficacy and corresponding behaviour.

The quality of maternal scaffolding support emerged as a more consistent predictor of mastery motivation and competence than attachment security. Moreover, scaffolding effectiveness predicted later child competence better than later child motivation. For competence factors, ratings of maternal motivational scaffolding support were predictive in three or four significant regression equations, offering support for Vygotsky's (1978) view of adult assistance in bridging the child's zone of proximal development. However, our specific prediction that the quality of maternal technical support would facilitate later competence was not confirmed.

Scaffolding contributed most to the prediction of expressive aspects of mastery motivation. The maternal sensitivity that underlies highly effective scaffolding may promote increased expressiveness in children. It is also likely that expressive toddlers give clearer feedback about their emotional state while working on difficult tasks than non-expressive toddlers. This would allow their mothers to modify the pace and type of their assistance quickly and better facilitate their child's positive response to challenge. In addition, this study provides interesting evidence that maternal scaffolding effectiveness may be mediated by the security of the mother–child attachment relationship. A secure attachment may be a prerequisite for the most effective levels of scaffolding.

Finally, our prediction that a stressful marital relationship would adversely affect toddler mastery motivation was generally not confirmed. Hence, our results suggest that the parent–child relationship is a more powerful influence on child mastery motivation and competence than qualities of the marital relationship and general family climate. However, the limited nature of our marital and family measures requires that we view our results in this area as preliminary. Research involving thorough assessments of family and marital dynamics will yield a more complete picture of the influence of the early social environment on developing mastery motivation and competence.

NOTE

This research was funded by grants from the John D. and Catherine T. MacArthur Foundation Research Network on the Transition from Infancy to Early Childhood, the Developmental Psychobiology Research Group, and the Graduate School of the University of Wisconsin at Madison. We are grateful to the mothers and children who participated in this study. We wish to thank Beth Blazek, Carol Buxton, Janet Kask, Kathy McBride, Cheryl Richards and Maggie Sauer for their help with data collection, and Virginia Cross, Donald Gutentag, Sook Ryong Kim, Charlynn Prentiss, Judy Seybold, Jean Svedman, Linda Szabo and Linda Wilcox for their help with data scoring. Reprints are available from the first author at Rocky Mountain Marriage and Family Center, 1302 South Shields St, Fort Collins, CO 80521.

REFERENCES

Ainsworth, M. D. S., Blehar, M. C., Waters, E. and Wall, S. (1978) *Patterns of Attachment: A Psychological Study of the Strange Situation*, Hillsdale, NJ, Erlbaum.

Barrett, K. C. and Morgan, G. A. (in press) 'Continuities and discontinuities in mastery motivation in infancy and toddlerhood: a conceptualization and review', in R. H. MacTurk, and G. A. Morgan (eds) *Mastery Motivation: Conceptual Origins and Applications*, Norwood, NJ, Ablex.

Bates, J. E., Freeland, C. A. B. and Lounsbury, M. (1979) 'Measurement of infant difficultness', *Child Development* 50, 794–803.

Bayley, N. (1969) *The Bayley Scales of Infant Development*, New York, Psychological Corporation.

Bowlby, J. (1982) *Attachment and Loss. Vol. 1: Attachment*, 2nd edition, New York, Basic Books.

Bretherton, I. (1984) 'Representing the social world in symbolic play: reality and fantasy', in I. Bretherton (ed.) *Symbolic Play: The Development of Social Understanding*, New York, Academic Press.

Bretherton, I. (1985) 'Attachment Theory: retrospect and prospect' in I. Bretherton and E. Waters (eds) 'Growing Points of Attachment Theory and Research', *Monographs of the Society for Research in Child Development* 50, (Serial No. 209).

Bretherton, I. (1988) 'Scale to assess engrossment in free play with toys at 18 and 25 months', unpublished manuscript, available from the author at the Department of Child and Family Studies, University of Wisconsin, Madison WI 53705.

Bretherton, I. and Wilcox, L. (1988) 'Scale for the assessment of combinatorial play at 18 and 25 months', unpublished manuscript, available from the first author at the Department of Child and Family Studies, University of Wisconsin, Madison WI 53705.

Bretherton, I., Wilcox, L., Prentiss, C. and Szabo, L. (1988) 'Scale for the assessment of pretend play at 18 and 25 months', unpublished manuscript, available from the first author at the Department of Child and Family Studies, University of Wisconsin, Madison WI 53705.

Buss, A. H. and Plomin, R. (1984) *Temperament: Early Developing Personality Traits*, Hillsdale, NJ, Erlbaum.

Carey, W. B. and McDevitt, S. (1978) 'Revision of the infant temperament questionnaire', *Pediatrics* 61, 735–9.

Frodi, A., Bridges, L. and Grolnick, W. (1985) 'Correlates of mastery-related behavior: a short-term longitudinal study of infants in their second year', *Child Development* 56, 1291–8.

Hazen, N. L. and Durrett, M. E. (1982) 'Relationship of security of attachment to exploration and cognitive mapping abilities in 2-year-olds', *Developmental Psychology* 18, 751–9.

Main, M. (1983) 'Exploration, play and cognitive functioning related to infant–mother attachment', *Infant Behavior and Development* 6, 167–74.

Maslin, C. A. (1987) 'Scales for assessing maternal scaffolding effectiveness', unpublished manuscript, available from the author at Rocky Mountain Marriage and Family Center, 1302 South Shields St, Fort Collins, CO 80521.

Maslin-Cole, C. A. and Spieker, S. J. (1990) 'Attachment as a basis for independent motivation: a view from risk and non-risk samples', in M. T. Greenberg, D. Cicchetti and E. M. Cummings (eds) *Attachment in the Preschool Years: Theory, Research, and Intervention*, Chicago, University of Chicago Press.

Matas, L., Arend, R. A. and Sroufe, L. A. (1978) 'Continuity of adaptation in the second year: the relationship between quality of attachment and later competence', *Child Development* 49, 547–56.

Morgan, G. A., Busch-Rossnagel, N. A., Maslin-Cole, C. A. and Harmon, R. J. (1992) *Mastery motivation tasks: Manual for 15- to 36-month-old children*, available from the second author at Department of Psychology, Fordham University, Bronx, NY 10458.

Morgan, G. A., Harmon, R. J. and Maslin-Cole, C. A. (1990) 'Mastery motivation: definition and measurement', *Early Education and Development* 1, 318–39.

Nicolich, L. M. (1977) 'Beyond sensorimotor intelligence: assessment of symbolic maturity through analysis of pretend play', *Merrill-Palmer Quarterly* 23, 89–100.

Olson, D. H., Portner, J. and Bell, R. (1982) *Family Adaptability and Cohesion Scale II*, available from the first author at Family Social Science, University of Minnesota, 297 McNeal Hall, St Paul, MN 55108.

Olson, D. H., Sprenkle, D. H. and Russell, C. S. (1979) 'Circumplex model of marital and family systems I: Cohesion and adaptability dimensions, family types and clinical applications', *Family Process* 18, 3–28.

Plomin, R. (1986) *Development, Genetics and Psychology*, Hillsdale, NJ, Erlbaum.

Redding, R. E., Morgan, G. A. and Harmon, R. J. (1988) 'Mastery motivation in infants and toddlers: is it greatest when tasks are moderately challenging?', *Infant Behavior and Development* 11, 419–30.

Rowe, D. C. and Polmin, R. (1977) 'Temperament in early childhood', *Journal of Personality Assessment* 41, 150–6.

Scarr, S. (1981) 'Testing for children: assessment of the many determinants of intellectual competence', *American Psychologist* 36, 1159–66.

Spanier, G. B. (1976) 'Measuring dyadic adjustment: new scales for assessing the quality of marriage and similar dyads', *Journal of Marriage and the Family* 38, 15–20.

Sroufe, L. A. (1979) 'The coherence of individual development', *American Psychologist* 34, 834–41.

Sroufe, L. A. and Waters, E. (1977) 'Heart rate as a convergent measure in clinical and developmental research', *Merrill-Palmer Quarterly* 23, 3–27.

Thomas, A. and Chess, S. (1977) *Temperament and Development*, New York, Bruner/Mazel.

Ulvand, S. E. (1980) 'Cognition and motivation in early infancy: an interactionist approach', *Human Development* 23, 17–32.

Vygotsky, L. S. (1978) *Mind in Society: The Development of Higher Psychological Processes*, in M. Cole, V. John-Steiner, S. Scribner and E. Souberman (eds), Cambridge, MA, Harvard University Press.

Waters, E. and Deane, K. E. (1985) 'Defining and assessing individual differences in attachment relationships: Q-methodology and the organization of behavior in infancy and early childhood', in I. Bretherton and E. Waters (eds) 'Growing points of attachment theory and research', *Monographs of the Society for Research in Child Development* 50 (1–2, Serial No. 209).

White, R. W. (1959) 'Motivation reconsidered: The concept of competence', *Psychological Review* 66, 297–333.

Wood, D., Bruner, J. S. and Ross, G. (1976) 'The role of tutoring in problem solving', *Journal of Child Psychology and Psychiatry* 17, 89–100.

Yarrow, L. J., Klein, R., Lomonaco, S. and Morgan, G. (1975) 'Cognitive and motivational development in early childhood', in B. Z. Friedlander, G. M. Sterritt and G. E. Kirk (eds) *Exceptional Infant: Assessment and Intervention*, New York, Bruner/Mazel.

Yarrow, L. J. and Messer, D. J. (1983) 'Motivation and cognition in infancy', in M. Lewis (ed.) *Origins of Intelligence*, 2nd edition, Hillsdale, NJ, Erlbaum.

Yarrow, L. J., Morgan, G. A., Jennings, K. D., Harmon, R. J. and Gaiter, J. L. (1982) 'Infant's persistence at tasks: relationships to cognitive functioning and early experience', *Infant Behavior and Development* 5, 131–42.

Chapter 12

Mastery motivation in 3-year-old children with Down syndrome

Penny Hauser-Cram

Exploration of the environment is considered to be a critical aspect of the development of competence in all children. For the very young child, a substantial part of exploration involves playing with objects; such play results in the eventual understanding that actions produce effects (Piaget 1952). The motivation to master such understanding is regarded as an intrinsic and integral part of human development (White 1959). As with other fundamental human characteristics, however, individual differences exist in the motivation to master an understanding of physical objects. We are only beginning to understand the origins and extent of such differences.

Theories of motivation suggest that cognitive ability, at least in part, explains differences in motivation. Theorists have conceptualized the cognition-motivation relation in a variety of ways. White (1959) contends that motivation in the young child manifests itself as an 'urge toward competence' that results in broad knowledge and skill in understanding the world of physical objects. In this regard, motivation may be considered the servant of cognition. A complementary perspective of motivation was conceptualized by Berlyne (1966), who contended that individuals engage in problem solving when experiences are discrepant from those anticipated. Thus, motivation stems from cognitive activity. Finally, Hunt (1971) implied an integrated relation between cognition and motivation in his proposal that motivation is a critical aspect of information processing. In this view, cognition and motivation are colleagues. All three theorists are united in their perspective that motivation and cognition are critically linked.

Although none of the theorists mentioned above used the term 'mastery motivation', all described behaviours that individuals display when mastering challenging problems. Mastery motivation has been conceptualized as 'the psychological force that stimulates an individual to attempt independently, in a focused and persistent manner, to solve a problem or master a skill which is at least moderately challenging to him or her' (Morgan *et al.* 1990: 319). Mastery motivation has been operationalized most frequently in the research literature as persistence on problem-posing tasks that are performed independently and that are moderately challenging (Morgan *et al.* 1990).

The relation between cognition (as measured by performance on a standardized developmental assessment) and mastery motivation (as measured by persistence on a challenging problem-posing task) in young children has been examined in a number of studies. In general, the relation between cognition and motivation differs according to the developmental stage of the children being studied. Yarrow and Pederson (1976) and Scarr (1981) suggest that cognition and motivation may be intricately intertwined during infancy. Reasonably high correlations between cognition and motivation have been reported in most studies of infants (Morgan and Harmon 1984). In interpreting these findings, Morgan *et al.* (1990) have speculated that the high correlations may be due to the difficulties of measuring each construct independent of the other.

Departure of motivation from cognition appears in studies of normally developing children during the pre-school years, where low to moderate concurrent correlations between the constructs have been reported. For example, whereas Redding *et al.* (1988) found high correlations between intelligence and persistence at 12 months, the correlations were close to zero at 24 and 36 months. In a study of 2 ½-year-olds, Messer *et al.* (1987) reported a moderate correlation between problem engagement on mastery motivation tasks and the General Cognitive Index (GCI) of the McCarthy Scales of Children's Abilities.

One way to test the relation between cognition and motivation is to examine their association in populations that are on the extreme end of either scale. What is the relation between motivation and cognition for children who exhibit unusually advanced cognitive abilities or delayed development? To date, very few studies have tested the cognition–motivation relation in atypical populations. Vietze *et al.* (1983) studied attention and exploration in 1-year-olds with Down's syndrome. They found moderate to high correlations between the Mental Development Index (MDI) on the Bayley Scales and task-directed behaviour on effect-production tasks ($r = 0.87$) and problem-solving tasks ($r = 0.66$). In a study of 2–3-year olds with mental retardation Schwethelm and Mahoney (1986) reported moderate correlations (ranging from $r = 0.40$ to $r = 0.55$) between developmental age and task persistence. Harter and Zigler (1974) reported lower scores on a series of motivation tasks for school-aged children with more severe levels of mental retardation. In contrast, Jennings *et al.* (1985) found low and non-significant correlations between the McCarthy GCI and persistence on mastery motivation measures in pre-school children with physical (but not cognitive) disabilities ($r = 0.24$) and in non-disabled children ($r = 0.08$). Finally, Gottfried and Nordquist (1989) studied school-aged children with unusually advanced cognitive skills, and reported greater academic intrinsic motivation (on the basis of a questionnaire) in that group compared to children with more modest abilities. Although the data on the extent of the relation between cognition and motivation are somewhat inconsistent, the studies indicate that these two domains of development often overlap – but are not redundant – in children developing normally or atypically during the pre-school and early school years.

Since cognitive status is an insufficient predictor of children's mastery motivation, other aspects of children's development need to be considered when explaining individual variation in mastery motivation. Current models of development emphasize the importance of the ecological niche in which the child grows and learns (Bronfenbrenner 1979) and the formative value of the transactions within the child's environment (Sameroff and Chandler 1975; Vygotsky 1978). Aspects of the care-giving environment can be characterized in two distinct ways: proximal – that is, the 'microsystem' in which the child's needs are met and in which parents establish the immediate context for caregiving (Bronfenbrenner 1979); and distal – that is, the qualities of family life that define the broader context in which the care-givers function (Schneewind 1989).

Proximal characteristics include both direct parental involvement in the child's social and learning experiences, and indirect parental influence through the provision of challenging play objects. Accumulating evidence has indicated the importance of the quality of the parent–child relationship in promoting optimal development (Bee et al. 1982; Clarke-Stewart 1973; Rogoff et al. 1984). Research has also pointed to the important role of indirect parental influence on children's development for example, through the provision of appropriate play materials (Bradley, Caldwell et al. 1989).

Distal characteristics include the degree to which the family functions as a cohesive and adaptive unit. The emotional cohesiveness among family members and the ability of the family as a system to adjust to situational or developmental stressors constitute essential elements of families that function well (Olson and Lavee 1989). Evidence suggests that such elements are predictive of more positive outcomes for children as well as for parents (Mink et al. 1983; Sameroff and Seifer 1983).

In 1978, Harter suggested that the role of socialization agents be examined in understanding individual differences in motivation, yet only a few studies have done this. For the most part, these studies have focused on the mother's psycho-social well-being or skill in interacting with her child. Redding et al. (1990) found that maternal depression was related to lower task competence and persistence in toddlers. Yarrow et al. (1984) found parental stimulation to be associated with persistence in problem solving of infants at 6 months, but to have less consistent associations with problem-solving persistence at 12 months. Maslin-Cole et al. (this volume,

Chapter 11) found positive relations between maternal scaffolding effectiveness (i.e. behaviours that support and encourage mastery attempts)
and children's task persistence at 18 months, but fewer relations at 25
months. Wachs (1987) reported that high levels of parent mediation
predicted object mastery for children with low activity levels, yet in-
terfered with object mastery for children with high activity levels.
Lutkenhaus (1984) reported that specific aspects of maternal cooperative
behaviour related to mastery motivation in 3-year-old children. In a study
of children with cerebral palsy, Blasco et al. (1990) found positive aspects
of maternal involvement were related to children's independent mastery
performance, measured in a spontaneous play situation.

In summary, when aspects of the care-giving environment have been
investigated directly, they appear to aid in the prediction of children's
mastery motivation. The studies, however, are limited by a focus on
maternal characteristics and, with few exceptions, have not examined the
extent of the relation between aspects of the care-giving environment and
mastery motivation in children who are not developing according to a
typical timetable. Is the relation between cognition and motivation so
strong in children with mental retardation that the facilitative features of
the environment lack potency, or do such features aid in understanding
individual differences in mastery motivation in children with differing
cognitive abilities?

Questions about the sensitivity of young children with atypical development to environmental effects on mastery motivation comprise a critical
realm of inquiry. Children who have repeated experiences with failure
often tend to be less motivated to attempt the most challenging tasks
(Diener and Dweck 1978) and in this way, limit their own ability to learn.
Research (e.g. Weisz 1979) suggests that children with mental retardation
exhibit high rates of 'learned helplessness' when presented with challenging tasks. Thus, investigation of aspects of the environment that maximize
motivation in children with mental retardation, and thus minimize the
opportunities for the development of 'learned helplessness', may yield
suggestions for programmatic intervention.

The analyses reported in this chapter were designed to examine several
aspects of mastery motivation in 3-year-old children with Down syndrome. First, the analyses addressed the question of the extent to which
mastery motivation (as measured by persistence on problem-posing tasks)
is a unitary phenomenon across tasks. Second, they examined the relation
between three aspects of children's functioning (cognitive performance,
adaptive behaviour, and independent play skills), each measured between
3 and 36 months, and mastery motivation at 3 years. And finally, they
tested the extent to which distal and proximal aspects of children's early
care-giving environment were associated with their subsequent mastery
motivation.

Table 12.1 Descriptive characteristics of the sample

Characteristics	Percentage/number
Child characteristics:	
Percentage female	58.8%
Percentage with a cardiac anomaly	41.2%
Percentage firstborn	35.3%
Percentage living with both parents	91.2%
Percentage white	82.4%
Family characteristics:	
Percentage of mothers with at least some college education	61.8%
Maternal age at child's birth (years)	30.8 years
Percentage of employed mothers	54.5%
Percentage of families with incomes above $20,000	70.6%

Note: $n = 34$.

THE STUDY SAMPLE

The study sample was drawn from a larger sample of children and families who participated in the Early Intervention Collaborative Study (EICS), a longitudinal study of young children with disabilities or developmental delays (Shonkoff *et al.* 1992). All children with Down syndrome who demonstrated at least one solution on each of the two mastery motivation tasks presented at 3 years of age were included in the final sample ($n = 34$). Descriptive characteristics of those children and their families are presented in Table 12.1. The children's cognitive performance, based on the MDI of the Bayley Scales of Infant Development (Bayley 1969) or the GCI of the McCarthy Scales of Children's Abilities (McCarthy 1972), averaged 51.4 (SD = 10.1) administered at 3 years of age. The majority of the sample were moderately mentally retarded.

DATA COLLECTION

Children were participants in a longitudinal study that involved a series of home and school visits during the early childhood years. Data were collected during three home visits conducted during infancy (M = 3.5, SD = 2.3 months), shortly after 1 year of age (M = 15.5, SD = 2.3 months), and at 3 years of age (M = 36.6, SD = 1.2 months). The home visits were conducted by two research field staff unfamiliar with the study's hypotheses. Parents were interviewed by one staff member while another assessed the child.

During the first home visit, a parent completed a form on family demographics and was asked to sign a consent form, allowing release of the child's medical records (which were used to determine the presence or absence of a cardiac anomaly). Mothers also completed a measure of family functioning, the Family Adaptability and Cohesion Evaluation Scales (FACES II: Olson *et al.* 1982). The FACES is a questionnaire that measures two dimensions of the family environment, cohesion and adaptability. Cronbach's alpha for the EICS sample on these subscales was 0.86 for cohesion and 0.79 for adaptability.

Children were assessed during the first home visit (and each subsequent visit) on the Bayley Scales of Infant Development, the Vineland Adaptive Behavior Scales (Sparrow *et al.* 1984) and the Belsky–Most Play Scale (Belsky and Most 1981). The Vineland Scales are based on a semi-structured interview with a parent to identify skills the child demonstrates on a regular basis. It includes four domains – communication, daily living skills, socialization, and motor skills – and also yields a standard composite score. The Cronbach's alpha coefficient was 0.96 for the EICS sample on the composite score.

The Belsky–Most Play Scale is a fourteen-step scale that reflects an ordinal developmental sequence of play, ranging from simple sensori-motor manipulations through complex symbolic pretence play. The child is observed for twenty minutes while playing independently with two standard sets of toys. The investigator records the highest level of play using a fifteen-second time-sampling period. The Guttman scale analysis of this play scale yielded a coefficient of reproducibility of 0.95 and a coefficient of scalability of 0.77.

During the 1-year home visit, the field staff completed the Home Observation for Measurement of the Environment (HOME: Caldwell and Bradley 1984). The HOME is an observational measure designed to assess the quality of a young child's care-giving environment. Administration requires a semi-structured interview with the mother in the home, and items are completed through observation and maternal report. The Cronbach's alpha reliability coefficients were 0.62 for the provision of play materials sub-scale and 0.64 for the parent involvement sub-scale. These alpha coefficients are slightly lower than those reported by Bradley, Rock *et al.* (1989) in research on families with children who have disabilities.

Data collection: mastery tasks

When children were 3 years old, they were presented with two mastery motivation tasks. The method of presentation was based on techniques developed by Morgan *et al.* (1992). Two types of problem-posing toys were used: those involving cause and effect (e.g. slide a lever for a figure to appear) and those involving puzzles. The cause-and-effect toys were commercially produced items and formed the following hierarchy: (1) a typewriter; (2) a surprise box; (3) a cash register; and (4) a tape-recorder. The puzzles were also commercially produced and formed five levels of difficulty: (1) a balloon puzzle with eight identical pieces; (2) a traffic light puzzle with six pieces; (3) a traffic signs puzzle with five pieces; (4) a transportation puzzle with eight pieces; and (5) a three-pigs puzzle with eleven interlocking pieces. For each task, the examiner selected one toy out of the hierarchy described above that was moderately challenging for the child (i.e. one in which the child could complete one, but not all solutions within 1½ minutes). If the child was unable to complete one solution within the established time period, a less challenging toy was selected; if the child completed all solutions within the time period, a more challenging toy was selected. The order of presentation of the two tasks was counterbalanced across subjects.

For both tasks, the examiner presented the toys and demonstrated two predetermined solutions. After giving the child the direction, 'Now, you try it', the examiner began scoring the child's modal level of behaviour

Table 12.2 Definitions of behaviours observed on the mastery motivation tasks

Behaviour	Definition
Child's activities:	
Task-directed	Child attempts to solve the problem posed by the toy.
Apparatus-directed	Child manipulates the toy in a simple, exploratory, non-goal-oriented way.
Own task	Child develops his or her own way of playing with the toy.
Looks	Child visually attends to the toy but does not manipulate it.
Mother-oriented	Child's attention is focused on his or her mother.
Examiner-oriented	Child's attention is focused on the examiner.
Uninvolved	Child's attention is not focused on the toy, mother or examiner.
Perseverative	Child duplicates the same response three or more times in succession.
Reset	Child disassembles toy.
Child's performance:	
Achieves solution	Child successfully solves one problem posed by the toy.
Completes all solutions	Child successfully solves all possible problems posed by the toy.
Child's affect:	
Positive	Child smiles, laughs, claps upon achieving a solution.
Negative	Child frowns, grimaces, cries upon achieving a solution.
Neutral	Child displays no noticeable affect upon achieving a solution.

within 15-second blocks for a total of 4 minutes per toy (yielding a total of 16 intervals). For each 15-second interval, the examiner recorded the child's activities, the child's performance, and the child's affect (see Table 12.2).

For each child, the following summary scores were calculated on each task:

1 the percentage of solutions that were accompanied by positive affect (termed 'affect');
2 the percentage of intervals in which the child displayed simple exploration of the toy (i.e. non-goal-oriented behaviour with toy) (termed 'exploration');
3 the percentage of intervals in which the child displayed task-directed problem-solving activity with the toy (termed 'persistence');
4 the percentage of possible solutions successfully achieved, adjusted by the level difficulty of the toy (termed 'competence').

Of the four summary scores described above, exploration is considered to be a negative indicator of mastery motivation, whereas the other three, especially persistence, are considered positive indicators. Inter-rater reliability for the two tasks was $r = 0.72$, $r = 0.88$, $r = 0.87$ and $r = 0.94$ for the cause-and-effect tasks, and $r = 0.74$, $r = 0.86$, $r = 0.89$ and $r = 0.96$ for the puzzle tasks on the measures of affect, exploration, persistence and competence, respectively.

MASTERY MOTIVATION AT THREE YEARS

The means and standard deviations for the mastery motivation measures are presented in Table 12.3. As the table indicates, children showed greater persistence, higher levels of competence, and a tendency to display more affect on the cause-and-effect tasks. On both tasks, children showed higher levels of persistence than of exploration, a result similar

Table 12.3 Means and standard deviations of mastery motivation measures on two tasks

Measure	Cause-and-effect tasks	Puzzle tasks	Paired t-test value
Affect[a]	19.4 (28.0)	9.7 (22.0)	1.89[+]
Exploration[b]	7.9 (2.4)	7.0 (10.2)	0.30
Persistence[b]	56.8 (31.1)	32.9 (21.9)	4.14**
Competence[c]	365.2 (93.6)	250.5 (81.3)	7.48***

Notes: [+] $p < 0.10$. ** $p < 0.01$. *** $p < 0.001$.
[a]Scores are based on the percentage of solutions accompanied by positive affect. [b]Scores are based on the percentage of intervals in which the behaviour was observed as the modal behaviour. [c]Scores are based on the percentage of possible solutions successfully completed, weighted by level of difficulty of task.

to that reported by Hupp and Abbeduto (1991) in a study of mastery motivation in very young children with cognitive delays. Children in this sample demonstrated low levels of simple exploration on both tasks and relatively low levels of affect, especially on the puzzle tasks. Less than 10 per cent of the solutions achieved on the puzzle tasks were accompanied by positive affect. Only 15 children displayed at least one interval of positive affect (when achieving a solution) on the cause-and-effect tasks, and 8 children showed positive affect with solutions on the puzzles.

The intercorrelation matrix of the mastery motivation measures is presented in Table 12.4. Persistence and affect were not correlated, a finding predicted by current theorizing (see Barrett *et al.*, this volume, Chapter 5). The two measures of persistence were not significantly correlated in this sample. Persistence on each task, however, was moderately related to competence on that task, a finding that is consistent with that reported by MacTurk *et al.* (1985) in a study of mastery motivation of infants with Down syndrome. Finally, competence on the two tasks was significantly related.

CORRELATES OF MASTERY MOTIVATION: CHILDREN'S FUNCTIONING

Analyses were conducted to test different correlates of mastery motivation. The first set of correlates were children's demographic and health variables, including firstborn status, gender, and the presence or absence of a cardiac anomaly. No differences were found in mastery motivation for children with and without a cardiac anomaly, and only two significant differences were found for the demographic variables. First, a higher proportion of males demonstrated positive affect with solutions on the cause-and-effect toys ($t = 2.13$, $p < 0.05$). Second, firstborn children had significantly lower levels of simple exploration on the cause-and-effect tasks ($t = 2.44$, $p < 0.05$).

The second set of analyses examined the extent to which aspects of children's functioning at three age points correlated with mastery motivation at 3 years of age. The descriptive statistics of the three measures of children's functioning are presented in Table 12.5.

As the table indicates, children's cognitive performance and adaptive behaviour, as measured on a standardized scale, diminished (relative to their peers) over time. At the time of the age 3 assessment, the average mental age of children in this sample was 19.1 months, indicating that they were still operating within the sensorimotor period of development. As expected, their play skills increased from simple gazing during the infant assessment, to simple manipulation of objects at the 1-year-old assessment, to functional-relational play with objects at age 3 years.

Table 12.4 Correlations among the mastery motivation measures

| | Cause-and-effect tasks | | | | Puzzle tasks | | | |
	Affect	Exploration	Persistence	Competence	Affect	Exploration	Persistence	Competence
	(1)	(2)	(3)	(4)	(5)	(6)	(7)	(8)
1	–	0.01	-0.08	-0.19	0.29	0.13	-0.13	-0.12
2		–	-0.30	-0.02	-0.21	-0.07	0.08	-0.13
3			–	0.60*	0.26	-0.09	0.23	0.56*
4				–	0.002	-0.26	0.08	0.49*
5					–	-0.02	0.33	0.19
6						–	-0.11	-0.24
7							–	0.49*
8								–

Note: * $p < 0.01$.

Table 12.5 Descriptive statistics on measures of children's functioning at three age points

Assessment	Mean	Standard deviation
Infant:		
Cognitive performance[a]	70.6	13.4
Adaptive behaviour	94.3	5.7
Independent play	0.4	0.4
Age 1:		
Cognitive performance[b]	45.0	14.3
Adaptive behaviour	77.2	6.0
Independent play	2.3	0.6
Age 3:		
Cognitive performance[c]	51.4	10.1
Adaptive behaviour	60.4	6.0
Independent play	4.8	1.3

Notes: Cognitive performance was measured by the Bayley Scales, adaptive behaviour by the Vineland Adaptive Behavior Scales and independent play by the Belsky–Most Play Scale. [a]Mental age: M = 2.2 months, SD = 1.8. [b]Mental age: M = 9.7 months, SD = 2.4. [c]Mental age: M = 19.1 months, SD = 3.1.

With only one exception, the measures of children's functioning assessed during the first few months of life failed to correlate with the mastery motivation measures at age 3 (Table 12.6). The single exception was that children who had higher levels of adaptive skills tended to display less simple exploration at age 3. In general, early infant assessments were poor predictors of later mastery motivation.

The assessments performed after 1 year of age showed stronger and more consistent relations with later mastery motivation. Cognitive performance correlated with later persistence on both tasks, and with affect and competence on the puzzle tasks. Adaptive behaviour correlated with persistence on the cause-and-effect tasks and with competence on both tasks. Independent play showed consistent negative relations with simple exploration on both tasks; children who demonstrated higher levels of independent play at 1 year of age displayed less simple exploration on mastery motivation tasks at 3 years of age.

Contemporaneous correlations between children's functioning at age 3 and their performance on mastery motivation indicate that cognitive performance was more highly related to behaviour on the puzzle tasks than on the cause-and-effect tasks. Cognitive performance was correlated negatively with simple exploration and positively with persistence and competence on the puzzles. Adaptive behaviour correlated only with competence on the puzzle tasks. Independent play was the only significant correlate of persistence on the cause-and-effect tasks, and was correlated with competence on both tasks.

In summary, measures of children's functioning during the first few

Table 12.6 Correlations between mastery motivation measures at age 3 and children's cognitive performance, adaptive behaviour and independent play at three time points

Assessment	Mastery motivation measures							
	Cause-and-effect tasks				Puzzle tasks			
	Affect	Exploration	Persistence	Competence	Affect	Exploration	Persistence	Competence
Infant:								
Cognitive performance		0.27				−0.30		
Adaptive behaviour		−0.44**						
Independent play						−0.22		−0.25
Age 1:								
Cognitive performance		−0.27	0.36*	0.21	0.39*	−0.33	0.35*	0.37*
Adaptive behaviour			0.42*	0.40*	0.21		0.29	0.49**
Independent play		−0.36*	0.24	0.22		−0.42*		
Age 3:								
Cognitive performance	−0.20		0.25	0.30	0.27	−0.43*	0.44**	0.47**
Adaptive behaviour			0.32	0.32		−0.26	0.26	0.53**
Independent play			0.50**	0.42*		−0.33	0.22	0.50**

Notes: Only correlations ⩾ 0.20 are included in this table. * $p < 0.05$. ** $p < 0.01$.

months of life appear to be poor predictors of later mastery motivation. However, when children reach the mental age of 9–10 months, cognitive performance may be predictive of later persistence. The infant who operates at the 9–10-month age is probably reaching stage 4 of the sensorimotor stage of intelligence. At this mental age, the infant is beginning to understand simple cause-and-effect sequences, and his or her behaviour on developmental assessments that include some cause-and-effect items, such as the Bayley, may be more predictive than behaviour on cognitive tests at earlier stages. Moreover, the pattern of contemporaneous correlations at age 3 years suggests that persistence on the two tasks may have different sets of relations. Performance on the puzzle tasks is related to general cognitive skill, whereas performance on the cause-and-effect tasks is related to children's independent ability to play skilfully with toys.

CORRELATES OF MASTERY MOTIVATION: MEASURES OF THE FAMILY ENVIRONMENT

A final set of analyses was designed to help in understanding the extent to which different aspects of the family environment, measured during the early stages of life, correlated with children's later mastery motivation. Four measures were selected, as they define the family environment in distinct ways and have demonstrated power in predicting children's functioning for the preschool ages. First, maternal education, a traditional demographic measure, was used. Next, a measure of family functioning, the FACES II, was chosen as a means of describing the distal care-giving environment – families who score within the 'balanced' range on the FACES have specified levels of cohesion and adaptability. Finally, two different aspects of the proximal care-giving environment were selected: provision of play materials, and parent involvement (sub-scales of the HOME). Parents can be involved indirectly with a child's learning through providing appropriate toys and games; they can also be involved directly through providing specific instruction or assistance in structuring play.

Partial correlation analyses (controlling for children's cognitive performance: see Table 12.7) suggest an interesting pattern of relations between aspects of the care-giving environment and children's mastery motivation. Maternal education had no significant relation with any of the mastery motivation measures. In contrast, family functioning was negatively related to simple exploration on the cause-and-effect tasks and had a modest relation with persistence on that task. It was also positively related to affect and had a modest negative relation to exploration on the puzzle tasks. In general, families that displayed higher levels of functioning (i.e. were more balanced in their levels of cohesion and adaptability) had children who later engaged in less low-level performance

Table 12.7 Partial correlations between mastery motivation measures and characteristics of the family environment, controlling for children's cognitive performance

Family characteristics	Mastery motivation measures							
	Cause-and-effect tasks				Puzzle tasks			
	Affect	Exploration	Persistence	Competence	Affect	Exploration	Persistence	Competence
Maternal education								
Family functioning		−0.50**	0.25+		0.31*	−0.25+		
Provision of play materials							0.37*	0.29+
Parent involvement			−0.40*	−0.30*				−0.35*

Notes: Only correlations ≥ 0.20 are included in this table. + p < 0.10. * p < 0.05. ** p < 0.01.

(i.e. simple exploration) when mastering tasks. These children also tended to be more persistent and display more positive affect when successful on certain tasks.

The two measures of the proximal care-giving environment revealed different patterns of relations. The provision of play materials was positively related to higher levels of persistence and competence on the puzzle tasks. In contrast, high levels of parent involvement were negatively related to persistence on cause-and-effect tasks and to competence on both tasks (even when level of cognitive performance was controlled). Together, these findings suggest that the indirect role parents play by selecting appropriate learning materials was associated with more positive effects for children's independent mastery motivation, whereas the more direct role taken by some parents in structuring children's activities was associated with less advantageous outcomes.

IMPLICATIONS

The results of this study indicate that an underlying relation between cognition and motivation, especially on perceptual-motor tasks such as puzzles, exists in children with Down syndrome. Moreover, the findings suggest that the predictive power of cognitive performance for later motivation emerges by the fourth stage of the sensorimotor period. In general, the moderate relation between cognitive performance and mastery motivation indicate that cognition and motivation are related – but not redundant – domains of development in children with mental retardation.

The low levels of affect associated with task solution found for this sample are consistent with prior studies on children with Down's syndrome. For example, Thompson et al. (1985) reported that toddlers with Down syndrome displayed diminished affect, in comparison to their peers, during episodes of separation in the 'strange situation'. They suggest that the quality, rather than the organization, of emotionality differs for children with Down syndrome. Larger samples and longitudinal study will illuminate our understanding and the extent to which children with Down syndrome display increasingly positive affect in mastering problem-posing tasks as they mature developmentally (see Jennings, this volume, Chapter 3).

The results of this study further indicate that persistence on tasks is not a unitary phenomenon for young children with Down syndrome. In this way, the findings of this study do not depart from those of children with normal development, where low correlations across tasks have been reported and the multidimensional nature of the construct of mastery motivation has been underscored (Morgan et al. 1990). Assuming that persistence is a valid measure of motivation, these findings indicate that motivation is task specific in young children with Down syndrome. The contemporaneous correlations suggest that different aspects of children's functioning correlate differently with motivation on the two tasks. Children who are able to engage in higher levels of independent play (i.e. play with toys without adult involvement) display higher levels of motivation on cause-and-effect tasks. Children with higher general cognitive skills engage in higher levels of persistence on puzzle tasks. This finding suggests the need to understand better the various propensities exhibited by children with Down syndrome and how individual differences in skills and individual differences in motivation are related.

Finally, the analyses conducted in this study suggest that mastery motivation in children with Down syndrome is not impervious to environmental influence. The children in this sample were within the sensorimotor period of development, a stage of development that is often considered to be resistant to modest differences in the care-giving environment (McCall 1979). Indeed, environmental differences during the sensorimotor period of development in young children with disabilities appear to have little relation to traditional cognitive outcomes (Shonkoff et al. 1992). In contrast, mastery motivation appears to be sensitive to the early care-giving environment. Even distal aspects of the family environment, such as the general level of family functioning, relate to some aspects of children's later mastery motivation. Families that exhibit balanced relationships in terms of cohesion and adaptability provide a more nurturing environment for children to exhibit persistence and display pleasure in tackling challenging tasks.

Proximal measures of parental influence appear to have important and differing relations to mastery motivation. In general, these findings support the thesis put forward by Wachs (1987) that the effects of the early environment on children's mastery motivation are not unitary, simple or global. Parents who provide appropriate toys and games for their child have children who later display more persistence in accomplishing puzzle tasks. Thus, the opportunity for independent engagement with a wide range of play materials may provide a supportive setting for children and stimulate children's independent persistence on certain tasks, such as puzzles.

The findings of this study also indicate, however, that high levels of direct parent engagement in structuring children's play may lead to less active independent motivation. At first glance, this may appear to be a counter-intuitive finding; but the mothers of children in this sample as a whole displayed an unusually high level of parental involvement in contrast to studies of families of children without disabilities (Caldwell and Bradley 1984). This finding is consistent with results of other studies of children with disabilities, which have indicated that parents appear to be highly directive in their interactions with children (Buckhalt et al. 1978; Eheart 1982; Jones 1977). Stoneman et al. (1983) noted that parents of young children with Down syndrome took on the role of helper, manager and teacher significantly more often than parents of normally developing children in their play with children.

Studies of the qualities of parent–child interaction that promote high levels of mastery motivation in normally developing children stress the importance of parents' ability to encourage autonomy in young children. Grolnick et al. (1984) found that infants whose mothers supported autonomous attempts at mastering challenging tasks were more persistent than infants whose mothers were more controlling. Lutkenhaus (1984) reported that specific qualities of maternal cooperation appear to relate to children's mastery motivation. In particular, unobtrusive assistance and affective sharing have positive relations to children's mastery attempts, whereas physical intrusion has negative influences upon mastery motivation. Heckhausen (this volume, Chapter 4) further delineates the critical role of parents as guides, rather than didactic instructors, in the child's striving for self-reliance. Thus, parents who are highly involved in direct structuring of their child's independent play may not give their child the opportunity or support for sufficient autonomy to engage in independent, persistent, problem-solving activity. This suggests that the nature of parent involvement with children with mental retardation should be examined carefully, and that the characteristics of such involvement may offer a clue to the later 'learned helplessness' found in many children with mental retardation.

In conclusion, even in a population where families are functioning adequately in their care-giving roles and where children have biological constraints on their development, modest variations in the care-giving environment may have important implications for children's later learning. Although the analyses in this study do not indicate whether specific changes in the care-giving environment will promote increased mastery motivation, the relations found here suggest that this question be explored further. We need to understand whether critical intervention points exist and the ways in which parents and other care-givers can enhance (rather than impede) children's motivational behaviour (Hauser-Cram and Shonkoff, in press). As a whole, these findings point to the value of applying the transactional model of development to children with disabilities (Sameroff and Fiese 1990) and to the need to understand more fully the restrictive and facilitative power of children's environments.

NOTES

Special thanks to Marty Wyngaarden Krauss, George A. Morgan, Jack P. Shonkoff, and Carole C. Upshur for their comments on this chapter.

Support for the preparation of this chapter was provided by Grant No. MCJ-

250583 from the Maternal and Child Health Bureau (Title V, Social Security Act), US Department of Health and Human Services.

REFERENCES

Bayley, N. (1969) *The Scales of Infant Development*, New York, Psychological Corporation.

Bee, H., Barnard, K., Eyres, S., Gray, C., Hammond, M., Spietz, A., Snyder, C. and Clark, B. (1982) 'Predictions of IQ and language skill from perinatal status, child performance, family characteristics, and mother–infant interaction', *Child Development* 53, 1134–56.

Belsky, J. and Most, R. (1981) 'From exploration to play: a cross-sectional study of infant free play behavior', *Developmental Psychology* 17, 630–9.

Berlyne, D. E. (1966) 'Curiosity and exploration', *Science* 153, 25–33.

Blasco, P. M., Hrncir, E. J. and Blasco, P. A. (1990) 'The contribution of maternal involvement to mastery performance in infants with cerebral palsy', *Journal of Early Intervention* 14, 161–74.

Bradley, R. H., Rock, S. L., Caldwell, B. M. and Brisby, J. A. (1989) 'Uses of the HOME inventory for families with handicapped children', *American Journal of Mental Retardation* 94, 313–30.

Bradley, R. H., Caldwell, B. M., Rock, S. L., Barnard, K. E., Gray, C., Hammond, M. A., Mitchell, S., Siegel, L., Ramey, C., Gottfried, A. W. and Johnson, D. L. (1989) 'Home environment and cognitive development in the first 3 years of life: a collaborative study involving six sites and three ethnic groups in North America', *Child Development* 25, 217–35.

Bronfenbrenner, U. (1979) *The Ecology of Human Development – Experiments by Nature and Design*, Cambridge, MA, Harvard University Press.

Buckhalt, J. A., Rutherford, R. B. and Goldberg, K. E. (1978) 'Verbal and nonverbal interaction of mothers with their Down's syndrome and nonretarded infants', *American Journal of Mental Deficiency* 82, 337–43.

Caldwell, B. and Bradley, R. (1984) *Home Observation for Measurement of the Environment*, Little Rock, University of Arkansas at Little Rock.

Clarke-Stewart, K. A. (1973) 'Interactions between mothers and their young children: characteristics and consequences', *Monographs of the Society for Research in Child Development* 38 (6–7, Serial No. 153).

Diener, C. I. and Dweck, C. S. (1978) 'An analysis of learned helplessness: II. The processing of success', *Journal of Personality and Social Psychology* 39, 940–52.

Eheart, B. K. (1982) 'Mother–child interactions with nonretarded and mentally retarded preschoolers', *American Journal of Mental Deficiency* 87, 20–5.

Gottfried, A. W. and Nordquist, G. C. (1989) 'Intellectual giftedness', paper presented at the Biennial Meeting of the Society for Research in Child Development, Kansas City, MO.

Grolnick, W., Frodi, A. and Bridges, L. (1984) 'Maternal control style and the mastery motivation of one-year-olds', *Infant Mental Health Journal* 5, 72–82.

Harmon, R. J., Morgan, G. A. and Glicken, A. D. (1984) 'Continuities and discontinuities in affective and cognitive-motivation development', *Child Abuse and Neglect* 8, 157–67.

Harter, S. (1978) 'Effectance motivation reconsidered: toward a developmental model', *Human Development* 21, 34–64.

Harter, S. and Zigler, E. (1974) 'The assessment of effectance motivation in normal and retarded children', *Developmental Psychology* 10, 169–80.

Hauser-Cram, P. and Shonkoff, J. P. (in press) 'Mastery motivatism: implications for intervention' in R. H. MacTurk and G. A. Morgan (eds) *Mastery Motivation: Conceptual Origins and Applications*, Norwood, NJ, Ablex.

Hunt, J. McV. (1971) 'Intrinsic motivation and psychological development', in H. M. Schroeder and P. Suedfeld (eds) *Personality Theory and Information Processing*, New York, Ronald Press.

Hupp, S. C. and Abbeduto, L. (1991) 'Persistence as an indicator of mastery motivation in young children with cognitive delays', *Journal of Early Intervention* 15, 219–25.

Jennings, K. D., Connors, R. E., Stegman, C. E., Sankaranarayan, P. and Mendelsohn, S. (1985) 'Mastery motivation in young preschoolers: effect of a physical handicap and implications for educational programming', *Journal of the Division for Early Childhood* 9, 162–9.

Jones, O. H. M. (1977) 'Mother–child communication with pre-linguistic Down's syndrome and normal infants', in H. R. Schaffer (ed.) *Studies in Mother–Infant Interaction*, San Francisco, Academic Press.

Lutkenhaus, P. (1984) 'Pleasure derived from mastery in three-year-olds: its function for persistence and the influence of maternal behavior', *International Journal of Behavioral Development* 7, 343–54.

MacTurk, R., Vietze, P. M., McCarthy, M. E., McQuiston, S. and Yarrow, L. J. (1985) 'The organization of exploratory behavior in Down syndrome and nondelayed infants', *Child Development* 56, 573–81.

McCall, R. (1979) 'The development of intellectual functioning in infancy and the prediction of later I.Q.', in J. Osofsky (ed.) *Handbook of Infant Development*, New York, Wiley.

McCarthy, D. (1972) *McCarthy Scales of Children's Abilities*, New York, Psychological Corporation.

Messer, D. J., Rachford, D., McCarthy, M. E. and Yarrow, L. J. (1987) 'Assessment of mastery motivation behavior at 30 months: analysis of task-directed activities', *Developmental Psychology* 23, 771–81.

Mink, I. T., Nihira, K. and Meyers, E. (1983) 'Taxonomy of family life styles: I. Homes with TMR children', *American Journal of Mental Deficiency* 87, 484–97.

Morgan, G. A. and Harmon, R. J. (1984) 'Developmental transformations in mastery motivation: measurement and validation', in R. N. Emde and R. J. Harmon (eds) *Continuities and Discontinuities in Development*, New York, Plenum Press.

Morgan, G. A., Harmon, R. J. and Maslin-Cole, C. A. (1990) 'Mastery motivation: definition and measurement', *Early Education and Development* 1, 318–39.

Morgan, G. A., Busch-Rossnagel, N. A., Maslin-Cole, C. A. and Harmon, R. J. (1992) *Individualized Assessment of Mastery Motivation: Manual for 15 to 36 Month Old Children*, Bronx, NY, Fordham University Psychology Department.

Olson, D. H. and Lavee, Y. (1989) 'Family systems and family stress: a family life cycle perspective', in K. Kreppner and R. M. Lerner (eds) *Family Systems and Life-span Development*, Hillsdale, NJ, Erlbaum.

Olson, D., Bell, R. and Portner, J. (1982) *Family Adaptability and Cohesion Scales (FACES II)*, St Paul, MN, Family Social Science.

Piaget, J. (1952) *The Origins of Intelligence in Children*, New York, International Universities Press.

Redding, R. E., Harmon, R. J. and Morgan, G. A. (1990) 'Relationships between maternal depression and infants' mastery behaviors', *Infant Behavior and Development* 13, 391–5.

Redding, R. E., Morgan, G. A. and Harmon, R. J. (1988) 'Mastery motivation in infants and toddlers: is it greatest when tasks are moderately challenging?', *Infant Behavior and Development* 11, 419–30.

Rogoff, B., Malkin, C. and Gilbride, K. (1984) 'Interaction with babies as guidance in development', in B. Rogoff and J. V. Wertsch (eds) *Children's Learning in the 'Zone of Proximal Development'*, San Francisco, Jossey-Bass.

Sameroff, A. and Chandler, M. (1975) 'Reproductive risk and the continuum of caretaking casualty', in F. Horowitz (ed.) *Review of Child Development Research. Vol. 4*, Chicago, University of Chicago Press.

Sameroff, A. J. and Fiese, B. H. (1990) 'Transactional regulation and early intervention', in S. J. Meisels and J. P. Shonkoff (eds) *Handbook of Early Intervention*, New York, Cambridge University Press.

Sameroff, A. and Seifer, R. (1983) 'Familial risk and child competence', *Child Development* 54, 1254–68.

Scarr, S. (1981) 'Testing for children: assessment of the many determinants of intellectual competence', *American Psychologist* 36, 1159–66.

Schneewind, K. A. (1989) 'Contextual approaches to family systems research: the macro–micro puzzle', in K. Kreppner and R. M. Lerner (eds) *Family Systems and Life-span Development*, Hillsdale, NJ, Erlbaum.

Schwethelm, B. and Mahoney, G. (1986) 'Task persistence among organically impaired mentally retarded children', *American Journal of Mental Deficiency* 90, 432–9.

Shonkoff, J., Hauser-Cram, P., Krauss, M. W. and Upshur, C. C. (1992) 'Development of infants with disabilities and their families', *Monographs of the Society for Research in Child Development* 57 (Serial No. 230).

Sparrow, S., Balla, D. A. and Cicchetti, D. V. (1984) *Vineland Adaptive Behavior Scales: Expanded Form Manual*, Circle Pines, MN, American Guidance Service.

Stoneman, Z., Brody, C. H. and Abbott, D. (1983) 'In-home observations of young Down syndrome children with their mothers and fathers', *American Journal of Mental Deficiency* 87, 591–600.

Thompson, R. A., Cicchetti, D., Lamb, M. E. and Malkin, C. (1985) 'Emotional responses of Down syndrome and normal infants in the strange situation: the organization of affective behavior in infants', *Developmental Psychology* 21, 828–41.

Vietze, P., McCarthy, M., McQuiston, S., MacTurk, R. and Yarrow, L. (1983) 'Attention and exploratory behavior in infants with Down syndrome', in T. Field and A. Sostek (eds) *Infants Born at Risk: Perceptual and Physiological Processes*, New York, Grune & Stratton.

Vygotsky, L. S. (1978) *Mind in Society: The Development of Higher Psychological Processes*, Cambridge, MA, Harvard University Press.

Wachs, T. D. (1987) 'Specificity of environmental action as manifest in environmental correlates of infant's mastery motivation', *Developmental Psychology* 23, 782–90.

Weisz, J. R. (1979) 'Perceived control and learned helplessness among mentally retarded and nonretarded children: a developmental analysis', *Developmental Psychology* 15, 311–19.

White, R. W. (1959) 'Motivation reconsidered: the concept of competence', *Psychological Review* 66, 297–333.

Yarrow, L. J. and Pederson, F. (1976) 'The interplay between cognition and motivation in infancy', in M. Lewis (ed.) *Origins of Intelligence*, New York, Plenum Press.

Yarrow, L. J., MacTurk, R. H., Vietze, P. M., McCarthy, M. E., Klein, R. P. and McQuiston, S. (1984) 'Developmental course of parental stimulation and its relationship to mastery motivation during infancy', *Developmental Psychology* 20, 492–503.

Name Index

Subject Index